OPEN
ORGANIZATIONS

Developing
& Managing
OPEN ORGANIZATIONS

A Model and Methods for
Maximizing Organizational Potential

Oscar G. Mink
James M. Shultz
Barbara P. Mink

SOMERSET
CONSULTING GROUP, INC.

Library of Congress Cataloging in Publication Data

Mink, Oscar G
    Developing and managing open organizations.

    Bibliography: p.
    1. Organization.   2. Organizational change.
I. Shultz, James M., joint author.   II. Mink,
Barbara P., 1945– joint author.   III. Title.
HM131.M543   301.18'32   79–10195
ISBN 0–89384–045–9

Distributed by
    Somerset Consulting Group, Inc.
    1208A Somerset Avenue
    Austin, TX 78753

Edited by Karen I. Stelzner

Jacket design by Suzanne Pustejovsky
Book design and composition by Mary Ann Noretto

DEDICATION

To leaders who cope successfully with a rapidly changing environment

And to those who inspire confidence during uncertainty,

especially Tom Cottingham, Professor
Appalachian State University, Boone, North Carolina

Carl Heinz, President
Joy Machinery Company, Pittsburgh, Pennsylvania

Fred Taylor, President, and the staff
College of the Mainland, Texas City, Texas

Contents

Foreword

When Sigmund Freud was asked to state the two most important aspects of life, he replied, "Lieben und arbeiten" (To love and to work). Probably in these simple words lies the key to why people are restless today. Work without love produces a fractured life. Love without work may irresponsibly deny a love of humanity. Perhaps love and work are essential in combination. And perhaps the most advantageous ratio of one to the other is as individualistic and unduplicatible as a fingerprint. The promise of open organizations, as described in this book, is to provide for the accommodation of both.

"But what about our society's basic need to produce?" skeptics ask. "Can our institutions today meet the demands for improved delivery of products and services as well as for higher quality of work life for employees? Can they achieve organization goals and still enable employees to discover and realize their individual love and work ratios?"

Government organizations are facing turbulence caused by the complexity of their sociotechnical functions and the many revolutions in society. Not only is this true for government agencies, it applies equally to industries, communities, educational institutions, and others at all levels. Strains are exerted also by similar and even more dynamic interrelationships and increased interdependence among these. Such forces must be met. Systems and processes of organization renewal, adaptation, planning for change, and other innovations are sorely needed.

Most organizations are not initiating such processes. Why? I think in most instances we are working from an inadequate model or concept of an organization. Many organizations still indirectly value and practice the *power view* of organization that traces back to Machiavelli's (1515) view of people:

> Because of Man's rebelliousness and uncooperative behavior, he must be strictly and ruthlessly controlled. (Knowles and Saxberg, 1971, p. 103)

According to this way of thinking, organizations are controlling and inhibiting systems. Many modern organizations, both profit and nonprofit, prefer the *economic view* of man as advocated by Adam Smith (1760):

> Under the laws of supply and demand and by pursuing his self interests, each individual can further not only his own fortune, but that of society as a whole. (Knowles and Saxberg, 1971, p. 105)

While power and economics are realistic and understandable organizational frames of reference for managing our institutions, the most predominant one has been the *mechanistic view* as advocated by Frederick Lewis Taylor (1910):

> The employee is (1) a constant in the production equation, (2) an inert adjunct of the machine, prone to inefficiency and waste unless properly programmed, (3) by nature lazy, (4) and his main concern is self-interest. He must therefore be tightly controlled and externally motivated in order to overcome his natural desire to avoid work unless the material gains available to him are worth his effort. (Knowles and Saxberg, 1971, pp. 107–108)

This view has led to all the advantages and traps of bureaucracy. The principles of planning, organizing, controlling, and specializing have led to a model of supposed efficiency that all too often stumbles over its multiple mechanisms and blocks effectiveness.

In the midst of this century, the *human relations* model of organizations came into vogue. Its chief advocate, Douglas MacGregor (1960), challenged the old models when he said:

> If employees are lazy, indifferent, unwilling to take responsibility, intransigent, uncreative, uncooperative, this is due to the traditional assumptions and methods of organization and control. (Knowles and Saxberg, 1971, p. 116)

This human relations model, however, was often seen as paternalistic, not goal-oriented, and too "soft."

Where does this leave us as we approach the end of a century of study and application of methods of organization functioning?

Erich Fromm, in *The Revolution of Hope* (1968) predicts a once more dehumanized society in A.D. 2000. He agrees with Lewis Mumford who says that the age of *megamachines* will be upon us. He foresees that work, as well as personal environment, will be dominated by impersonal social systems of negative impact on the individual. He anticipates a society that more and more stresses quantity and consumption and measures progress by increases in things rather than by quality of life. He sees workers becoming pathologically passive, without capacity for individuality and creativity:

> Are we confronted with a tragic, insolvable dilemma? Must we produce sick people in order to have a healthy economy, or can we use our material resources, our inventions, our computers, to serve the ends of man? Must individuals be passive and dependent in order to have a strong and well-functioning organization? (p. 2)

Three interrelated conditions have piqued management interest in how to combat this tendency and how best to better the quality of life of those working:

1. In the well-fed society in which we live, with almost full employment and rapid technological changes and challenges, it is ever more possible for a person to make the choice of where he or she will work. The choice can be based upon his or her own needs and goals.

2. Ever more importance is attached to human dignity in our society. Ever greater recognition is forthcoming that work must be so organized and managed as to take human dignity fully into account.

3. Ever more findings from the behavioral sciences show that work suited to individual needs as well as organization requirements tends to produce the greatest productivity and the highest quality of work.

The dilemma for an organization's leaders then is this: "How can we create conditions that will mobilize human effort for achieving our goals while making work meaningful and rewarding enough that employees *want* and *love* to produce and receive personal satisfaction from their efforts?" This brings us to the contributions and values of a *systems view* of organization. While some interpreters of this field focus on complex mathematical models, the systems views are generally broader, more comprehensive, and potentially more divergent or creative than those of operations research. Recent contributions to this concept include M. Beer and E. F. Huse (1972), J. W. Forrester (1961, 1968, 1969, 1971), E. J. Miller and A. K. Rice (1967), J. G. Miller (1955, 1965a, 1965b), and E. L. Trist (1968).

The idea behind sociotechnical systems is that any production or service system calls for both a technology and a work relationship structure relating human to technological resources. That is, an organization's total system has a complete set of human activities plus interrelationships to the technical, physical, and financial resources and to the processes for turning out products and delivering services. Thinking about an organization as a sociotechnical system helps us accept the human-machine relationships of today's society.

All organization systems include in their makeup many elements and processes. This is true for all, including subsystems, the smallest groups (or dyads), and the most complex multigroup structures of the international organization. When no attention is paid to the elements and processes of the system, it cannot function effectively.

A systems view may suggest that other models of organization operating as parts of that organization only serve to contribute to its complexity. The relevance test for systems models is how appropriate the response is to them in terms of the interaction between the individual, organization, and environment. Organization openness, as described in this book, may be construed as an energy exchange system.

The organization openness model presented in this book assumes that people have a great capacity for being creative, inventive, and ingenious. It recognizes that an inner energy exists within the individual, ready to be turned on and in turn to release that creativity, inventiveness, and ingenuity. It also recognizes individual needs for survival and security and that we tend to rush past the line that divides us from the lower order of animals, seeking satisfaction of our higher needs. Organization openness calls for restructuring work to provide opportunities for the worker to express initiative, responsibility, and competence—elements that contribute to the higher need for self-fulfillment. If the desire for self-fulfillment triggers creativity, inventiveness, and ingenuity, the worker's self-fulfillment results in both high personal satisfaction and greater output.

Such an improvement in the quality of working life depends on four factors:

1. *The work itself*—generating high levels of accountability and responsibility through organization openness, which encourages direct feedback on performance, clear work goals, fewer controls with more accountability, and appropriate involvement in decision making.

2. *The individual*—growing personally and professionally under organization openness through work roles and relationships, which are fostered and consistently improved by processes of role clarification, through opportunities for individualization, self-identity, and learning; through linking individual, work, and life goals; and through tangible support from superiors.

3. *The work output*—improving quality as a result of organization openness, which enlarges responsibilities, calls for intergroup collaboration, requires completion of work in units rather than in fragments, rewards quality and innovation, and provides for measurable goal attainment.

4. *The organization's functions and structures*—providing through organization openness a climate for creativity, two-way communication, an overall perspective, respect for the individual, and ongoing organization development.

The need to initiate moves toward such organization openness, then, arises partly from changes in our technological environment—from the hardware through which we wander every day. It also arises, and more significantly, from the changes in philosophy that have moved the worker from a victim of serfdom to a victim of scientific management, an evolution in the software of work that has progressed from complete coercion and threat to nearly complete collaboration and reason. The potential of organization openness is within ourselves. Yet making the most of that potential is as much a problem for the top executive as for the least paid employee. Realizing the potential for openness is not measured by how much money we have, how much floor space, how much production, how much profit. It lies in how much meaning we realize in our work, how much personal satisfaction, how much peace of mind. It is demonstrated by our belief in the desire of people to live in the full measure of their capabilities and still reach beyond them. Only then can we say that we have an open organization, that organization renewal is taking place.

GORDON L. LIPPITT

Preface

This book is addressed to anyone involved in organizational enterprise who is interested in more effective ways of identifying and releasing organization potential. We hope to offer a fresh view of the possibilities of organizations for flexibility, creativity, and productivity, through the perspective of an open organization model. We are not presenting a finished theory or specialized technique, but rather, a practical working model originally derived from general systems theory and writings about organization openness. The model was further developed and refined during our work with business, industry, government agencies, educational institutions, and other organizations. In addition to the model, we also present some procedures, tools, and instruments which may be used to apply the model systematically for organizational growth. Case studies drawn from our work with organizations are used to illustrate these applications.

We believe the book will be of both philosophical and practical value to managers, organization development practitioners, and students—in short, to anyone receptive to the notion that maximizing human and organization potential is required for future economic and social progress, and not just an appealing view to include in an employee benefit package.

An effective framework for organization change must provide at least provisional responses to two fundamental questions: "What is the healthy state of an organization?" and "How does an organization reach that state?" If the state of health is defined too narrowly in terms of one condition, such as efficiency, the diagnosis and interventions based upon the definition may have little effect, or an entirely different effect than intended. What is needed is a comprehensive theory of healthy organizations—a systematic, operational description that takes the complexities of people and organizations into serious account. We regard the open organization model as a step in this direction. As a framework for change, the model's value is twofold. First, it presents an ideal standard against which to evaluate the current status of any organization, regardless of its size or purpose. And further, the model pinpoints areas in which a given organization needs to grow in order to move toward greater health. Thus, it provides a vision of organization potential, permits systematic diagnosis of organization growth needs, and allows room for a wide repertoire of methods for releasing that potential.

We have been trained in diverse disciplines—psychology, sociology, and educational administration. Yet we have been moving toward some common assumptions about requirements for successful organization changes. During the years we have worked with organizations, we have struggled with the inability to predict whether or not particular interventions would succeed, and to analyze why. Probably, as many of our efforts worked as not, but successes were attributable to chance as much as to principle or plan. From these experiences, we have reached several conclusions. First, you must work through the existing organizational structure; working around the structure carries a high risk of failure. Second, you must learn to use social influence and power appropriately to achieve the results you want in the organization. Third, you must generate energy for change among members of the organization. Finally, and perhaps most important, you must have a model from which to work, even if it is relatively unsophisticated to begin with. A model helps you determine what data to gather, how to organize the data, and by what criteria to analyze the effectiveness of actions.

Our greatest need has been to find a way to organize and interpret information to get a more comprehensive picture of the complex dynamics of an organization. Of little use were methods of analysis that study each person in the organization and the organization in the context of each person's dynamics. We needed an approach that would clarify the relationships between individuals composing work groups, between work groups composing the organization, and between the organization and its environment.

The open organization model enables us to study the entire organization: its internal dynamics at various levels, and its relationship to the environment. Further, we have been able to identify and bring about needed changes on several levels within the organization—in individuals, in working groups, among working groups, and in the whole organization. Application of the model has permitted purposeful, systematic, positive control of our interventions. Since we developed the model, we have worked with almost every type of profit and nonprofit organization, including multinationals, heavy manufacturing, mining and petrochemicals, hospitals, professional associations, universities, and human service agencies. Collectively, we have served more than three hundred organizations over the past seven years. We estimate our success rate at better than ninety percent. We are convinced that managers and others can apply this approach with similar success.

The open organization model also provides a comprehensive perspective from which to critique, select, and integrate the profusion of management concepts, systems, styles, and improvement techniques that have sprung up in the past ten years. The model provides a corrective to the general tendency to promote narrow gains through short-term treatments or specialized techniques. It is especially helpful in counteracting "either-or" and fragmented approaches to organization change. Here we will briefly indicate three types of narrowness in current thought and practice which the model seeks to overcome. First is the indiscriminate application to both profit and nonprofit organizations of models and assumptions drawn mostly from business practices. While profit and nonprofit organizations share certain fundamental characteristics, they also have very distinct differences in goals and processes. An approach is needed which can correct the bias toward applying business-derived notions to all organizations.

A second type of narrowness is the attempt to solve system problems by arbitrarily applying specialized techniques, such as team building, management by objectives, T-groups, management training, attitude surveys, and conflict resolution. These techniques are highly effective when directed singly or in combination at carefully identified organizational needs and definite priorities. But they can also be abused as magical, packaged answers to organizational ills. Under such circumstances, they may actually worsen the situation by distracting attention and energy away from the solution of an actual, crucial problem. What is needed is a diagnostic framework that distinguishes between problems of different kinds and magnitudes at various levels of an organization.

A third example is the tendency to view established structures and processes as inherently opposed to the realization of human values. Much of the literature criticizing bureaucracy, one mode of organization, has resented and generally rejected established ways of organizing human effort. Although not the intent of original scholars like MacGregor, this view is clearly held by many involved in humanistic psychology and applied behavioral science, and it seems to permeate much management practice in organization development. In our view, established structures and processes are a fact of modern life, and can be a resource *for* people and not against them. The assumption that organization per se is pitted against human potential results in blindness to what can be done by and for people through organizations. Since organizations will probably continue to be a dominant force in modern life, they need to be more appropriately organized, not less organized. What is needed is a framework that will let us move toward a synergic relationship between individual human potential and organization potential.

Organizations today confront a proliferating advice market and a wide variety of training and intervention programs. Often consultants build remunerative practices by writing books popularizing highly specific techniques, such as MBO or grid OD. Such methods may or may not be useful to a particular organization. The professional community of consultants has not yet achieved sufficient unity to provide definitive guidelines for the services, education, and certification of consultants. Management consulting cuts across many fields and varied professional groups—the Association for Creative Change, International Association of Applied Social Sciences, National Training Laboratories, Organization Development Network, and Organization Development Division of the American Society for Training and Development, to name a few. Given the lack of clear professional guidelines, quality control falls back upon the client. The generic perspective of organizations presented in this book can serve clients well in sorting through organization needs and choosing among available kinds of intervention.

The book is divided into four sections. Part I, **"Toward Open Organizations,"** describes the concept of organization openness and the components of the open organization model, presented within a historical perspective. Part II, **"Foundations of the Open Organization,"** presents key theories, concepts, and research necessary to understand the philosophy and practice of open organizations. Part III, **"Action Steps,"** describes a sequence of interventions by which an organization can develop its potential openness. The sequence parallels the process of development, which can be characterized by four questions:

- Where are we now? Marshaling resources, appraising the present situation in comparison with organization potential (chapters 5 and 6)
- Where do we want to go? Setting goals and objectives (chapter 7)
- How do we expect to get there? Strategies (chapters 8, 9, and 10)
- How will we know when we have arrived? Evaluation—if at first you don't succeed, refine, redesign, and try again (chapter 11)

Part IV, **"Action Tools,"** presents instruments we have found useful. Some are adapted; others are our own creation.

We have not felt constrained to tie each point into formal literature; however, basic sources are cited in the list of references. The case studies are described from the view of the external consultant. Ideas and techniques from other sources have often been synthesized into our own, to the extent that the origins can no longer be identified. In some cases there is no single source.

OSCAR G. MINK
JAMES M. SHULTZ
BARBARA P. MINK

Acknowledgments

In producing a book of this magnitude, we have drawn steadily on the energy and expertise of a multitude of friends, colleagues, and clients. It is difficult to single out a few names from the many professional, caring individuals who have suggested ideas, stimulated our thinking, and helped organize and critique the manuscript. These contributors have added elbow grease, inspiration, and delight to our journey from the initial conception to the book you see here.

Over a period of years, we have worked with many individual and organizational clients to help improve their working environments and managerial skills. We are particularly grateful for the opportunity they have given us to develop and refine the ideas, processes, and instruments contained in this book.

Several persons not recognized in the text have made important substantive contributions to various drafts of the manuscript. Gene Jensen, an excellent methodologist with a firm grip on systems theory, was extremely helpful in drafting portions now contained in the preface and first two chapters. We are grateful to George J. Wilkerson for his early version of the chapter on values entitled "Open Minds, Values, and Beliefs." Nora Comstock and Jerry Snow deserve credit for stimulating dialogue and contributing to ideas. Jerry also contributed material for a literature review of the diagnostic study process.

We owe a debt of special gratitude to Gordon Lippitt, Leslie This, Jerry Harvey, and David Bradford, who took time from busy schedules to read earlier drafts and to give us suggestions and ideas for improving the quality of the book. We are grateful, too, to Bob Formosa, a practical-minded manager of human resource development at Joy Manufacturing, who contributed to the overall sense of the manuscript. In addition, Mary H. McCaulley, Director of the Center for Application of Psychological Types, provided helpful feedback and constructive suggestions to the chapter on values.

Acknowledgment is made to the International Transactional Analysis Association for permission to reprint a sequence from Pamela Levin's article entitled "A 'think structure' for feeling fine faster," from the *Transactional analysis journal*, 1973, 3 (1), 38–39.

Several persons provided support and editorial services that made possible the publication of this book. In the early stages, Beverly Moore provided valuable editorial expertise and insights. Besides interviewing various authors and developing the case study material, Ann Linquist handled permissions correspondence, editorial queries, and other detailed tasks necessary to prepare the manuscript. She receives a large share of the credit for the completion of the book. Karen Stelzner made a substantial contribution to the quality of the final product; she is one of the most competent and dedicated editors with whom we have worked.

PART I

Toward Open Organizations

1

THE OPEN ORGANIZATION MODEL

ONE TASK OF organization management has always been maintaining equilibrium between stability and change in response to both internal and environmental pressures. This task has intensified as organizations have moved into a post-industrial age of rapid social change and increasing complexity. The values, assumptions, and management processes of bureaucratic organizations that have served us well in the past are now becoming problematic. The accountability—even the survival—of bureaucratic organizations is being challenged because of their inability to respond flexibly and appropriately to the needs of their employees, beneficiaries, and environment.

We believe an open systems model offers the needed alternative to bureaucracies. An open systems view does not reject being organized as a condition of modern human enterprise. Rather, it presents a way of understanding and developing organizations so that management processes and individual human potential work together instead of against each other. This model can enable organizations to become more flexible both internally and externally, while maintaining stability and purpose.

A New Direction For Organizations

THE BUREAUCRATIC HERITAGE

Bureaucracies became the usual dominant form of organization during the industrial age. A bureaucracy may be characterized as an organizational pyramid with wealth, power, and control concentrated at the top. Leaders are concerned with determining who belongs and rewarding those whom they like. In the early 1920s Max Weber (1957) identified the following elements of a bureaucracy:

- Division of labor based upon functional specialization
- Well-defined hierarchy of authority
- System of rules defining the rights or duties of members, employees, or participants
- System of "standard operating procedures," for dealing with work situations

Classic bureaucratic theory and practice assumed a relatively stable, predictable environment. This assumption was grounded in the world view of physicist-philosopher Isaac Newton, who saw the world and all its components as mechanistic, a network of causes producing inevitable effects. People were considered inherently weak, lazy, avaricious, lustful, and disposed to evil. Therefore, they had to be organized to work in a reliable, predictable fashion to achieve chosen organization goals.

Bureaucracies were intended to ensure order and fairness through hierarchical control, regulations, and norms of personal conduct. To codify acceptable behavior and guarantee results, standard operating procedures were devised. Another means of control was promotion of the ethic of the impersonal specialist. Products and services were delivered to client or consumer groups by experts specializing in various fields. These persons would be fair and impartial in their work. As conceived by Max Weber (1957), bureaucracies could overcome problems such as nepotism, arbitrariness, and lack of competence.

Diverse workforce. One predictable element of the working environment through the late 1950s was a relatively uniform employee value system. We had emerged out of an agrarian era in which, if you did not work, you did not eat. Workers were goal-oriented, willing to subject their identities to the goal of production in return for material survival. However, by the time of Sputnik's launch in 1957, we achieved a prosperity that caused young people to experience another orientation. They said, "First I've got to establish my own identity—find out who I am. Then I'll choose my work." Workers from this generation tend to take adequate wages and fringe benefits for granted. They expect jobs to fulfill personal needs and to propel them toward objectives. Robert N. Form, manpower utilization director for American Telephone and Telegraph, depicts these workers as persons who refuse to be bored. If their work is not interesting, he says they demand more responsibility, quit, or retire on the job (Herzberg, Mausner, and Snyderman, 1959; Ford, 1969).

As we enter the post-industrial period, more workers fit Abraham Maslow's description of "self-actualized" people. He characterized such people as uniformly devoted to some task, calling, vocation, or beloved work (Maslow, 1967). They place meaningful tasks above wage, and satisfying relations with coworkers above fringe benefits. They prefer responsibility, freedom, creativity, and supportive relationships to economic security and bureaucratic conformity.

At the same time, more women and minorities are working, bringing a wide variety of expectations, orientations, backgrounds, and problems. Some are primarily identity- or self-oriented; others are still production- and survival-oriented. These diverse values and motivations have profound implications for organizational planning, development, and operation. Organizations can no longer count on the work ethic and the profit motive to provide cohesiveness and direction for everyone. The quality of life and the challenge and satisfaction of jobs must also be taken into account.

A changing world. Authoritarian institutions, such as monarchies and hierarchical organizations, are capable of some responsiveness to constituents. Few monarchs thought they could completely neglect constituents and survive long. Typically, monarchs used hearings as the mechanism of responsiveness and responsibility toward their subjects. At specified times and places, rulers would listen to subjects' complaints and supplications, and then pass judgment. Both monarchs and bureaucracies also negotiate with recognized powers and marshal resources quickly to meet crises. There have always been means of learning public opinion, whether from spies or market research.

Although various forms of bureaucracy did not eliminate nepotism and other inequities, they helped develop the United States into an industrial giant. The traditional hierarchy of authority used by army engineers to build the American railroads become a model for other organizations. With all their imperfections, bureaucratic organizations have given us competent public servants, quality goods and services, and one of the best transportation and distribution systems in the world. Bureaucratic organizations have effectively accomplished the enormous task of planning, organizing, implementing, controlling, and evaluating the use of our rich natural resources.

Although most formal organizations in the United States today will tend toward a hierarchical, bureaucratic pattern, new patterns are needed to meet the changing conditions and demands of post-industrial society. We can no longer assume that we deal with a world of order and certainty or a work environment that is predictable. Nor can we assume organizational stability through standard operating procedures and control concentrated atop a pyramid. Bureaucracies today experience three difficulties: a tendency toward dysfunctional internal rigidity, increasingly diverse workers, and a complex, rapidly changing environment.

Internal rigidity. As organizations grow, bureaucratic methods result in procedural build-up, departmental territoriality, and stalemates among vested interests. Formal procedures and rules war with invisible norms. To observe how these rigidities work, let us follow the development of a small organization.

It begins as a small movement, community, or partnership. Communication is open, and there is common goodwill and trust. Power and obligations are fairly equally distributed among departments. In time, however, communication channels become monopolized, power unequally distributed, and previously shared resources the province of particular departments. Rights once common are systematically withdrawn. The organization becomes more complex by dividing labor into specialties, geographic areas, or types of use assigned to departments or divisions.

At first, these splits are useful; the standard operating procedure is not the culprit. However, employees become more concerned with completing paperwork than fulfilling clients' needs or meeting the organization's goals. This happens simply because employees get more rewards and recognition for the former. Nourishing each subunit becomes an end in itself. Knowledge, rights, and resources become organized around department structures whose goals conflict with the organization's primary goals. Workers use the rules to maintain their roles, positions, and vested interests.

Interdepartmental communication is restricted to a formal chain of command. Departments become like islands, fragmented, rigid, and isolated from the organization's purposes. Each department has little sense of contributing to the whole; top management keeps power for decision making. Attempts to make the organization more responsive threaten the status quo of both departments and upper-level decision makers. Yet, as rigidity and increasing control become the primary means of insuring organizational stability, lack of adaptability threatens the system with extinction.

Yet historically, many authoritarian systems have failed to respond adequately to changing environments. Two examples are Hitler's underestimation of Soviet geography, will, and strength when invading Russia in 1941, and Rome's ignoring the growing power of the barbarians at the end of the Roman era. American railroads furnish a dramatic modern example of a nonresponsive organization in a rapidly changing environment. We have already noted the remarkable success of the railroads and the hierarchical model they set for others. With the help of federal land grants, railroads spanned the continent, grew, and prospered for several decades. However, when trucking and air travel developed, the railroad industry continued to focus on building technically improved railroads rather than creating services for the transportation needs of various groups.

Today organizations are confronted with a magnitude and complexity of world change that strains the coping mechanism of bureaucracies. We face rapid technological advances, knowledge explosion, struggles of women and minorities for political and economic enfranchisement, limited raw materials, increasing environmental and social blight, inflation, shifting third world politics, and collisions of diverse values and philosophies. The world view upon which bureaucracies are based is no longer functional. The Newtonian world view and the bureaucratic system have outlived their triumphs. This decay has been a long time in coming: Alfred North Whitehead in 1933 wrote, "Systems, scientific and philosophic, come and go. In its prime, each system is a triumphant success: in its decay, it is an obstructive nuisance" (p. 34). We must now seek an alternative way to organize human energies toward common ends.

THE FUTURE

The organization of the future will be based upon the principle of adaptability rather than predictability. It will be an "open" organization that considers process more important than structure, and free human interaction more effective than impersonal, chain-of-command hierarchy. Swiss developmental psychologist Jean Piaget defines intelligence as adaptability (Piaget, 1950). So, we are talking about developing an intelligent, adaptable organization—one that can respond to shifts in the changing social environment.

The philosophical perspective and operating principles of an open organization are provided by the process philosophy of Alfred North Whitehead and by general systems theory. Process philosophy views human life as organic and fluid, not mechanistic, dependent upon personal and group relationships rather than simple cause-and-effect relationships, and intuitive as well as rational. Systems theory de-emphasizes structure as the basis for organization, and focuses on the goals, functions, and processes of self-organization.

By distinguishing between *open* and *closed* organizations, general systems theory provides a helpful framework for effective organizations. Kast and Rosenzweig (1972) have presented the open systems view:

> Systems can be considered in two ways: (1) closed or (2) open. Open systems exchange information, energy, or material with their environments. Biological and social systems are inherently open systems; mechanical systems must be open or closed. The concepts of open and closed systems are difficult to defend in the absolute. We prefer to think of open–closed as a dimension; i.e., systems are relatively open or relatively closed. (p. 448)

In this view, the ultimate measure of adaptability is the capacity of an organization to respond to its environment. A closed organization is self-contained, but an open one interacts with its environment. Feedback is the key operating principle. In a relatively closed situation, interaction and feedback among various parts is similar to the controlled chemical reaction which takes place in a sealed test tube. No extraneous factors affect it or are affected by it. In a relatively open situation, the organization expects some uncertainty and plans responses to environmental change.

Lawrence and Lorsch (1967, 1969, 1970) propose that a primary task of an organization is developing strategies which enable it to identify and cope effectively with significant areas of uncertainty in the environment. Planning should be continuous; roles and functions should adapt to new conditions as they arise.

Not all parts of an open system need be highly responsive to external conditions, however. An assembly line, for example, may function best when it remains closed and well-defined, while a research and development unit may alternate between a closed phase of developing products and an open phase of market testing. Similarly, organizations vary in the amount of environmental uncertainty encountered. Some may experience little outside pressure, while others will be pressured by external forces to adopt a more open strategy in order to be effective. Nevertheless, open systems logic assumes that any organization will be affected to some degree by variables, both internal and external, outside its immediate control. The *capacity* for response is essential.

The open systems view also defines adaptability in terms of the capacity for internal responsiveness. Organization planning must take account of diverse motivations and values, perspectives and resources of employees. In the bureaucratic hierarchy these decisions are made at the top and passed down. The thought given to views and aspirations of personnel at lower levels depends on the wisdom and personalities of the authorities. The open systems approach, on the other hand, demands that planning be organization-wide and ongoing. All members provide input and feedback, with the group recognizing the special competencies of individual members, and with competence serving as the crucial element in decision making.

The challenge of adaptability will be to maintain responsiveness to external and internal diversity and change, while achieving the unity of purpose and cohesiveness necessary to act effectively. In other words, organizations must develop balance between flexibility and stability. The open systems view presents an understanding of organization dynamics that will enable us to achieve this balance. Feedback, planning, and self-initiated change is possible because the network of interdependencies within and outside an organization enable it to assimilate new information and to modify its goals and structures. An organization must work toward balancing differentiation and integration of its parts (Lawrence and Lorsch, 1969), so that cohesive subunits can cooperate successfully. The open organization model presented in the next section will clarify the various components of an open system and their dynamic relationships.

Characteristics of an Open Organization

The model presented here is of a system in its healthiest state—an ideal to evaluate relative openness and a guide to greater effectiveness of a given organization. The model, based on general systems theory, looks at a person, group, or organization as a system composed of subsystems located within a larger system. The model allows us to determine how well these systems function internally, in relation to each other, and in relation to the environment.

The concept of this model is the organization as an energy exchange system:

> There is an input of energy from the environment, and a patterned internal activity that transforms the energy into output, which in turn provokes a new energy input. The organization is thus seen as an open system engaged in constant transactions with its environment, which can be visualized as a system of systems. These systems include the sub-systems within the corporations (divisions, departments) which are constantly engaged in energy exchanges, and the systems operating outside the organization, but affecting it—other members of the same industry, members of competing industries, suppliers, government institutions, etc. (Fabun, 1967, p. 12)

Unity and internal and external responsiveness are normative for healthy systems, small (a cell, a person) or large (a group, organization, or society). In the model these characteristics are inherently interrelated, overcoming the dichotomies of system and components, or system and environment. Particular organizations will show some of each characteristic, on a continuum between extremely open and extremely closed systems.

AN INTEGRATED WHOLE

The first property of a system is coherence or unity. Unity is the process of centering. It is the organizing dimension of any biological life or physical form, like the nucleus of the amoeba or the eye of a hurricane. Many terms have been used to label this centering process—self-concept, ego, identity, ego states, self, perceived self, persona, personality, syntality (group personality), organizational mission, purpose. These terms represent various ways of describing how a person, group, or organization shows consistent, unifying, and purposive behavior in varying environments.

Unity in an open organization is not achieved at the price of internal fragmentation or being closed to the system's environment. It permits and promotes awareness of self, other components, and the external world. It is the essence of being and becoming, enabling adaptability or intelligence. In open organizations, unity is maintained and enhanced by consistently focusing energy on the definition and achievement of purposes and goals, rather than around power issues. Organization purpose is sharpened and modified through shared information and consensus-creating activities. Leaders build credibility through their ability to use a system-wide perspective to solve problems, symbolize organization purposes, and persuade others to these purposes. They rely only secondarily upon legal and economic coercive authority.

INTERDEPENDENT COMPONENTS

In an open system all parts are responsive to each other rather than being fragmented, rigid "empires." The parts of an open system are themselves open systems. For example, the organs of the human body are open, interdependent subsystems which exchange nutrients, oxygen, nitrogen, and other elements of biological functioning and life energy. When the free exchange and flow of life elements is blocked, disease results, as in a tumor or a blood clot in a vein. Human organizations also develop blocks, with closed, belligerent members or defensive departments. Transactional analysis has characterized closed couples, families, and organizations as having well-established games complete with victims, persecutors, and rescuers.

In an open organization, internal responsiveness is developed and maintained through collaboration rather than through authority. Focused on achievement of accepted goals, this collaboration involves managers and staff participating together in planning and implementation. This process assumes that people have the capacity for creativity, responsibility, and growth, given opportunities to develop.

INTERCHANGE WITH THE ENVIRONMENT

An open organization continuously interchanges activities, data, and energy with other systems in the environment which it serves or upon which it depends. This interchange is an ongoing series of planned transactions through which the organization represents its purposes to outside groups and gathers information that may affect decisions and goals.

An open system does not become unified or centered by fencing itself off from the outside. Unlike the fanatic who becomes secure in a closed, oversimplified world view, the open organization is unafraid of new data. It has the processes and skills to assimilate new data into planning and setting goals. It is proactive rather than reactive in its relationship to the external environment. An open system anticipates and prepares for changes, rather than making decisions after crises have developed. So it can maintain unity while remaining open both internally and externally.

INTERRELATING INDIVIDUAL, GROUP, AND ORGANIZATION

The three characteristics of unity, internal responsiveness, and external responsiveness may be used to describe the entire organization, or its subsystems. The open organization model looks at these characteristics at three levels: the individual person, the work group, and the entire organization. As shown in figure 1, the model also indicates the interchange among the three levels in terms of these characteristics. For example, a complementary relationship exists between the external responsiveness of an individual and the internal responsiveness of his or her work group. When a work group is composed of people with high involvement and concern for one another (external responsiveness), the group's internal responsiveness will be high. Conversely, if a group suffers low internal responsiveness, individual members need to develop greater involvement and commitment to the group.

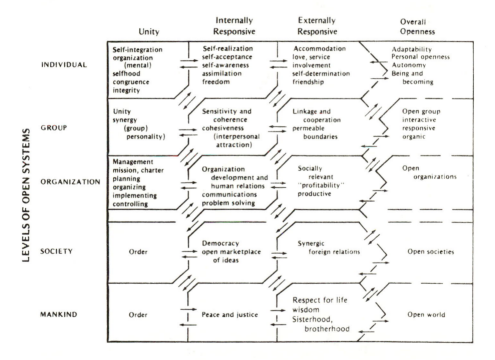

NOTES: Columns one to three present three characteristics of openness. Column four defines the overall degree of openness. The first three horizontal levels represent an organization composed of group and individual subsystems. The words in each square describe qualities manifested in that aspect of the organization. The model may also be extended; levels four and five represent societal and world systems. You may wish to experiment with descriptive words that have meaning for you at these levels.

Horizontal arrows represent the balance maintained among the three characteristics at each level. The vertical arrows indicate complementary relationships between different levels.

Figure 1.   Defining Characteristics of Open Systems

To understand more concretely the characteristics at each level and the relationships between levels, let us trace the structure of an organization represented by figure 2. Consider the portion of the diagram labeled A1 as a single individual who is a member of a team (B1) and is also employed in the organization (C). Unity for an individual is self-concept—"I know who I am and appreciate my uniqueness." Internal responsiveness on the individual level is awareness of one's wants and needs and permission to fulfill them. External responsiveness on the individual level is defined as interaction with others in the environment which produces mutually beneficial results. In figure 2, two-way arrows between A1, A2, and A3 illustrate interaction with members of the work group. External responsiveness on the individual level is reaching out, listening, responding, being open, attraction, positive stroking in transactional analysis terms, or old-fashioned affection and love.

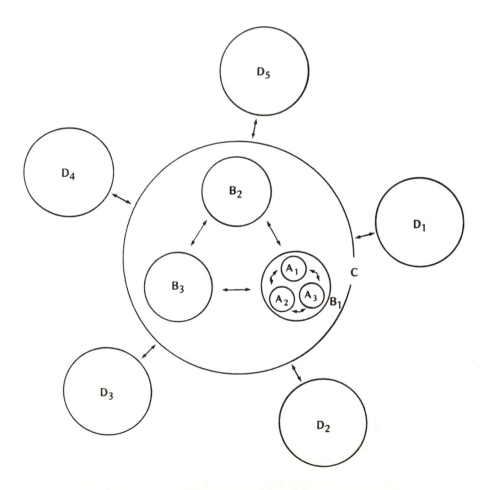

Figure 2. Interrelating Individual, Group, and Organization

If we consider the basic unit as the team instead of the individual, unity involves concern with team goals. Are all team members moving in the same direction? Are there team goals and objectives? Are team members committed to these goals? Internal responsiveness on the team level means members of the team are aware of one another. Are team members sensitive to other members' needs and wants? Are there good relationship skills in the team? External responsiveness on the team level is cooperative interaction with other teams or components within the organization. Does the team link with other teams? Does the team gather information relevant for team problem solving from other sources? Does the team support institutional goals?

Achieving unity on the organizational level (C) involves organizing according to purpose. Is there a sense of where the whole organization is moving? Internal responsiveness on this level is the way different components within the organization interact. Do departments gather information from other departments? Do they share data? Do units seek relevant information from outside sources to help in solving problems? External responsiveness on the organizational level is the way the organization interacts with the larger community. Does the organization gather information from its environment for planning and setting goals? Does it provide data to other organizations? Does the organization provide relevant services to constituent groups?

Table 1 summarizes behavior and characteristics that maintain and enhance open systems at each level of an organization.

Moving Toward Open Organizations

According to Warren Bennis and Philip Slater (1968), the open organic system is an embodiment of the democratic process. This process is the root requirement for survival of a post-industrial society. An open system with full interaction among all its parts and with its environment has resources for renewal. In a changing environment this system must also be purposive, working toward specific short- or long-term goals.

The goal of development, then, is organizational and societal renewal. Renewal will occur through developing organizations which deal effectively with uncertainty, diversity, and complexity. An open organization has been characterized as a healthy system with mechanisms for organizing around purposes and information flow, rather than preordained centers of power. Such an organization values its history and develops a shared view of future direction, strengths, and weaknesses. It incorporates internal and external mechanisms for obtaining and responding to feedback.

TABLE 1
Open Organization Behaviors

	UNITY	INTERNAL RESPONSIVENESS	EXTERNAL RESPONSIVENESS
INDIVIDUAL	Identification of my basic beliefs; who I am; my uniqueness; self-concept, perceived self. Values: Am I open and other-oriented or closed and self-oriented? A	Awareness of myself, my feelings, my needs, my defenses; freedom to fulfill my wants and needs. B	Hearing and responding to others; active listening; openness to ideas, experiences, persons; love—ability to enter into and establish enduring relationships; interpersonal attraction and involvement. C
GROUP	Identification of team goals and objectives; building the team. Group achieves syntality (personality) and synergy (group output is greater than the sum of individual outputs). D	Interpersonal skills; facilitation of interaction among team members; process observation; sensitivity and coherence; interpersonal attraction or cohesiveness develops. E	Gathering and relating external information relevant to task of team; linkage with other individuals and groups; cooperation for achievement of common purpose with other systems. F
ORGANIZATION	Development of common goals of organization; management according to purpose and mission. G	Ways components within organization react to and impact each other; data sharing; organization development and human relations. Linkages between individuals and groups. H	Organization responsiveness to larger community; social relevance, profitability. I

PLANNING FOR CHANGE

Moving from bureaucratic to open organizations will require more than tinkering with present beliefs, methods, and structures. Often, organization survival and growth may require a fundamental reorientation. As Watzlawick, Weakland, and Fisch (1974) have noted, "There are two different types of change, one that occurs within a given system which itself remains unchanged, and one whose occurrence changes the system itself" (p. 10).

We will refer to these as first- and second-order change. For example, the crew and passengers of the Titanic might have been so busy rearranging the deck chairs on the ship that they were unaware of the impending collision with the iceberg. They would have been involved in first-order change. If, however, they had altered the Titanic's course to avoid the iceberg, they would have been carrying out a second-order change. Another example of nonproductive first-order change would be a person having a nightmare who attempts to escape a predicament by running, fighting, screaming, or jumping off a cliff. No change of dream behavior will help end the nightmare. The only way out of the dream involves a second-order change from dreaming to waking—reframing the situation from immediate terror to the realization that one has been dreaming. Waking is no longer part of the dream; it is an altogether different state (Watzlawick et al., 1974, p. 10).

Second-order change requires a fundamental change of the entire organization. It is usually brought about by outside people acting from a different perspective than that held by members of the organization. Power groups outside the organization, without professional guidance, can cause second-order change, often with negative results that may lead to institutional regression or even destruction. Outside consultants may also bring about second-order change which preserves the organization's strengths while enabling it to grow to meet new problems and opportunities.

The development of open organizations requires a change process that is significantly different from traditional approaches.

1. LEADERSHIP VERSUS AUTHORITY. An open organization does not rely on raw authority, policy making or incentives in the usual sense. Full use of informal influence, communication, and goal setting is assumed. Various constituencies are involved in decision making.

2. SOCIOCULTURAL DEVELOPMENT VERSUS TANGIBLE DEVELOP—MENT. Development in institutions tends to deal with tangible factors—developing finances and facilities—while putting less energy into changes in sociocultural and sociopolitical forms. The open organization focuses on change in the entire sociotechnical system. Any satisfactory development plan involves *total* institutional renewal in all major aspects.

3. FULL VERSUS PARTIAL CHANGE STRATEGIES. Typical change strategies focus on a single method or innovation, shifting personnel or units on the organizational chart, responding to immediate pressures or crises, or starting new units or programs. An open organization approach involves develop-

ment in an established institution as broad as would be required in starting a new institution.

4. KNOWLEDGE APPLICATION SYSTEMS VERSUS IDENTIFICATION WITH ONE BIT OF KNOWLEDGE. Knowledge about institutions has outstripped the ability of institutions to assimilate it. Instead of focusing on a single idea which may soon be obsolete, institutions are beginning to install systems and roles (e.g., research and development) for selecting, introducing, and adapting a wide variety of ideas and practices. There are countless advances in technology, media, and community organization. The most needed change, however, is the introducing of generic methods and mechanisms for using existing knowledge and tools. Two such methods, management science and organization development, will be described in chapter 5.

5. SOPHISTICATED VERSUS SIMPLE CHANGE MODELS. Changes are complex social processes. Major theories of political science, anthropology, sociology, social psychology, and psychology underlie literature on planned change. Planned change usually involves risk, conflict, and ambiguity during initial stages. The pain and danger accompanying such change is matched, however, by the cost of changes forced upon an unprepared institution. Paradoxically, organizations undergoing change will have more conflict, mobilization, and confusion, yet be better "managed" than organizations that don't deal with change.

6. CHANGE-WEIGHTED VERSUS STABILITY-WEIGHTED ORGANIZA-TIONS. Some consider concepts like "planned change" or "change agents" undesirable because they appear to value change itself. In our view, however, a bias toward change and creation of special mechanisms to promote it are necessary in order to have some control over the course of events. Organizations tend to drift toward an irrational and dangerous status quo reinforced by bureaucracy. Planned change assumes organizational lag and sets up mechanisms to counteract it. An ongoing capacity for constructive change is an important goal for the organization of tomorrow.

Despite the increasing problems of bureaucracies and the value of planning for change, most American institutions and industries remain trapped in a bureaucratic pyramid. Profit organizations have developed ways of periodically counteracting disadvantages of traditional structures. Nonprofit organizations have suffered visibly from inability to respond to environmental change. Both profit and nonprofit organizations cling to stability and certainty whenever possible, rather than risking the uncertainty of fundamental change.

Any organization intending a course of change will meet resistance from its members. For example, when an organization studies itself to reshape divisions, departments, and relationships between groups, a rash of destructive behavior is likely. Rumors may fly about the personal conduct of certain individuals. Those professing to favor a proposed change may work feverishly behind the scenes to protect the status quo. They fear change as punitive. They expect, often correctly, that change will create more work and more diffuse roles, the need to develop new skills, or the loss of power, status, and prestige. People in charge of planning for change are likely to be seen as villains. Resistance leaders will try to discredit them, and through them, proposed changes.

Under the stress of anticipated change, people who are usually rational may act in irrational, counterproductive ways. Their defensive behavior is often caused by fear of losing prestige, power, or control in the organization. In short, they assume that showing weakness will be threatening to others and destructive to themselves. They are probably wrong. People seldom compete in areas of recognized weakness; they are more likely to feel threatened by strengths rather than weaknesses of peers and subordinates. Usually, when secrets are out, the results are positive in the long run. People who open up enable others to know them better, appreciate their strengths, and reward them with acceptance and inclusion (Jourard, 1964).

ACTION STEPS FOR CHANGE

An organization, then, must prepare for the likelihood that initiating change will bring feelings of threat, fear of punishment, and defensive behavior among members. Such effects can be lessened and ultimately overcome, however, by understanding these aspects of human behavior and by introducing change gradually. This book offers a step-by-step approach to involving members of an organization in change toward greater openness. These steps are:

1. USE A THEORY OR A MODEL AS A BASIS FOR DIAGNOSIS, DECISIONS ABOUT INTERVENTIONS, AND EVALUATION OF PROGRESS. We have already emphasized the importance of having a framework to set boundaries and direction for change and have described the model we use.

2. IDENTIFY AND EXAMINE VALUES OF THE ORGANIZATION AND ITS MEMBERS. No person or organization can be value-free. Values are not only inherent in an organization's or person's perspective, but also have a profound influence upon goals and behavior. As noted earlier, today's workers have diverse and frequently conflicting values. Clarification of values is essential if the needs and wants of organizations, members, and the environment are to be integrated.

3. BUILD A CLIMATE OF TRUTH AND TRUST WITHIN WORKING GROUPS. Developing trust and open exchange of information within working units is a potent way to minimize stress and defensiveness toward organization change. It is also an essential foundation for openness throughout a system. Once trust and candidness have been built up, work units will gain the self-confidence and skills necessary to implement change on a continuous basis.

4. WORK THROUGH THE EXISTING POWER STRUCTURE. Leaders must make use of the power of official structures—board members, community and political leaders, and managers. In addition, leaders must involve unofficial power structure in gathering data and soliciting support for change.

5. TAKE ACCOUNT OF AND USE THE EXISTING MANAGEMENT STRUCTURES. Second-order change must embrace all facets of the existing structure—all subunits, operations, constituents, intergroup relationships, personal relationships, and organization identity. However, the opening-up process does not seek to eliminate all bureaucratic features, nor does it necessarily imply changes in formal organizational structures. Rather, it aims to help them function effectively to increase the organization's unity and internal and external responsiveness.

6. GENERATE ENERGY FOR CHANGE THROUGH SHARED GOAL SETTING AND PROGRESSIVE ACHIEVEMENT OF GOALS. Whatever the organization's needs, development begins by appraising where the organization is and where it wants to be, and by progressive accomplishment toward selected goals. Systematic progress is made by stepping carefully from one milestone to the next. In a changing environment some ideal goals will never be reached. However, failure to achieve goals is not tragic. What is tragic is failure to set goals and to renew, clarify, and systematically approach them.

7. USE ACTION RESEARCH TEAMS TO RESOLVE PROBLEMS AND MAKE CHANGES. An action research team is a group of key organization members selected to study a problem and initiate appropriate solutions. Its function is to define problems, collect data on them, interpret data, make recommendations, and implement or facilitate recommended changes. The action research team then evaluates results and uses this data as a basis for further planning.

Action research teams are a high-impact, low-cost vehicle for change. Team membership includes insiders closely involved with all significant aspects of the problem. They are likely to take seriously the data they have collected and shared. And as insiders, they have more immediate influence with peers affected by the problem than an external consultant would.

8. DEVELOP OPEN SYSTEM MANAGERS. The organization of tomorrow must learn to develop a supportive, flexible climate able to deal effectively with uncertainty. The challenge will not be management of a bureaucracy, but management of a more open system. In a complex, changing environment, capable leaders will be required to mobilize an organization's resources in accord with its purpose and, in the context, with data from all sources relevant to the organization. Leaders must be able to represent organization purposes in persuasive ways and to focus energies on achieving goals. They must also be able to involve both organization members and external constituents in constructive contributions to organization efforts. Strong, open leadership is an essential ingredient of lasting change.

GETTING STARTED

No organization is completely closed or open; these are simply the extremes of a continuum. Where is your organization on this continuum—how open are its people, structures, and processes? Figure 3 identifies some characteristic patterns of open and closed organizations. It can serve as a basis for reflection and discussion. You can also convert the list into a self-assessment instrument by placing each pair of items at the poles of a seven-point scale.

An Open Organization is more likely to:	A Closed Organization is more likely to:
• Treat top positions in the hierarchy as broader in scope and more integrative in function but not implying overall personal superiority;	• Treat occupants of top business as if they possessed overall personal authority (omniscience, omnipotence);
• Seek external feedback and respond flexibly in light of the organization's mission;	• Avoid external feedback so as to avoid inconvenient changes in the status quo;
• Base itself on higher motives (self-actualization, a desire to know and contribute);	• Base itself on lower motives (personal safety, comfort);
• Encourage an overlap in planning and implementing;	• Make a sharp distinction between planning and implementing;
• View top-level decisions as hypotheses subject to review and revision at lower echelons;	• View top-level decisions as final unless review is initiated by the top-level staff;
• Structure itself by temporary task forces, functional linkages, broad role definitions, mobile and regional property, brief amendable constitution;	• Structure itself by permanent departments and echelons, fixed property, permanent detailed constitution and and bylaws;
• Set an atmosphere which is goal-oriented, challenging yet informal;	• Set an atmosphere which is routine-oriented, deadening, formalistic;
• Manage through supportive use of authority, i.e., encourage experimentation, learn from errors, emphasize personnel development, use resources, tolerate ambiguity;	• Manage through intimidating use of authority, i.e., create caution and fear of errors, emphasize personnel selection, conserve resources, and avoid ambiguity;
• Communicate up, down and across— unlimited chain of command. Promote an interactive mode.	• Communicate one-way, downward through the chain of command–-all other communication viewed as insubordinate.

Figure 3. Patterns of Open and Closed Organizations

In Part IV, you will find two other tools useful for assessing the current situation of your organization: *A Leader Checklist*, on page 183, lists effective open systems behaviors. You can use the list to assess your present approaches to working with others. *A Self-Appraisal Form,* on page 184, identifies areas of personal growth which can lead to enhancing the work situation for managers, leaders, staff, employees, or clientele. The items are taken from Carl Rogers's (1961) chapter, "Characteristics of the Helping Relationship." They make an excellent checklist of the personal traits of an open person.

PART II

Foundations of the Open Organization

2

VALUES

NEITHER ORGANIZATION NOR personal openness exists in a vacuum. Both are based upon fundamental beliefs about what is "true" and "desirable" in personal life and in organized human enterprise. Openness is grounded in actively chosen values and directed toward the achievement of carefully selected goals: it is both purposive and sensitive to context.

The best organizations are more than means or tools to be used and disposed of at will. Like an elegant cathedral, or a well-planned city, they embody the greatest values of humankind. Their values are the basis of both unity and excellence.

Open organizations have certain core values that enable them to maintain unity and provide fulfillment for both members and the organization itself. Moving toward open organizations involves identifying and examining values as a part of clarifying goals. Planning goals and strategies for implementing them must then involve synchronizing individual and organization values.

This chapter will show how an organization's values relate to its unity and potential for openness. We will identify essential core values of open organizations, based upon biological and psychological research and upon systems theory. Then, we will identify dysfunctional and constructive values for managers and consultants moving toward open systems. Finally, we will introduce two self-assessment instruments to help group and organization leaders begin the process of clarifying values.

Values Have Power in Organizations

Values are beliefs about what is desirable and worthy in life; they are based upon our most fundamental understanding of the kind of world we live in.

In this book, we will define values as

> broad, fundamental norms which are generally shared by members of a society or sub-group, and which serve to integrate as well as to guide and channel the organized activities of the members, in part by giving rise to complexes of derivative norms regulating functionally important areas of life. (Gould and Kolb, 1964, p. 744)

Rokeach (1969) has distinguished between two different but related kinds of values, *instrumental* and *terminal,* which may be held by individuals, groups, or organizations.

An *instrumental value* is a single belief about a desirable general mode of conduct. It generally takes the following form: "I believe that such-and-such a mode of conduct (for example, honesty, ambition, or courage) is personally and socially preferable in all situations with respect to all objects." A *terminal value* is a belief about a desired end state of existence. It generally takes a comparable form: "I believe that such-and-such an end-state of existence (for example, a sense of accomplishment, salvation, national security, or a world at peace) is personally and socially worth striving for" (p. 160). We will refer to instrumental values as *process values* and to terminal values as *outcome values.*

An organization's understanding of its purpose or mission is based upon underlying beliefs about desirable outcomes of the organization's activities, and about worthy ways of accomplishing these outcomes. These beliefs constitute a set of values which may or may not be verbalized. When these values are understood and shared by members, they provide the basis for cohesive work groups and a unified organizational effort.

Different types of organizations have different sets of outcome and process values. Legal institutions espouse some conception of justice and order; hospitals a conception of health; schools a conception of truth and knowledge; churches a conception of salvation, brotherhood, and sisterhood; and industries a conception of profit or profitability. The outcome values of organizations usually point toward beneficiaries other than paid leaders and workers. For industry, the beneficiaries are customers; for hospitals, patients; for schools and colleges, students. For some commonwealth institutions, society is the presumed but somewhat vague beneficiary. Process values underlie an organization's conception of worker motivation and role, and its philosophy and strategies of management, as well as its use of material resources. An organization with high unity has consistent outcome and process values.

At their inception, organizations usually give much attention and energy to clarifying their purpose and underlying values, and to integrating organizational values with those of individual members. Eventually, however, an organization may lose the original meaning of the values in its basic mandate, charter, mission, or purpose. Without shared values, a large complex organization loses the basis for unifying its parts. The various parts become fragmented, each pursuing its own tasks and objectives. For example, a university may become a multiversity composed of isolated, competing departments, each with its own budget demands and notion of "higher education." In a private industry, manufacturing units and data processing units may be at war over the best ways to use data for solving problems and monitoring production rates and outcomes.

Along with the loss of unity and cohesion comes a tendency to forget the intended beneficiary. Justice gives way to the convenience of lawyers, judges, and clerks; industry to profit at the expense of environmental and consumer needs; patient health and well-being to the convenience of doctors, nurses, and technicians; student learning to the career ambitions of teachers. The organization no longer responds meaningfully to its environment.

To perceive and describe these tendencies is not to judge a particular person or occupation. Healthy organizations do not come about automatically. Complex human systems for cooperation and consensus must be continually reintegrated because unity of human effort is an achievement—a product of unifying structures and values.

Organizations, then, have underlying values, and the question of the worth of an organization's goals can never be value-free. Nor can the values themselves be evaluated upon some objective, scientific basis. Although values may be studied scientifically, in organizations a consensus on values is not achieved through scientific proof (unless the overriding value of that particular organization is scientific precision, in which case it will have to convince members that the values were "scientifically" arrived at). Clarifying and improving values for individuals and organizations involves subtle processes of symbolizing, communicating, and persuading.

For centuries, organizations have found buildings, pictures, ceremonies, rituals, songs, and banners as necessary as written documents, if not superior to them. The values of an organization may also be partially expressed or embodied in its leader—not so much in the particular person as in the symbolic nature of his or her office. The embodiment of values in a leader is not necessarily self-serving; it can be an effective way to build an organization's unity by gaining consensus about values.

Values in Open and Closed Organizations

Given that values have an ever-present and powerful impact on organizational functioning, what kind of values are most characteristic of open organizations? Our best clues come from a comparative study of human personalities at both extremes of the open and closed continuum, and from research on modes of human perception and thought, as well as from the principles of organizational dynamics derived from general systems theory.

OPEN AND CLOSED PERSONALITIES

In 1972, A. P. MacDonald correlated a list of thirty-six process and outcome values identified by Rokeach (1969, 1973) with measures of rigidity, authoritarianism, and ambiguity tolerance. He discovered that certain values correlated positively with the closed personality characteristics of rigidity and authoritarianism and others with the open personality characteristic of ambiguity tolerance.

High cognitive *rigidity* was found to be significantly associated with placing a higher value on being ambitious, capable, clean, honest, logical, obedient, polite, responsible, and self-controlled, and a lower value on broad-mindedness. High cognitive rigidity was also significantly associated with placing a higher value on family security and salvation, and a lower value on an exciting life.

High *authoritarianism* was found to be significantly correlated with placing a higher value on being ambitious, clean, obedient, and polite, and a lower value on being broad-minded. High authoritarianism was also associated with valuing a comfortable life, family security, national security, salvation, and social standing, and with placing a lower value on equality.

High *tolerance for ambiguity* was found to be significantly associated with placing a higher value on being broad-minded and imaginative, and a lower value on being ambitious, capable, clean, obedient, polite, and responsible. Also, high tolerance for ambiguity was negatively associated with desires for having a comfortable life, family security, national security, and salvation (MacDonald, 1972).

SELF-ACTUALIZATION AND BEING-VALUES

Much of what early psychology learned about motivation and personality came from experiments with animals or the mentally ill. Abraham Maslow determined to study outstanding personalities to learn more about the positive potential of human beings. His study of the continuum of human needs underlying personal values sheds more light upon values characteristic of open and closed persons and organizations.

Maslow (1943) developed a *need hierarchy* theory of human motivation. This theory holds that as human beings, we have certain basic needs which must be fulfilled if we are to survive and grow normally. He arranged these needs in a pyramid with the most essential need category, the physiological (food, water, rest, elimination, air), at the bottom. His hierarchy is presented in figure 4. Human beings faced with the need for physiological survival are bound to place a high value upon the material means of ensuring survival. When basic needs at this level are met satisfactorily, however, they become aware of needs for love and self-esteem, and act to meet these needs.

Maslow went a step further than Freud and the behaviorists, proposing that there are still higher levels of needs and values that go beyond love and esteem. He identified these needs by studying the special characteristics of great persons whom he called *self-actualizers.* These persons developed a human potential far beyond what is considered "normal"—not related to high IQ, but to being fully human. They represented the best human specimens, not the average. They seemed to focus less upon survival values and more upon intrinsic values such as beauty, uniqueness, justice, and the like. Maslow called these *being-values* (B-values) because they are related to intrinsic experiences of being fully alive as opposed to mere assurance of bodily and psychic survival (Maslow, 1971). A complete list of being-values appears in table 2, at the end of this chapter.

Being-values are not only characteristic of self-actualizing people, but also of *peak experiences,* moments of sudden insight, ecstasy, and inner peace experienced by most persons at various times through life. Being-values are also characteristics of great art and religion. They are what we all deeply yearn for, the ultimate satisfiers, and the highest source of a sense of fulfillment. They may be discovered through meditation or psychotherapy. And they are expressed in some human organizations more than in others.

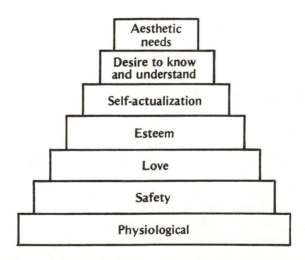

Figure 4. Maslow's Need Hierarchy

Reprinted from "A theory of human motivation" by A. H. Maslow, *Psychological review,* 1943, *50,* 370–396

Unfortunately, most popular usage of the need hierarchy stops with the levels of belonging and self-esteem, with only vague reference to self-actualization, as though it were equivalent either to "doing your own thing," or to an elite spirituality unrelated to daily realities. On the contrary, the self-actualizing people studied by Maslow were not self-centered, idealistic social isolates or selfish pleasure seekers. They had a combination of characteristics similar to those of open organizations: a strong sense of commitment to a calling or purpose based upon being-values, awareness of internal motivations and feelings, and active involvement with the events and people about them. In terms of MacDonald's personality traits, self-actualizers have a high tolerance for ambiguity. They are open to a diversity of ways to achieve higher needs. As the being-value "dichotomy-transcendence" (table 2) indicates, they value the creative synthesis of opposites into a new whole, rather than feeling forced to choose one and reject the other.

While the people whom Maslow studied were a minority in the population, they represent a potential toward which ordinary individuals can grow through the stages of self-discovery, self-fulfillment, and self-actualization. Indeed, as Maslow observed, many frustration illnesses of modern people do not arise from deprivation of lower needs—not even self-esteem—let alone of physiological needs. Rather, we suffer from fixation on lower or more primary needs, so we are prevented from moving on to higher needs. Maslow called the fixation upon a lower need a *metapathology*. (See table 2 for a list of metapathologies.) These are a major cause of sickness or failure in our lives.

BRAIN RESEARCH AND INTUITIVE THINKING

The kind of thinking characteristic of Maslow's subjects went beyond analysis to include creative ways of combining things which seem very different. His work has been corroborated by recent brain research, which has thrown more light upon the human potential for creative thinking and problem solving.

Since 1950, neurological researchers have been studying how specialized mental functions are localized in various areas of the brain. Their research has indicated that the left and right hemispheres differ in their styles of information processing, in the way they "see" and "think."

The left hemisphere of the brain not only seems to specialize in language, but also to perform linear, analytical, mathematical, sequential, and logical computations. Bogen (1977) called this hemisphere the "propositional" side of the brain. It seeks out details rather than perceiving wholes. It thinks in terms of categories and cause-effect relations in methodical steps. As David Galin (1977) points out, this

> verbal-analytic style is extremely efficient for dealing with the object world. Our modern technology, standard of living, and scientific achievements depend heavily on highly developed linear, analytic methods. (p. 29)

The right hemisphere, in contrast, has been dubbed the "appositional" hemisphere, since it appears to think nonlinearly and holistically in terms of "pictures" or gestalts:

> It is particularly good at grasping patterns of relations. This mode of thinking seems to integrate many inputs simultaneously, rather than operating on them one at a time, sequentially, like the analytic mode. This is important for the many situations in which the essential meaning is given by the overall pattern of relations between the elements, not by the elements themselves.... The holistic mode of information processing is very good for bridging gaps; we can perceive a pattern even when some of the pieces are missing. In contrast, a logical, sequential mode cannot skip over gaps. Since we are usually trying to operate in this world with incomplete information, we very badly need to have the capacity to perceive general patterns and jump across gaps in present knowledge. (Galin, 1977, p. 30)

Left hemisphere thinking has been of great value in enabling the personal, individual survival of human beings, the most pressing need for most of our history. It has led to the development of advanced industrial and technological societies in which the availability of food and shelter and the biological survival of the race have become technically assured. At the same time, the great emphasis in western societies upon left brain activity has resulted in a general cultural devaluation of right brain activity—of intuition, creativity, and holistic thinking about the world as a network of interdependent relationships. The philosophy accompanying this emphasis could be summed up as "every man for himself, and it will all come out all right." As we have noted, this kind of closed thinking is now being challenged by societal and world-wide problems that can only be solved by a collaborative, other-oriented approach. What is now needed, according to Robert Ornstein (1976) is

> a shift in mode of consciousness by many people away from the egocentric, individual focus toward one geared more to overall relationships between entities. Such an "emergent" consciousness could convey a more comprehensive perspective of the life and action of an individual and of a group, as well as the relationship among seemingly disparate activities and systems. (p. 34)

Creative, holistic thinking and problem solving is a potential in everyone. This potential must be tapped in order to solve the complex problems facing modern organizations. We are not saying that right brain thinking is the only kind needed for development of open organizations. We need both kinds of thinking; they are complementary, and they can work together to help us plan for the future. However, in view of the past devaluation of intuitive thinking, an organization moving toward openness needs to give special emphasis to this mode of thinking, encourage its development through training, and its application to appropriate situations and problems.

ORGANIZATION VALUE PROFILES

Like individuals, organizations base their values on fundamental understandings of the nature of people, the world, and human enterprise. The typology of three organization value profiles, Theories X, Y, and Z, will illustrate this point. These are three belief and value systems of organizations which have been identified by MacGregor (1960) and Maslow (1971). *Theory X* views employees as unmotivated to productivity, averse to taking responsibility, working only for monetary reward, and needing close supervision. Given the disposition of the employees, managers must impose their values of order and productivity if the organization is to function effectively. *Theory Y*, by contrast, views employees as self-motivated and creative under the right conditions, willing to share in and be involved with the organization's values and goals. Given the capacity of workers for active participation, managers must provide mechanisms for shared consensus building and decision making that will make most effective use of employees as a resource.

Theory Z views both employees and managers as capable of working together, based on shared values and common purpose. It has characteristics of both X and Y. Like X, the Z manager is a strong leader, but the basis for leadership is different. This manager leads by virtue of special competencies and the ability to elicit and represent the system's core values. Like Y, the Z manager takes into account the values of the people with whom he or she is working, but may or may not emphasize open debate, consensus building, voting, or the like. The key is consent of employees to the purpose and values of the organization and their roles in it. By leading according to shared values and a common purpose, the Z manager has access to the full range of leader behaviors and selects from them according to the specific situation. Table 3 summarizes the characteristics of these three organization value orientations.

CORE VALUES OF AN OPEN ORGANIZATION

What, can we conclude, must be the core values of an open organization? According to our model, open organizations operate on the basis of two core values: the "worthiness" of outcome goals and "openness" of process goals.

Worthiness. As we have seen, the basis for organization unity in an open system is a well-defined and worthy mission, with an accompanying set of agreed-upon goals. A weakness of many managerial goal-setting processes is the assumption that a goal will be effective if it is clearly expressed in written language. To be operationally effective, however, goals must also be perceived as worthy by members: they must be felt, embodied, symbolized, visualized. They are feelings as well as ideas. Effective goal setting includes not only procedures such as management by objectives which enable clarity, but also measures which permit sharing and symbolizing of underlying values which give meaning to goals.

TABLE 3
Types of Leaders and Organizations

	Theory X	Theory Y	Theory Z
Needs	Physiological, safety, security	Belonging, esteem	B–values, meta-needs
Process depended upon	Power	Leadership	Devotion to B–values
Employee's orientation	Obedience, personal dependency	Task performance and participation in decision making	Admiration for and acceptance of leader's superior devotion or competence
Morale measure	Compliance	Motivation	Commitment to B–values

Adapted from *The farther reaches of human nature* by A. H. Maslow. New York: Viking Press, 1971

Open organizations also tend toward the formulation of multidimensional outcome goals including both survival values and higher being-values which respond to the needs of the environment. That is, they are not simply reducible to a single, quantifiable bottom line. Certainly, effective voluntary and service organizations work toward multidimensional outcomes that enhance the quality of life for their clients and society. In contrast, profit-making organizations depend upon profit as a quantifiable, univariable outcome measure of their effectiveness. Yet, even in the private sector, an open organization acknowledges other important values such as delivery of quality products and services, contributions to the well-being of local communities, maintenance of the natural environment, and funding of cultural or educational enterprises. These broader concerns run through United States history. For example, the people who developed the midwestern "breadbasket" built farms, colleges, and churches almost simultaneously. Even today, Iowa still supports thirty-three private colleges and thirty-two public colleges—a legacy of entrepreneur farmers' concept of profit. Peter Drucker (1968) incorporates within his notion of "profitability" this possibility of formulating goals that include a number of higher values.

Even when an organization does choose one bottom line, it should be carefully evaluated and well measured. Examples of univariable outcomes that went astray include body counts as a measure of success in Vietnam and the gross national product as a measure of quality of life. In most cases, a univariable outcome is no substitute for multidimensional measures continuously evaluated by a responsible group or person.

Openness. For an open organization, openness is an essential value underlying all others. It is reflected in tolerance for diversity and creativity in setting and achieving goals. Referring to table 4, we see the being-values "richness" and "simplicity." Though these seem to be opposites, we would expect to find that both are permitted at various times within an open organization. By contrast, a closed system tends to focus on one process value, such as simplicity. In an organization, simplicity might be equated with efficiency, which leads to a single outcome goal such as profit.

Openness as a core value leads to formulation of process goals which take the developmental needs of workers and of the organization into account. An excellent example is the unit method of production used by Volvo. This method satisfies the needs of employees for responsibility, mastery, and pride in their work, while also meeting organization needs for efficient production. A number of other companies such as Roche Pharmaceuticals and Sony are known for similarly innovative job enrichment methods.

Values Harmful and Helpful in Moving Toward Open Organizations

The integration of organization and individual goals and values is a prime means of moving toward fully developed organizations which are both productive and highly satisfying to employees. People seeking to develop such organizations must work toward core values of worthiness and open process. What personal and professional values will enable them to bring about effective change? First we will look at some values that hinder progress. Then, we will describe constructive process values for consultants and managers and the kinds of interventions they require.

DYSFUNCTIONAL INTERVENTION VALUES

1. PRESERVING A NONVALUE VALUE. Some consultants or leaders try to be value free. In staying at the supposedly operational or practical level, they force the organization to be unconscious of its purposes and values—and of their values as well. The organization accepts their values uncritically and compliantly. This situation leads the members to a declining sense of worthiness in their work. Often the only values that remain are preservation of existing organization structures and processes, and personal economic success.

2. MAINTAINING AN ANTIORGANIZATION VALUE. Typical of outsiders, nonmanagers, or psychologists, this view tends to equate the realization of human potential with freedom from formal organization structures and processes. Supposedly, the smaller the organization and the more personal the relationships, the more "human" the situation. This view prevents making the organization synergic with human potential. Organization structures and procedures can be either positive or negative in their impact on various human values such as health, cooperation, intellectual development, and social life. Much literature criticizing bureaucracy seems to be attacking organized enterprise as such. What we need is not less organization, but more humanistic and suitable organization—that is, open systems.

3. OVERVALUING HIERARCHY AS THE LOCUS OF ORGANIZATIONAL IDENTITY. The authority structure of an organization is only one facet of its identity. That structure may take several forms; a chain of command is only one possibility. Except in rare cases, such as a charismatic movement or a one-owner company, it is faulty to locate organizational identity exclusively in the offices or people at the top. The identity of a healthy organization has many facets—legal, historical, social, economic, and cultural.

4. VALUING PROCESS OVER CONTENT. In the early practice of organization development, behavioral scientists thought they could identify and deal separately with human relations, attitudinal, communication, and team-building processes. Others, such as lawyers, industrial engineers, architects, economists, and planners, could deal with product, mission, structure, facilities, and the work itself. No longer can we maintain such a distinction between process and content. No separable "human" side of the organization exists. The entire organization, including its most tangible and technical aspects, is a human creation embodying human values. It will ultimately be evaluated for its significance to human beings. Furthermore, all human relations and attitudes depend on the task and work context. It is especially dangerous to separate content and process if the organization's product is a human resource or human development service in such fields as health, education, welfare, religion, and government. This principle is also applicable to profit-making corporations, although to a lesser extent. Thus, to diagnose an organization accurately, we must take into account its particular products, missions, technical systems, structures, and markets. No one process indicator—no management style or climate—is appropriate to all organizations.

5. TAKING EITHER STABILITY OR CHANGE AS AN UNQUALIFIED VALUE. We stated in chapter 1 that the movement toward open organizations should be weighted in favor of change, in the light of the demands placed on modern organizations by a rapidly changing environment. Nevertheless, constructive organization development also involves appreciating, conserving, and strengthening whatever is authentic in the present organization. This involves both change and preservation. Change is not necessarily needed in every situation. And changes can be negative as well as positive. Thus we cannot equate open systems with newness. Nor is the effective manager or

consultant necessarily a "change agent." Some organizations have been decimated and confused by providing themselves as guinea pigs for too many change agents and change programs.

6. IMPOSING PRIMARY GROUP VALUES ON ORGANIZATIONS. If someone wants primarily to help individuals, he or she can find individual clients. However, if an organization is the client, the task is to help it and thereby help individuals. A typical error of those in personnel or training is to overplay personnel factors and personality characteristics.

Just as the popular press tends to personify the United States government in the presidency, we often fantasize: "If we could just get rid of manager X and have Y instead." Often we are dismayed when the new person produces little improvement. Perhaps we should consider structural factors. Another related error is to overplay aggregate individual attitudes, such as morale. Though important, these are not synonymous with a healthy organization.

7. RELYING EXCLUSIVELY ON A SINGLE VIEW, SYSTEM, OR TECHNIQUE. One danger is to value a single answer to all organization problems. There are many fields and persons who specialize in the care and feeding of organizations. Since all seek niches for their products, organizations are in danger of being dominated by a single segment. The panorama of advice is too valuable to ignore altogether, and too expensive and inconsistent to be followed in its entirety.

8. VALUING A SINGLE, QUANTIFIABLE OUTCOME MEASURE. We have already mentioned that a profit-making organization can appropriately slant all effort to a single, quantifiable outcome—at least as a measure of economic accountability to stockholders. This use of a single measure may come under more challenge in the future, but for the present, it is of primary importance in the profit sector. Unfortunately, this approach is patently not applicable in the nonprofit sector. In an effort to simplify planning and management, voluntary and service organizations may attempt to define their goals in unidimensional, quantifiable terms. Such an attempt only causes rigidity or confusion.

9. VALUING DISPENSABILITY OF ORGANIZATIONS. Those who hold this value, a particular form of antiorganization bias, see a given organization as a temporary means to an end in pursuit of a larger agenda held by a cadre of organizers. Although this view may be appropriate for a small, short-lived or letterhead organization, it can be destructive when an organization has developed special assets and a unique heritage. For example, when two organizations merge into a new organization, unique and valuable assets tied to the old identities may be lost.

CONSTRUCTIVE VALUES FOR CONSULTANTS

Originally the term *organizational development* (OD) was closely connected with laboratory training, a method. As the meaning of OD has evolved, it has come to include a panorama of concepts and intervention methods drawn from management science and behavioral science. Though its public image remains more restricted, in the generic sense OD means all approaches for developing organizations.

Whatever their concepts and methods, organization development practitioners have tended to have common values. They have been prone to question the bureaucratic model. In emphasizing integration of people needs and organization needs, they have often focused on the personally constraining or deadening aspects of bureaucracies. Tannenbaum, Davis, and Schmidt (1970) have summarized values shared by many practitioners in the form of direction "away from _____" and "toward _____." They express the ideal OD practitioner's values this way to emphasize that they are tendencies, not outcome goals. These are in summary the beliefs of practitioners holding the ideal basic values necessary to successful OD leadership:

- People can be trusted, are intrinsically good, and are simply human beings, all continually growing.
- All people possess individual differences that can be accepted and used both in personal life and on the job.
- Appropriate expression of feelings should be permitted and effectively used, with authentic behavior encouraged.
- Status is useful for relevant purposes of the organization.
- Openness and confrontation in connection with relevant data are healthy, as is appropriate risk taking.
- Process work is essential to doing a job effectively, particularly when competition is eliminated to favor collaboration.

How do consultants express and advocate open systems values in working with client organizations, without undermining the active role organizations play in solving their own problems? Gordon and Ronald Lippitt (1978b) have addressed this issue by distinguishing between content and process advocacy. They characterize a *content advocate* as one who will "attempt a conscious influence on choice of goals and means," whereas a *process advocate* is one who

> will attempt a conscious influence on the methodology underlying the client's problem-solving behavior. For example, a process advocate might suggest an open meeting rather than a closed one, in order to increase trust in the system. In this sense, the advocate-consultant is less concerned with what is specifically said at the meeting than with the general method or approach to the meeting itself. (p. 32)

When working for the development of open organizations, consultants function primarily as process advocates by modeling and by teaching an open-systems approach to diagnosis, communication, problem solving, planning, and evaluation. They may teach by making an open process contract with the client organization, disclosing the open systems model as the rationale for process interventions, and training staff in requisite skills. The consultant models open processes by being an open-minded, other-oriented person tolerant of ambiguity and respectful of the culture and values unique to each institution. He or she can assume a number of different roles, some directive and some more passive, depending upon circumstances and the developmental stage of involvement with the client. The consultant believes that given sufficient information, trust, and skills, an organization can solve its own problems, define the worthiness of its own mission, and set its own goals. However, this consultant does not contract to work with an organization which only seeks reinforcement of a closed situation or set of values.

MANAGER VALUES AND STYLES

Making behavior congruent with values requires involvement, growth, and commitment of people. It requires not only an attitude of consent, but also the necessary knowledge and skills. For example, many managers affirm in principle the organization development values of trust, collaboration, risk taking, confrontation, and authenticity, but they need to develop skills to practice these values in specific daily organization situations.

Leaders are often constrained by what they think is a required style. In our consulting relationships, we have noticed that managers tend to value realistic, down-to-earth approaches and to feel a strong need to control others. We have used many psychological tests to help managers become more aware of their styles and underlying values, and to explore other options. Two especially useful instruments have been the *FIRO-B* (Schutz, 1958) and the *Myers-Briggs Type Indicator (MBTI)* (Myers, 1962).

The FIRO-B and Manager Needs. The *FIRO-B* assesses interpersonal behavior in terms of needs which are being fulfilled. It measures six needs: needs to express control, inclusion and affection toward others, and needs to receive control, inclusion and affection from others. Having tested many groups of managers, we have noted that the typical manager scores unusually high on the need to control others and low on all five other needs, particularly affection needs. This unusual emphasis upon one need to the exclusion of the others suggests a new look at leadership styles.

High control is appropriate when the situation calls for mastery of the subject matter, values, roles, and competencies—as with the Theory Z leader. But if, as in the case of the Theory X leader, the high control is simply a personality need, it is more likely to be dysfunctional to the organization and the people in it. Although control may indeed be important, why should other equally legitimate needs be neglected? We need to distinguish between a control need which is required by the situation and one which is part of a personality imbalance within a manager.

Myers-Briggs Type Indicator and the Manager Personality. The *Myers-Briggs Type Indicator* is designed to help people identify preferred ways of perceiving, thinking, and problem solving (Myers, 1962, 1976, in press). The *MBTI* is based on C. G. Jung's theory of psychological types which states that individuals choose among different ways of taking in information and different ways of making decisions (Jung, 1971). There are certain modes they prefer to use, although they are capable of using all the modes. There are two ways of *perceiving,* which Jung calls sensing and intuition. Then there are two ways people organize and make decisions about their perceptions—thinking (analytical) and feeling (personal value assessment). Of these four modes of processing information, any given individual will choose one primary mode— one preferred way of perceiving or organizing data. He or she will also choose one second favorite mode known as an *auxiliary* process. One of the favorites will be chosen from the sensing–intuition pair, and the other from the thinking–feeling pair.

People also choose from two ways of relating to their world—*extraversion* or *introversion,* and two styles of life—*judging* (control through planning), or *perception* (flexible, spontaneous adaptation to events). Thus, the *MBTI* presents four pairs of preferences from which sixteen different personality types may be formed. The preference pairs are summarized in figure 5.

FOUR PREFERENCES ARE SCORED TO ARRIVE AT A PERSON'S TYPE

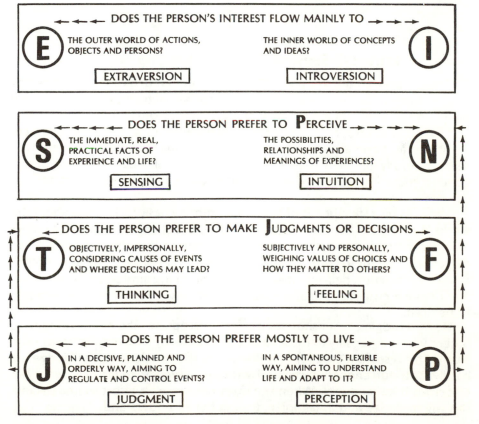

Figure 5. *MBTI* **Preference Pairs**

From "Myers-Briggs type indicator: understanding the type table," copyright© 1976 by Mary H. McCaulley, Director, Center for Applications of Psychological Type, Gainesville, Florida. Reprinted by permission of Mary McCaulley

Chief executive officers and other managers, expecially in the fields of business and economics, are often ESTJ or ENTJ types—preferring extraversion, sensing or intuition, thinking, and judgment. On the other hand, artists, writers and psychotherapists are often the INFP type—preferring introversion, intuition, feeling, and perception. This is only a tendency, as all sixteen types are found in occupations when sizeable samples have been studied. However, every field attracts some types more than others. Although ESTJ and ENTJ qualities are valuable in management positions, these managers can benefit greatly from appreciating and using the resources of other psychological types. When team members have contrasting preferences in gathering and processing information, work may be accomplished more creatively and productively. Table 4 summarizes some benefits of cross-type interactions.

Composite summary descriptions of a typical manager type ESTJ and an opposite type INFP follow. As you read them, think of the strengths and weaknesses of each type combination, and how they can complement each other.

Extravert–Sensing–Thinking–Judging (ESTJ)*

The extraverted thinker uses thinking to run as much of the world as may be hers to run. She has great respect for impersonal truth, well-thought-out plans, and orderly efficiency. She is analytic, impersonal, objectively critical, and not likely to be convinced by anything but reasoning. She organizes facts, situations, and operations well in advance, and makes a systematic effort to reach carefully planned objectives on schedule. She believes everybody's conduct should be governed by logic and governs her own that way as far as she can.

She lives by a specific set of rules that embody basic judgments about the world. A change in her ways requires a conscious change in rules. She enjoys being an executive and puts a great deal of herself into the job. She likes to decide what ought to be done and to give requisite orders. She abhors confusion, inefficiency, half-way measures, and anything aimless and ineffective. She can be a crisp disciplinarian and can with ease fire someone who ought to be fired.

Being a judging type, she may neglect perception. She needs to listen to others' views, especially to those under her authority who may not respond as freely. This is seldom easy for her. But unless she can do it, she will judge too hastily, without enough facts, and without sufficient regard for what her associates think and feel. When she does not make an effort to understand, she will misjudge and antagonize. It pays her to understand.

*Adapted by permission from *The Myers-Briggs type indicator manual*, copyright© 1962 by Isabel Briggs Myers. Princeton, N.J.: Educational Testing Service

TABLE 4
Mutual Usefulness of Opposites

INTUITIVE NEEDS A SENSING TYPE:	SENSING TYPE NEEDS AN INTUITIVE:
To bring up pertinent facts	To see the possibilities
To remember things that weren't relevant at the time they happened	To supply ingenuity on problems
To read over a contract	To deal with a complexity having too many imponderables
To check records, read proof, score tests	To explain what another intuitive is talking about
To notice what ought to be attended to	To look far ahead
To inspect (stay with something into real depth)	To furnish new ideas
To keep track of detail	To "spark" things that seem impossible
To have patience	

THINKER NEEDS A FEELING TYPE:	FEELING TYPE NEEDS A THINKER:
To persuade	To analyze
To conciliate	To organize
To forecast how others will feel	To find the flaws in advance
To arouse enthusiasm	To reform what needs reforming
To teach	To weigh "the law and the evidence"
To sell	
To advertise	To hold consistently to a policy
To appreciate the thinker himself	To stand firm against opposition

Adapted from *The Myers-Briggs type indicator manual*, copyright© 1962 by Isabel Briggs Myers. Princeton, N.J.: Educational Testing Service. Used by permission

Feeling (the direct rival of thinking) is her least developed and least manageable process. If too much is suppressed, feelings gradually build up pressure and explode unexpectedly upon slight provocation. A thinker's feeling needs some positive outlet. The most serviceable one is appreciation of the qualities of others. Appreciation is harder for a thinker than for other types, because she is naturally critical. But she *can* develop it if she will make a rule to try. She will find it valuable on the job and in personal relationships.

Introvert–Intuitive–Feeling–Perceiving (INFP)*

An introverted feeling type cares deeply about a few selected things. He has warmth inside (like a fur-lined coat); it may hardly show until you get past his reserve. He is faithful to duty and obligations. He chooses his final values without reference to the judgment of outsiders and sticks to them with passionate conviction. He finds these inner loyalties and ideals hard to talk about, but they govern his life.

His outer personality is mostly traceable to his auxiliary process, intuition, and so is perceptive. He is tolerant, open-minded, understanding, flexible, and adaptable (though when one of his inner loyalties is threatened he will not give an inch). Except for his work's sake, he has little wish to impress or dominate. He prizes people who understand his values and goals.

He is twice as good when working at a job he believes in, since his feeling for it puts added energy behind his efforts. He wants his work to contribute to something that matters to him, perhaps to perfecting some product or undertaking. He wants to have a purpose beyond his paycheck, no matter how big the check. He is a perfectionist wherever his feeling is engaged, and is usually happiest at individual work involving personal values. With high ability, he may be good in literature, art, science, psychology, and any kind of teaching.

His problem is that he may feel so marked a contrast between inner ideal and outer reality as to feel inadequate, even when he is being quite as effective as the other types. If he finds no channel of expression for his ideals, he becomes too sensitive and vulnerable, losing confidence in life and in himself. If he does find active expression for his ideals, they may give him a high, self-confident drive.

Being intuitive, he sees possibilities. He likes to concentrate on a project and dislikes all details not relevant to any deep interest. He has insight and long-range vision, curiosity about new ideas, interest in books and language. Probably he has a gift of expression, especially in writing. Finally, he is ingenious and persuasive on the subject of his enthusiasms, which are quiet but deep-rooted.

*Adapted by permission from The Myers-Briggs type indicator manual, copyright© 1962 by Isabel Briggs Myers. Princeton, N.J.: Educational Testing Service

OPEN SYSTEMS MANAGERS

People who want to promote organizational openness must also confront life as candidates for self-actualization. Managers who are closed and defensive will be neither efficient nor effective. In essence, they cannot model a level of personal being or encounter which exceeds their level of psychological functioning.

No manager can possess all strengths and capabilities that exist in human potential. We have seen that managers, like everyone else, tend to have preferred styles of perceiving and relating. However, open systems managers are committed to developing capacities within themselves to which they may previously have given little attention. They collaborate with others who have complementary strengths and resources. Such a manager controls, but at the same time facilitates group creative effort. The ideal characteristics of "human development facilitators" have been identified by O'Banion (1971):

> They tolerate ambiguity; their decisions come from within rather than from without; they have a zest for life, for experiencing, for touching, tasting, feeling, knowing. They risk involvement; they reach out for experiences; they are not afraid to encounter others or themselves. They believe that man is basically good, and given the right conditions, will move in positive directions. (p. 5)

Assessing Organization Values—Some Tools

What are your values? Your organization's values? Profiles can be identified with the help of two instruments derived from the work of Rokeach, MacDonald, and Maslow. The *Values Survey,* located in part IV (pp. 187–190), was created by A. P. MacDonald (1972) from lists of instrumental (process) and terminal (outcome) values developed by Rokeach (1969, 1973). Each value on the survey is ranked for its relative importance in your life. Individual scores can be averaged to obtain a values profile for your work group or organization. Self- or group-evaluation of profiles can be initiated by noticing any apparent inconsistencies in the value rankings.

A profile can also be created from Maslow's list of being-values. The profile identifies the pattern of values in an organization or in the career of an individual. Figure 6 shows how this can be done. The seven-point scale is marked to indicate the importance of each being-value in your life or in the life of your entire organization. A wide rating spread on individual values will indicate areas of possible value conflict. Comparison of two profiles can also reveal the general degree of self-actualization. In figure 6, for example, individual or organization Y not only has a different profile from X, but is also a more self-actualizing system, as shown by the location of the entire profile closer to the high importance end of the scale.

B-VALUE

SCALE

| | Low Importance | | | | | | High Importance |

B-Value	1	2	3	4	5	6	7
Truth, honesty	1	2	3	4	5	6	7
Goodness, generosity	1	2	3	4	5	6	7
Beauty	1	2	3	4	5	6	7
Unity, wholeness	1	2	3	4	5	6	7
Dichotomy transcendence	1	2	3	4	5	6	7
Aliveness	1	2	3	4	5	6	7
Uniqueness	1	2	3	4	5	6	7
Perfection	1	2	3	4	5	6	7
Completion	1	2	3	4	5	6	7
Justice, order	1	2	3	4	5	6	7
Simplicity	1	2	3	4	5	6	7
Richness	1	2	3	4	5	6	7
Effortlessness	1	2	3	4	5	6	7
Playfulness	1	2	3	4	5	6	7
Self-sufficiency	1	2	3	4	5	6	7
Meaningfulness	1	2	3	4	5	6	7

Individual or Organization "X"   Individual or Organization "Y"

Figure 6.   Sample Being-Values Profiles

TABLE 2
B-values and Specific Metapathologies

B-Values	Pathogenic Deprivation	Specific Metapathologies
1. Truth	Dishonesty	Disbelief; mistrust; cynicism; skepticism; suspicion.
2. Goodness	Evil	Utter selfishness. Hatred; repulsion; disgust. Reliance only upon self and for self. Nihilism. Cynicism.
3. Beauty	Ugliness	Vulgarity. Specific unhappiness, restlessness, loss of taste, tension, fatigue. Philistinism. Bleakness.
4. Unity; Wholeness	Chaos. Atomism, loss of connectedness.	Disintegration; "the world is falling apart." Arbitrariness.
4a. Dichotomy-Transcendence	Black and white dichotomies. Loss of gradations, of degree. Forced polarization. Forced choices.	Black-white thinking, either/or thinking. Seeing everything as a duel or a war, or a conflict. Low synergy. Simplistic view of life.
5. Aliveness; Process	Deadness. Mechanizing of life.	Deadness. Robotizing. Feeling oneself to be totally determined. Loss of emotion. Boredom (?); loss of zest in life. Experiential emptiness.
6. Uniqueness	Sameness; uniformity; interchangeability.	Loss of feeling of self and of individuality. Feeling oneself to be interchangeable, anonymous, not really needed.
7. Perfection	Imperfection; sloppiness; poor workmanship, shoddiness.	Discouragement (?); hopelessness; nothing to work for.
7a. Necessity	Accident; occasionalism; inconsistency.	Chaos; unpredictability. Loss of safety. Vigilance.
8. Completion; Finality	Incompleteness	Feelings of incompleteness with perseveration. Hopelessness. Cessation of striving and coping. No use trying.
9. Justice	Injustice	Insecurity; anger; cynicism; mistrust; lawlessness; jungle world-view; total selfishness.
9a. Order	Lawlessness. Chaos. Breakdown of authority.	Insecurity. Wariness. Loss of safety, of predictability. Necessity for vigilance, alertness, tension, being on guard.
10. Simplicity	Confusing complexity. Disconnectedness. Disintegration.	Overcomplexity; confusion; bewilderment, conflict, loss of orientation.
11. Richness; Totality; Comprehensivenss	Poverty. Coarctation.	Depression; uneasiness; loss of interest in world.
12. Effortlessness	Effortfulness	Fatigue, strain, striving, clumsiness, awkwardness, gracelessness, stiffness.
13. Playfulness	Humorlessness	Grimness; depression; paranoid humorlessness; loss of zest in life. Cheerlessness. Loss of ability to enjoy.
14. Self-sufficiency	Contingency; accident; occasionalism.	Dependence upon (?) the perceiver (?). It becomes his responsibility.
15. Meaningfulness	Meaninglessness	Meaninglessness. Despair. Senselessness of life.

From *The farther reaches of human nature* by A. H. Maslow, pp. 318–319. Copyright© 1971 by Bertha G. Maslow. New York: Viking Press. Reprinted by permission

3

TRUTH AND TRUST

DEVELOPING AN OPEN organization requires focusing people's energies productively around commonly held purposes and goals. Organization openness becomes a reality only as face-to-face work groups achieve a team identity based upon shared goals, objectives, processes, and skills. These agreements provide the context within which the team can exchange information, discover their real purpose, settle power issues, make decisions, and evaluate results. Without a team identity, goals are diverse and work output is relatively low. Work output increases as the group achieves internal responsiveness and unity.

Trust is the key to developing effective work groups. In an open organization, teams are characterized by high personal involvement, shared information, problem-solving skills, and above all, trust. At their best, teams achieve *synergy*, a situation in which the energy flow and work output of the group surpasses in quality and quantity the sum total of the energies and resources of individual members of the group. While group members are able to work effectively at common goals, they also fulfill individual needs and values, such as self-esteem. People learn to solve their problems by understanding themselves better, and they learn to make choices that yield valued payoffs. They express themselves honestly, accept and fulfill responsibilities, and define and pursue rational goals. Groups like these have a dynamism managers dream of but seldom experience.

This chapter will explore the meaning of trust and the determinants of its development in groups. Some tools for assessing the trust level of a group will be introduced.

The Importance of Truth and Trust

From the beginning of the organization development movement, trust has been considered an essential ingredient in constructive change. Bennis (1971) aptly summarizes the importance of trust to the development of groups.

> If there is enough trust, and enough truth, most changes can take place.... [The small group model of change] relies on three things: participation of the people involved in the change...trust in the people who are the basic proponents or advocates, or leaders of the change; and thirdly, clarity about the change. (pp. 3–4)

Our experience in helping groups function effectively has shown the importance of establishing clear, operational definitions and behavior norms for the concept of trust. The lack of a consistent definition of words like *trust* may well be a reason for the failure of groups to develop cohesion.

Trust is a person's confident expectation that another person's behavior will be consistently responsive and supportive to the mutual interests of both persons. It is a belief that the other person is able and willing to act in accord with mutual norms and agreements. Two types of trust have been identified. We will define these types operationally and indicate their roles in building teams.

Contractual trust is an essential ingredient of any ongoing relationship. Rotter's concept of contractual trust is presented succinctly by MacDonald, Kessel, and Fuller (1972) as

> "an expectancy held by an individual or a group that the work, promise, verbal or written statement of another individual or group can be relied upon" (Rotter, 1967, p. 651). This definition, and the wording of the Rotter Interpersonal Trust Scale items suggests that the "trust" involved is of a contractual nature. In other words, it seems to be largely restricted to the direct or indirect, real or imagined interaction of at least two parties on at least two occasions. The first interaction involves a commitment from Party A to Party B. The second involves the fulfillment or lack of fulfillment of that commitment. (p. 144)

In Rotter's view, we trust another when we expect that if someone says he or she will do something, that person will in fact do it. In working with groups, we call this kind of trust *responsibility*—defined operationally by Glasser (1965) as the willingness to make and keep simple agreements. Contractual trust is developed through the collaborative making of task-oriented and social behavior contracts. It is relatively low risk, since it focuses upon external behavior and tangible results rather than upon attitudes, beliefs, feelings, and values. Contracting will be discussed in greater detail in chapter 8.

MacDonald, Kessell, and Fuller (1972) also identified a second type of trust, called *disclosure trust*. This kind of trust has been explored by Sidney Jourard (1964):

> A choice that confronts everyone of us at every moment is this: shall we permit our fellow men to know us as we now are, or shall we seek instead to remain an enigma, an uncertain quantity, wishing to be seen as something we are not? (p. *iii*)

Disclosure trust is the expectation that if a person communicates feelings, opinions, and values to others, they will listen with respect and caring and will not use the information to hurt the teller. There are degrees of disclosure, ranging from relatively low-risk expression of opinions and tastes to high-risk sharing of intimate beliefs and personal problems.

In certain settings such as T–groups, human relations training events, and psychotherapy groups, the disclosure of high-risk information is both appropriate and desirable. In the words of Carl Rogers (1970):

> A climate of mutual trust develops out of this mutual freedom to express real feelings, positive and negative. Each member moves toward greater acceptance of his total being—emotional, intellectual, and physical—as it *is*, including its potential. . . . With individuals less inhibited by defensive rigidity, the possibility of change in personal attitudes and behavior, in professional methods, in administrative procedures and relationships, becomes less threatening. (p. 7)

However, in work group situations where the leader exercises organization authority, it is generally appropriate to develop norms around two low-risk levels of disclosure. *Friendship* is sharing personal information that allows development of positive personal involvements in the group. This kind of involvement is emphasized by Glasser (1969, 1972) as a necessary ingredient to facilitate personal and group problem solving. *Task and problem input* involves sharing information and feelings directly relevant to job issues or tasks. We refer to this type of trust as *honesty*. As a group norm, honesty is defined operationally as willingness to share information, either of fact or of feeling, that may contribute to group problem solving.

When defined in terms of behavior, the trust notions of *responsibility* (making and keeping simple agreements), *involvement* (personal relationships), and *honesty* (task-related self-disclosure) can become useful norms for group members during the process of building a cohesive team.

Determinants of Group Development

A number of theories provide understanding of the function of trust in group development. We will present three theories here as background for applying the team-building methods presented in chapter 8.

ROTTER'S SOCIAL LEARNING THEORY

Rotter (1954) developed a social learning concept of group functioning which identifies four conditions or determinants of the behavior of people in groups:

First, the potential for change is always present. Stated negatively, the only organisms that do not "behave" are dead ones. One could say there is no truth to the statement, "John isn't motivated." The major implication is that every person can do many things; no matter how hopeless a person may appear, he or she can change and grow. Behavior is learned, and what has been learned may be unlearned and relearned (Mink and Kaplan, 1970).

Second, people learn to expect that certain kinds of behaviors will lead to specific results in a given situation. Every act has a consequence, both biologically (internally) and environmentally (externally). People learn to expect these consequences or payoffs, but differ in their beliefs about whether or not they have direct control over them. These differing beliefs clearly influence behavior and in large measure determine a person's movement from "can" to "will" action.

Third, behavior leading to valued consequences occurs more often. A person places a certain degree of worth on the outcome or consequences of a behavior. The higher a person values the outcome, the greater the likelihood that he or she will act; hence, the value of individual involvement with the development of work and organization norms and payoffs is significant. People want to see the personal relevance of an activity.

Finally, people learn to trust others in a situation where positive consequences occur. The person trusts or has confidence in people and circumstances surrounding positive expectancy–behavior–payoff sequences. Everyone has had a wide variety of learning experiences, including at least some in which powerful people have manipulated payoffs arbitrarily or conditionally. Often, people suspect on the basis of past experience that organization leaders will be dishonest. This expectation is particularly true of minority group members (Rotter, Seeman, and Liverant, 1962).

When group development is understood as a social learning experience directed toward behavior change, the leader's challenge is to help each member focus on the relation between what he or she is doing and is getting out of it. The payoff must have value for the worker. And the leader must earn the worker's confidence in the setting within which performance occurs.

THE JOHARI WINDOW

The Johari window is a "graphic model of awareness in interpersonal relationships" developed by Joseph Luft and Harry Ingham (1969). It is helpful in understanding the dynamics of awareness and self-disclosure in a work group or organization.

The window has four panes or quadrants. The first represents the area of activity where behavior and motivation are known both to the person concerned and to other group members. The second is the "blind area." It includes those behaviors and motivations that others can see in the person but of which he or she is unaware. The third quadrant, the avoided or hidden area, is what the person knows about him- or herself, but does not choose to disclose to others. This could be a hidden agenda or a matter about which the person has sensitive feelings. The fourth quadrant, the area of the unknown, is behavior and motivation neither the person nor other group members are consciously aware of.

The Johari window is a dynamic model; the size of each quadrant grows or shrinks as the group or organization develops. In an immature work group, quadrant one is very small. In an atmosphere of growing trust, quadrant three (avoided or hidden area) shrinks as quadrant one grows larger. Quadrant two (blind area) takes longer to reduce in size, being dependent upon feedback and upon the willingness of people to accept sometimes painful information about their behavior. Quadrant four (unknown information) takes the longest to affect. People near someone needing insight into an unknown area tend to collude unconsciously with that person to maintain the status quo. If the entire organization is unaware of a particular fact, an outside observer may be required to identify the "missing piece."

This model is useful in understanding what happens when people feel threatened by imminent change in their organization. Fear tends to lower the

	Known to SELF	Not known to SELF
Known to OTHERS	1 OPEN	2 BLIND
Not known to OTHERS	3 HIDDEN	4 UNKNOWN

Figure 7. The Johari Window

level of disclosure trust. As a result, quadrant one shrinks as group members increasingly hide their thoughts and feelings, and refrain from giving honest feedback to others.

In terms of the Johari window, the group leader's challenge is to increase quadrant one (open) and simultaneously decrease quadrant three (hidden) by encouraging self-disclosure relevant to solving group problems and accomplishing objectives. As trust develops from improved performance on tasks, the leader attempts to reduce quadrant two (blind) by encouraging feedback. In a work group situation, the manager or consultant should probably avoid direct probing or interventions into quadrant four (unknown) of an individual. Sometimes life crises and other types of stress may call for the professional help of a counselor or psychotherapist. Under most circumstances, however, the fourth quadrant can be safely and indirectly affected by feedback to quadrant two, disclosure of quadrant three, and by carefully worked out, behavior-oriented action plans.

SEASHORE'S THEORY OF GROUP MEMBERSHIP

How does the group leader go about increasing the size of quadrant one in the Johari window? Charles Seashore (1977) provides some clues by focusing on one aspect of team building, the concept of group membership. He identifies three levels of intensity of membership. *Level one* is characterized by low information and low trust. He does not identify the type of trust, but seems to be referring to disclosure trust. *Level two* is defined as moderate intensity, some trust, and feelings of security. *Level three* is a state of high information and high trust, as between old friends or colleagues. Seashore indicates that each person has characteristic ways of behaving at each level. Table 5 presents a summary description of the three levels of group functioning.

When one is attempting to determine and influence what is happening in a group, it is important to focus on individual transitions between levels of membership. Some people seem to test slowly, like someone cautiously sticking a toe into a cold swimming pool; some just slide quietly into the group; and some plunge right in. Others dive deeply, withdraw, dive again, and withdraw. If we were to plot their behavior, we would find a jagged line of up and downs throughout the group's life. Seashore points out that transitions are triggered by such events as an emotional experience, a status change from member to leader or learner to tutor, the revelation of a new side of a person through a joke or part in a play, and cognitive learning. Note that it is normal for different members of the group to be at different levels of functioning, although the group as a whole might be at level one, two, or three.

The role of the group leader, then, is to determine the level of membership for individuals and for the group as a whole, to anticipate transitions toward deeper levels of involvement, and to facilitate these transitions.

TABLE 5
Seashore's Levels of Group Functioning

	Level 1	Level 2	Level 3
What *strategy* is the group following?	*Development of collusion* You talk about known topics like weather. You pretend you are really communicating something of yourself while carefully monitoring your behavior so as to give the impression you want to give.	*Confrontation* You're beginning to be bored with security and looking for some excitement. You extend yourself more, hoping for something unusual to happen, ready for some sandpaper along with the blankets.	*Collaboration*
What is the group *seeking?*	*Confirmation of self* You want to know that others have just the impression you meant to give.	*Surprise* As if walking in the woods at night, you feel somewhat vulnerable and somewhat guarded.	*Synergy* You are looking for something that's possible with others, that's not possible with just one person.
What is the *goal* if the strategy is followed?	*Security* You feel safe, can control the impression you are making.	*Some dissonance* You may have unearthed some conflict to struggle with or have some feedback to digest.	*Inquiry and search* Some security and some surprise are still needed, but the search has more direction.
What *learning* is possible?	*None*	*Some* You are partially open with some alert tenseness and defensiveness.	*Great*
What is the *state of the system?*	*Closed*	*Partially open* You may distort feedback because of alertness, over-reaction—A mouse in the bushes is a potential bear.	*Open*

Adapted from a presentation by Charles N. Seashore, Consultant, 4445 29th Street N.W., Washington, D.C. 20008. Reproduced by permission of the author

Assessing Group Trust Levels—Some Tools

Seashore (1977) frames several questions a consultant or leader might ask to assess group functioning:

> What strategy is the group following as a whole—are some in the group on different levels from the rest?
>
> In which direction is the movement in? Is the group building or dissolving?
>
> Are the group members capable of triggering their own transitions?
>
> What are the environment or climatic conditions under which need transitions can occur?
>
> Can other members of the group make the intervention I am thinking of if I wait for a while? (By interventions, I mean such actions as introducing time for processing, getting people to say how they're feeling about the group, getting people who need to make a transition to fishbowl, checking out your perception about the level of the group.

Group Membership Questions, located in part IV (pp. 193–194) is a simple instrument that a group can use to assess membership and disclosure levels, and patterns of communication and influence. Each member fills out the questionnaire. Then the group obtains a combined rating of all members and discusses the reasons for the ratings.

Rotter's *Interpersonal Trust Scale* (1967) can serve as a model for developing an instrument to measure the degree of contractual trust in a group. This instrument consists of forty statements of belief which the respondent rates on a scale from 1 (strongly agree) to 5 (strongly disagree). Examples of statements measuring trust-distrust are as follows:

> Most people can be counted on to do what they say they will do.
>
> Many major national sport contests are fixed in one way or another.
>
> Most repairmen will not overcharge even if they think you are ignorant of their speciality.

Fifteen statements are filler items to disguise the purpose of the scale. An example is:

> It is more important that people achieve happiness than that they achieve greatness.

Higher total scores indicate higher trust levels.

Deutsch's *Prisoner's Dilemma Matrix* (1960), is a game designed to allow individuals or groups to pair up into "trust" teams to test their disclosure trust of one another. The original version of the game, formulated and named by Albert W. Tucker, presents a hypothetical situation in which two men have been arrested for conspiring in an armed robbery. Not having sufficient evidence to convict the two men, the district attorney presents each prisoner with alternatives designed to encourage a confession at the expense of the other partner (Watzlawick, 1976). Both Deutsch's and MacDonald's modifications of this game use dollars rather than the freedom-imprisonment alternative as payoffs and penalties, but the dilemma is the same. The choices are structured so that both can profit by cooperating, but one person can profit slightly more by betraying the interests of the other. Thus, in making a decision, each person must test his or her trust in the other's willingness to make the one decision most advantageous for both. Persons who believe that others will betray them for a small advantage are not likely to disclose personal information that might render them vulnerable (MacDonald, Kessell, and Fuller, 1972).

Jourard's *Self-Disclosure Questionnaire* (1964) measures a person's degree of disclosure in relation to four others: mother, father, male friend, and female friend. The respondent is presented with a list of sixty topics of disclosure organized in the following categories: attitudes and opinions, tastes and interests, work, money, personality, and body (appearance, health). On each item, the respondent rates him- or herself 0 (no disclosure), 1 (general disclosure), 2 (detailed disclosure), or X (misrepresentation of self to the other). Topics from the work category include unenjoyable and satisfying aspects of one's work, personal strengths and weaknesses on the job, ambitions and goals, and how the person really feels about the people he or she works with. Numerical scores are summed to obtain the total self-disclosure score.

4

INFLUENCE AND POWER

EVERY ORGANIZATION HAS ITS own reservoir of social energy. Social energy is the cumulative momentum of constituents' ideas, feelings, and actions. It goes much deeper than attitudes revealed at any given moment in a particular situation. Rather, *constituents* include the founders, builders, and others who have had a hand in the creation and growth of an organization, and its collective artifacts—name, buildings, patents, position in the market or community, legal status, history, customs, morals, and policies. These are organization assets. Social energy also includes cooperation, cohesion, values, authority, power, anything that makes human behavior and artifacts cumulative and collective.

An organization's social energy is organized in an equilibrium between restraining forces that tend to maintain the status quo, and driving forces that tend to introduce change in the direction of new goals, structures, processes, methods, or leadership. This equilibrium of energies is subject to change, for there are always members or groups attempting to alter an organization, that is, to exert organizational influence. Influence may be used in ways that are constructive or destructive to the health of an organization.

Every step taken to release the potential of an organization toward greater openness inevitably means freeing some social energies for creative uses, lessening some restraining forces that champion the status quo, and establishing a new equilibrium between forces. An organization moving toward openness is learning not to reject stability, but rather to change the basis for stability from adherence to the status quo as a value in itself to commitment to shared purposes and goals subject to periodic review and revision.

Redefining the basis for stability is a difficult process to initiate and carry through successfully. It involves profound changes in organizational attitudes, values, and processes. It necessitates a wise use of both consentive and coercive influence by leaders in order to build a climate for change and to prevent the development of destructive, wasteful power struggles. Power, or the coercive use of social influence, is a necessary ingredient of organizational change. Yet unbridled use of power is incompatible with the nature of open organizations.

In this chapter, we will take the view that change based upon consent to shared values and ideas is ultimately more productive and more influential on people's behavior than ideas enforced through the use of power. Conflict can be productive if it centers around shared testing of ideas and values, but it is destructive if it becomes a win–lose struggle among warring factions.

We begin by examining three bases for influence in organizations, and contrasting coercive with consentive uses of these types of influence. We will emphasize the importance of analyzing organizational norms as carriers of influence, discuss the constructive uses of conflict and confrontation, and describe appropriate uses of influence by management and change specialists. The chapter introduces two instruments which may be used to assess current personal and organizational influence styles and strategies. We conclude with a case study illustrating the importance of getting the support of power groups to bring about successful change.

The Nature of Influence and Power

Influence may be defined as any method used by one party which in fact becomes a social force in the decision of a second party. The social energies of an organization are balanced in an equilibrium between driving and restraining forces. Every driving and restraining force which is valued by an organization as a determinant in making significant decisions becomes an influence. A force may wield an influence even though a system attempts to disregard it when making decisions. This situation occurs when the force is used to coerce the action of the system in a particular direction. *Power* is the coercive use of influence to affect a subordinate system against its will.

Influence is inherently neither good nor bad; its impact depends upon the situation and upon the manner in which the influence is wielded. Everyone in an organization exercises influence; its use is not limited to management. However, because of the authority of leaders, their use of influence is both necessary and legitimate in carrying out their charge to maintain and enhance the well-being of an organization.

The use of influence may be coercive or consentive. It may appeal to the lower or the higher values and motivations of people. Here we will distinguish among three bases of influence. Often these types of influence are exercised in combination, but it is useful to identify them separately to determine what constitutes an appropriate use of influence in an open organization.

VALUE-BASED INFLUENCE

This type of influence appeals to morals and values—to what is considered right or worthy in a given situation. Used constructively, value-based influence appeals to the conscience of individuals or to an organization's sense of its basic mission and goals. Backed up by a system of rewards and punishments, value-based influence may also be used coercively. One example is the practice of some churches in excommunicating members for moral deviation. An example in the business world is the punishment of employees for making personal long-distance telephone calls on business phones, or using company accounts and clerical help for personal enterprises. Similar situations occur in the public sector. In one state university some employees were indicted for misuse of state funds for practices that were common throughout the university. When the moral value being enforced is not widely shared, punishments like these often appear arbitrary and have little effect upon general practice except to increase caution. At best, coercive use of value-based influence is extremely complex and difficult to carry out effectively.

KNOWLEDGE- AND INFORMATION-BASED INFLUENCE

This type of influence appeals to beliefs about "how things really are" and "how things work best" in the world. Used constructively, knowledge-based influence creates greater awareness of the way an organization works, the need for defining problems more effectively, and the importance of solving problems through objective thinking and attention to relevant data. Backed by a system of rewards and punishments, knowledge-based influence may be used to coerce people to affirm beliefs they do not hold. A classic example is the trial of Galileo by the Holy Office in 1633. Galileo was forced to publicly "abandon the false opinion that the sun is the center of the world and immovable and that the Earth is not the center of the world and moves" because, in the view of some theologians, these ideas seemed contradictory to the nature of the world presented in scriptures (Santillana, 1955, p. 312). An example in the business world was the assumption of some managers in the nineteenth century that workers were motivated solely by the desire for making money. This narrow view left out other possible motivations, such as the desire for achievement and personal satisfaction in work, and established economic remuneration as the primary reward.

ECONOMIC- AND LEGAL-BASED INFLUENCE

This type of influence appeals to what is permissible in a given economic and political context, and to the right of a society to make laws and to govern its people. Used constructively, economic- and legal-based influence is used to vest leaders with the authority to govern others by broad consent. Authority is defined here as economic and legal power legitimized by a ruler's function as a society or organization leader. For example, our national government is authorized by the Constitution to make laws for the common welfare, to raise moneys through taxation, and to wage war. In organizations, managers have the authority to control job assignments and evaluate personnel based upon established criteria. Backed by a system of rewards and punishments, this kind of influence may also be used coercively. Sometimes coercion may be justified by the authorized role of a leader, as when a manager fires an employee after going through due process. As the founders of our country were very aware, however, economic and legal power may also be used tyrannically. Two examples are taxation without representation and firing an employee without cause.

The word *power* is most often associated with the coercive use of economic and legal influence. Power in traditional organizations has been defined as party A's ability to control party B against his or her will through incentives (pay) that satisfy survival needs (Maslow's hierarchy)—power comes from the top. Power from the bottom comes from such acts as sabotage, work stoppage, and collective bargaining for increased wages. Often power based on values or knowledge is reinforced by economic and legal power.

Norms as Carriers of Influence

In an organization, influence is channeled and maintained primarily through *norms*, group standards of behavior. Norms shape members' ideas about what is expected of them. The whole system of the organization has a set of norms; so does each subsystem. If in its behavior a subsystem supports the norms of the total system, the chance for change is slight. If, however, the subsystem norms vary from the total system norms, the chance of change depends on how much individual power is held by the subsystem leaders compared with that of people supporting system norms. Awareness of the patterns of norms in an organization allows us to assess the energy available for change.

VISIBLE AND INVISIBLE NORMS

There are two broad categories of norms. One embraces written, visible, or announced norms, and the other, unwritten, invisible, and unannounced. Visible norms include policy, procedures, guidelines, job descriptions, standards, and signs—all written communication in an organization telling members what is expected of them. Invisible norms stem from cultural mores of the organization. They are often not even known to exist until someone challenges them inadvertently. The matter of dress is a clear example. Organization norms on dress may be visible or invisible. A written dress code is enforced in some schools, colleges, and state agencies. Most organizations have an invisible norm on dress which a new member must discover by observing others.

Of the two kinds of norms, the invisible are by far the more powerful. They are inevitably encountered by someone joining an organization. Personnel handbooks of standard policies and procedures for new employees are often contradicted in real practice, as coworkers may verify.

Conflict between two different sets of invisible norms can destroy an organization, family, or friendship more quickly than conflict between visible norms. Often those involved do not realize they are dealing with a norm conflict because they can't imagine others having expectations different from theirs. For example, two couples spent the weekend together at a beach house. They developed a conflict over invisible norms when the first couple proposed an early morning dip. The second couple wanted to eat breakfast, wash dishes, and make beds before going swimming. Conflicting expectations about spontaneity and orderliness were never discussed, but they had a powerful impact on group behavior and enjoyment of the weekend.

IDENTIFYING AND ANALYZING NORMS

Often the clearest communication is not what an organization says it is doing but what indirect messages say. Thus, before attempting changes, it is important to notice not only procedures manuals and published organization goals found on managers' bookshelves, but also the organization logo, cartoons on bulletin boards, and bumper stickers on cars in parking lots. These provide clues to the organization's norms and priorities. In an organization with a history of reorganizing its members out of jobs, a member may hang the sign: "If you don't like what you're doing here, don't worry. Someone else will be doing it soon." In an organization involved with reorganizing or short-range planning, one might see signs and bumper stickers saying, "No amount of planning can replace dumb luck."

Because top management sets the tone for an entire organization, it is also imperative to observe what invisible norms are being enforced through the behavior of managers. For example, a consultant was hired to find out why the leader of a small parts manufacturing company kept losing her most promising subordinates to other companies. The consultant observed one of the regularly held staff meetings. He saw that she could pick able subordinates. He knew that in addition to being a manager, she was also a creative engineer, business entrepreneur, and enthusiastic customer representative all in one. Here is how the discussion at the meeting with her staff went. She said, "We've got a problem with Universal on widget 25. Customers are rejecting parts, and competitors are moving in on our most established customers. Any ideas?" Subordinate one said, "Why don't we . . . ?" She replied, "Yes, but . . . . " Subordinate two said, "Well, then, why don't we . . . ?" Her response was "Yes but . . . . " The invisible norm being enforced was clearly, "I'll think up the good ideas and you make them work. Don't confuse me with your suggestions." By videotaping and playing back a meeting, the consultant made her aware of this norm. As a result, she changed her behavior and staff turnover decreased.

After norms have been identified, they must be analyzed. Who sets them? Are those directly affected by them part of the developing process? Or does someone else develop visible and invisible norms affecting members of a work group? How negotiable are the norms? Are they continually open for examination and reality testing? Or are they solidified in policies and procedures and never tested against reality? Do the norms help or hinder those who must get the job done? If some norms help, awareness of them can become a basis for strengthening the organization. If norms that hinder are pinpointed, an organization can choose to dissolve them through problem solving. In a healthy organization, norms are set by those affected, are open for examination, and fit the reality of the organization.

Organization Norms that Affect You in part IV (see page 197) is an instrument that can be used to increase awareness of the norms that affect work life in your organization. You list norms and assess whether they are visible or invisible, who sets them, whether they are open to examination and reality testing, and whether they help or hinder the work of your organization.

Using Influence to Bring About Change

In an open organization, influence is grounded in shared values, beliefs, and goals of members. In the long run, ideas and values to which persons are committed by consent have more influence than ideas imposed by power. If enough minds share an idea, it can become a movement. A movement has great social energy; it is a source from which power is derived. But power is secondary to perceived truth and vitality of the movement's values and ideals.

At their best, large social groups are bound by more than economic self-interest, patriotism, or ethnic pride. They are held together by broad human values, such as morality, love, truth, justice, and worthy purpose. Nevertheless, social groups are often in danger of losing higher values and being reduced to a survival posture reinforced by coercive influences. For example, movements tend to become rigidified and doctrinaire as they age. Power becomes more and more primary and self-justifying. Leaders tend to base their authority on coercion and manipulation more than on the power of ideas and values. Disadvantaged and alienated groups may seize and abuse power out of self-righteousness and self-interest. Although power exercised by unions, revolutionaries, and saboteurs is neither good nor bad inherently, it encourages win–lose situations. Similarly, unbridled use of power by leaders or change specialists can cause destructive power struggles and backlashes.

For organization openness, power is used appropriately to open an organization to value- and knowledge-based influence processes, and to facilitate greater unity, internal responsiveness, and external responsiveness. Usually, power is used to start an organization's development, but the process itself must be as noncoercive as possible. To be successful, it must involve high trust, and be egalitarian and nonpunitive. Power is used appropriately to transcend itself, to restore an important role to value- and knowledge-based change.

Leaders of organization change must beware of the tendencies of power toward abuse and corruption. They should be careful to examine their motives, particularly when they are feeling righteous. They must resist the temptation to assume that being more powerful makes them right.

CONFLICT

One method of using influence to induce change is through conflict. If conflict becomes a power struggle, however, it tends to promote a win–lose situation that can become a lose–lose situation and waste both time and resources. Conflict can be healthy but it can also be particularly self-destructive when it becomes violent. Destructive conflict is based upon being the best, or winning over others regardless of cost or value. Winning or getting ahead can become a substitute for fulfillment of the organization's basic mission and gaining real personal satisfaction.

An open approach accepts conflict as a testing, not of the comparative powers of opposing groups, but of the merits of various ideas. Open organizations recognize the value of knowledge-based argument to a healthy system. Conflict is used to build unity around goals and methods, through the use of shared and fair information-seeking processes.

Knowledge-based conflict is of two kinds—differences between goals, and differences over strategies and methods for achievement of accepted goals. The most difficult conflict is that over goals. For example, the Roman Catholic church has struggled for over a decade over issues like celibacy of the clergy and divorce. Various groups debate about abortion. These basic differences in ideals are difficult to resolve and can create long-standing factions. Fortunately, organizations do not often encounter deep conflicts over missions and goals. When such disagreements are encountered, processes such as the Delphi technique described in chapter 7 may be applied. If agreement cannot be reached, disagreeing parties can go their separate ways.

Most conflicts in organizations are about means to achieve agreed-upon goals. They are amenable to solution under conditions of positive expectations ("I know you can resolve this.") and a problem-solving climate ("Conflict is OK around here. We expect conflict to occur in today's complex world."). For example, managers A and B disagree over the best way to manage others. Manager A is in favor of "Tell 'em!" Manager B wants to "Let the group decide." Usually their experiences and theoretical orientation differ. Manager A has come up from the old school and started out as a machinist in the shop. Manager B has a Harvard M.B.A. Each possesses strengths that the other can benefit from. They can be led to discover that no one management process can be established as clearly superior to another. Time, circumstance, the leader's personal qualities, the kind of employees, the nature of the task, available technology, and existing organizational structures are a few factors affecting the impact of management style. Resolution is possible through discussion, problem solving, learning, and third-party consultation. The consultant ensures accurate and specific feedback, generates alternatives, and establishes a problem-solving climate. Upper level managers should use their influence to set positive expectations for resolution. Management's stance should be "What caused the conflict?" rather than "Who caused the conflict?"

CONFRONTATION

During the late 1960s and early 1970s, the value of confrontation as a method of resolving differences between two disagreeing groups was debated between blacks and whites, then between generations, and then between doves and hawks. The purpose of confrontation is for opposing groups to meet face to face, explain their views, and clarity what they want. Confrontation is not a cure-all: it will work only if trust is first established between parties Both parties must be involved in the process, and both must eventually internalize new behavior to deal effectively with similar situations.

How does internalized change occur? In a study by the survey research center (Kahn, 1964) of a large manufacturing company, researchers found that directive, authoritarian supervisors with a power-based approach to their subordinates caused conforming responses rather than internalized change in subordinates. In related research, Peter Smith (1976) studied three kinds of influence processes—compliance, identification, and internalization—to determine which resulted in the most permanent behavior change benefits for participants in sensitivity training groups. The three influence processes are summarized in figure 8.

Influencer Characteristics				Results
Not attractive (coercive)	+	Confrontation	=	Compliance as long as behavior is observable
Attractive (reinforces concept of self)	+	No confrontation	=	Identification but not internalization
Attractive (similar values or attitudes)	+	Confrontation	=	Internalization

Figure 8. Smith's Three Types of Influence

Adapted from "Social influence processes and the outcome of sensitivity training" by P. B. Smith, *Journal of personality and social psychology*, 1976, 34, (6), 1087–1094. Reproduced by permission of the author

In a *compliance* relationship, B (the one being influenced) is a member of a system which she is not free to leave. B behaves in a way preferred by A (the influencer) in order to obtain a reward or avoid a punishment that A has the power to impose. Confrontation from A—challenging B's current behavior— does not result in changing B, however. B does not accept A's values and will revert to her preferred way of behaving when she is not being observed by A, or when A loses her power over rewards and punishments.

In an *identification* relationship, B is attracted to A and changes his behavior in order to please A. Maintaining a close relationship with A helps B to sustain a more certain concept of himself. A approves of B's behavior and does not confront B with demands for change. This kind of influence persists only as long as B remains attracted to A.

In an *internalization* relationship, B is attracted to A because of similar values or attitudes. At the same time, A's behavior is confrontive—it shows B's current behavior to be less effective than it might be. As a result, B begins to explore ways of changing. Peter Smith concluded that the internalization relationship produces the most permanent change because the influenced individuals feel personally responsible for their actions. They are internally controlled. That is, they attribute achievement of their goals to their own choice and actions rather than to the power of the influencer.

MANAGER INFLUENCE

Management did not begin in the modern age. The ancestor of the manager is the ruler. Rulers of humankind have been popes, kings, generals, explorers, bureaucrats, and corporation executives. The common denominator is the management of a large-scale enterprise. Although managers have the same basic roles and functions as the rulers of past centuries, the basis and scope of their authority have changed, as have methods available.

Rulers have always exercised some form of legitimized control over the fate of their constituents. Among rulers of the past, such as monarchs, the basis for authority was a claim to absolute knowledge and morality. Today we are far less likely to presume a moral or knowledge basis for management authority. Managers today have more limited influence as executors of material, financial, and other organizational assets. Their function is maintaining control over the economic fate of the organization and allocating the organization's resources to achieve its purposes. They have power over the career fates of organization members, but not the life-and-death hold of rulers of the past.

Despite the limited nature of managerial authority, managers are often seen as highly powerful. We easily use power language such as "my subordinates," "accountability," "performance review," "the boss," "the employee." This kind of language can be counterproductive, particularly if the manager does not exercise overwhelming power. Power language is especially inappropriate in organizations where actual power is diffused, as for example, among faculty members or the medical staff of a hospital.

Managers of today may need help in defining their roles so that they can tap other forms of social energy not amenable to a display of power. One strategy is to increase awareness of the negative aspects of the indiscriminate use of economic and legal power. Another is to demonstrate the benefits of leadership based upon pursuit of a cause or purpose with which followers can identify. It is impossible to be an open organization leader unless the organization itself has a mission seen as worthy by constituents. Moreover, upper level leaders must be unanimously committed to accepted goals if conflicts among subordinates are to be resolved constructively, and if the goals are to be implemented successfully. The case study at the end of this chapter illustrates what can happen when change is not supported by all top managers of an organization.

CONSULTANT INFLUENCE

Use of influence to alter an organization's social energy may come not only from its leadership but also from consultants. According to Bennis:

> The organization development consultant strives to utilize power that is based on and guided by rationality, valid knowledge, and collaboration and to discount power based on and channeled by fear, irrationality, and coercion. The latter kind of power leads to augmented resistance to change, unstable changes, and dehumanized and irrational conflicts. (Bennis, Benne, and Chin, 1969, p. 91)

The consultant's use of influence has several characteristics.

1. IT IS PRIMARILY KNOWLEDGE-BASED. Consultant influence is best based on knowledge and value. The consultant must play the role of facilitator rather than leader. He does not impose his own knowledge and values upon members of an organization, but rather helps to crystallize knowledge and values latent within the organization itself. To the degree that the consultant is seen as another boss, recipients of his services will be more cautious about revealing their thoughts and feelings. They will not want to be candid with someone who could influence their career.

2. IT IS A THIRD-PARTY ROLE. The consultant is neither a party in the struggle for results nor a member of the organization. She does not take sides. Rather, she uses conflict as an opportunity to "channel the aggressive energies of conflict and power toward the achievement of personal and social gain for all concerned" (Bennis, Benne, and Chin, 1969, p. 91).

The consultant must go to great lengths to prevent win–lose situations while encouraging healthy knowledge-based conflicts to proceed. She serves as a mediator in an effort to find a common basis for agreement.

3. IT IS COLLABORATIVE WITH MANAGEMENT BUT INDEPENDENT FROM MANAGEMENT. The consultant depends upon the authority of management to support and establish ground rules for change. However, he

is not involved with the normal organization controls over employees, and functions as an independent facilitator. Because of this independence, the consultant must be very careful not to abuse this privilege. He must realize that he sets an example, and avoid behaving in ways that others might emulate with disastrous results.

Ineffective or phony consultants are power hungry. They get satisfaction in winning over others as an end in itself. There are consultants who will openly brag about their use of power, seeing it as useful or necessary to their role. They do not realize that the consulting role involves knowledge rather than power. Others do not recognize or acknowledge their own power needs and exert camouflaged power. Such consultants can have a very damaging impact upon organizations faced with conflict.

Personal Influence Styles and Strategies

Regardless of job title or official status, every person in an organization exercises personal influence when accomplishing a job. This section will identify some of the styles and strategies people use to bring about changes in another person's behavior or in an organization as a whole. These methods and tactics may be used to varying degrees by people in an organization. Different people use various methods, and one may use several or most. Typically, members of organizations have not acquired the knowledge and skill to use a variety of methods appropriately and effectively. Most people limit themselves to traditional or direct influence.

Two instruments introduced here may be used to identify current individual and organizational patterns of influence, and to increase awareness of other options.

CHANGE EFFORT STYLES

Individuals often feel powerless to influence their supervisors, the management, or the organization in general. Leslie This has identified sixty methods of influence that could be used by an employee. The methods are grouped into six change effort styles:

STYLE A—TRADITIONAL TECHNIQUES. Style A uses rational and persuasive methods to sell a change effort to a supervisor or another person. Most managers regard the methods in this category as traditional, ethical, and the most desirable options. Examples are: present quality error-free work, demonstrate how the idea will cut costs or solve a current problem, and document the idea with research.

STYLE B—DIRECTLY ATTEMPTING TO INFLUENCE SUPERVISOR. This style includes strategies to influence the supervisor directly so that he will advocate or approve the idea directly. Methods in this category include getting the supervisor to attend a seminar that supports one's views and lobbying for an idea through the supervisor's friends.

STYLE C—MANIPULATING THE ORGANIZATIONAL SYSTEM. A person using this style recognizes formal and informal influence systems within an organization and uses these systems to bring about change. Methods in this category include using a routing slip to get visibility for one's ideas, using grievance procedures, and bypassing a supervisor to a person in higher authority.

STYLE D—AGGRESSIVE AND MILITANT STRATEGIES. This style uses confrontation and direct use of power to bring about change. Examples include demonstrations, slowdowns, and strikes.

STYLE E—RESOURCES EXTERNAL TO ORGANIZATION. These methods are normally used when becoming disillusioned with an organization's available internal means of change. They include asking congressmen or consumer groups to bring pressure, writing a letter to a newspaper editor, and using a consulting firm to recommend what one wants.

STYLE F—WAITING FOR ORGANIZATION MILIEU TO CHANGE. One might use waiting methods or arguments if an attempted change is repeatedly rebuffed. Examples are waiting for "blockers" to retire, and waiting for the situation to worsen so that others may be more open to change.

Methods and Tactics to Secure Organization Support for Change, located in part IV (pp. 198–203), is an instrument designed by Les This to help individuals examine their change effort styles and to consider additional options. The respondent rates each of the sixty methods of influence with one of the following letters:

a. I normally always use this technnique.
b. I use this technique occasionally.
c. I would use this technique only if I felt very strongly about the change effort.
d. I consider this technique unethical and would never use it.
e. This technique is not applicable to me in my job.

After responding to all items, record your responses in a matrix that groups them in vertical columns representing six change styles. By examining the matrix, you can see which styles you use most often.

For example, the responses of an internal change specialist in an educational setting are shown in figure 9. The matrix shows that of the ten instrument items measuring change effort style A, this person normally uses eight and occasionally uses two others. Of the ten items measuring change effort style F, she does not normally use any of them. She occasionally uses three of the tactics. Five other tactics she would use if she felt very strongly about the change effort. There are two tactics she considers unethical and would never use. By drawing a line across the matrix between "b" and "c," we can identify which styles this person tends to use more often than others. She normally or occasionally uses styles A, C, and E.

When asked about the meaning of this profile, the internal change specialist commented that it reflects her change style accurately. She normally uses traditional, rational approaches (style A), such as pointing out advantages of changes, demonstrating how the change will solve current problems, and generally doing detailed, quality work. She was undecided about the trust level between herself and her supervisor, thus the inconclusive data on style B. She is aware of organization mechanisms for effecting change and uses them (style C). She is uncomfortable with aggressive and militant strategies and chooses not to use them or regards them as not applicable to her job (style D). She is aware of people and resources external to the organization and has recently had success with this strategy (style E). She is impatient with the need for creating a responsive, open organization and does not often choose to wait for the organization to change (style F).

The change specialist depicted in our example may also decide whether she tends to use too limited a range of techniques and resources. Adding across rows, we can see that she normally or occasionally uses thirty-five of sixty possible methods and tactics listed in the instrument. Therefore, she is choosing *not* to use twenty-five available strategies. A careful review of items rated "C" may reveal some strategies that she has not used and could consider using in a future change effort.

Extent of Use	Change Effort Styles						
	A	B	C	D	E	F	
a – normally use	8	1	1	2	2	0	} 35
b – use occasionally	2	4	6	1	5	3	
c – only use if feel strongly	0	3	2	4	3	5	
d – method unethical, would never use it	0	2	1	1	0	2	} 25
e – not applicable to job	0	0	0	2	0	0	

Figure 9. Change Effort Styles of an Individual

The instrument can also be used to obtain a group profile. For example, twenty change specialists working in a welfare agency completed the instrument. Their group responses are shown in figure 10. The numbers in the matrix mean that all twenty in the agency always or occasionally choose the traditional style of influence (style A). Most do not attempt to influence supervisors directly, manipulate the organization system, use resources external to the organization, or wait for the organization milieu to change (styles B, C, E, and F). Aggressive and militant tactics are considered unethical (style D). They might use aggressive and militant methods if they felt very strongly about change. They are choosing to limit their effectiveness as a group by using only traditional ways to "sell" a change.

Extent of Use	Change Effort Styles					
	A	B	C	D	E	F
a and b – use normally or occasionally	20	2	6	0	2	6
c, d, and e – use rarely or never	0	18	14	20	18	14

Figure 10. Change Effort Styles of an Organization

RESOLVING DIFFERENCES

We have assisted Del Poling in developing another instrument that can be used to explore aspects of personal power. *Power Strategies for Impacting and Resolving Differences,* found in part IV (pp. 204–210), has evolved out of several years of work with people attempting to use influence in their day-to-day personal and organization life. Section I is a list of thirty-seven strategies to influence others, such as using status, controlling information, and obligating others. Check off influence behaviors you use in professional and in personal life. Section II asks you to select five power strategies used most often and to evaluate them for frequency of use, impact on your self-concept, and impact on others. Section III presents five questions for reflection or discussion about personal use of power and the effectiveness of various power strategies.

Case Study. The Difficulty of Change: A Study In Power*

The setting was a southeastern rural community college with a dynamic new president. We met with him as potential consultants to the college. "During the three years I have been here," the president confided, "I have stressed the open-door policy. That is, we have opened the doors of the college to the community, inviting anyone who wanted to learn or to continue learning to come." It was clear that he was proud of the strides made at Boondock Community College (BCC) during that period. And he had every right to be.

A tall man, lean and gray, he seldom sat still for long, but paced back and forth across the modest board room as he recalled his problems. "Located in a rural section of a southeastern state, BCC serves what has been designated an 'economically depressed area' by the U.S. Department of Commerce. The economy," he explained, "is basically agricultural and operated on a tenant farmer-landowner arrangement. Seventy percent of our students come from families who meet the poverty criteria set by the federal government."

He explained that most of the population belonged to a poor working class— black, white, Indian—who depended on agriculture for one paycheck a year when the harvest came in. These people were essentially tenant farmers, and the entire community a carry-over from antebellum times of the Old South. The farming people had until recently been dependent upon the downtown stores for their goods. They could use charge accounts for their needs all year and pay the bill when the harvest check was received. For this privilege they paid thirty to forty percent more for products than if they had bought the goods outright. The use of charge accounts by farmers was extremely profitable to local business and the town bank.

Although the school had been started with the hope that it might become a "little Harvard of the Southeast," an elitist institution, BCC's mission changed rapidly with the arrival of the president. He immediately established an open-door policy and matched this policy with the development of programs relevant and appropriate to students coming from various backgrounds. The courses had been designed to serve even the geographically and culturally isolated Crusoe Island people, an unusual community of about one hundred people who had been "lost" for three hundred years and spoke an Old English dialect. They had never had the opportunity for any kind of public exposure or education. The president responded by hiring a couple of them to come to teach crafts they knew well, such as making canoes out of cypress trees.

"We also organized a program called 'Developmental Studies,'" explained the president, "with a curriculum designed to remedy early lack of education such as poor reading skills." For many, this provided a new experience of success in an educational setting. Vocational education offerings had been expanded in order to develop new marketable skills for a population retarded by the hardships of the agricultural economy. The president also helped set up two federally funded programs to provide educational opportunities and extracurricular services for

*Case study written by Ann Linquist

disadvantaged students. A nonpunitive grading system was adopted. An effective student recruitment program was started.

To increase job opportunities for his students, the president also formed a local committee to attract industry to the area. In the previous three years, enough industry had moved in to reduce unemployment to zero. The entire power structure—cultural and economic—was shifting from a traditional antebellum society to a more balanced economy. As a result of new jobs and vocational training, upper lower and lower middle class groups began to emerge. These people held jobs in private plants and received weekly paychecks. Now, for example, a person could take a six-month welding course, get a job, and make six dollars an hour, cash. With new mobility and new buying power, he could shop wherever he wanted and avoid paying high interest rates on charge accounts.

We were much impressed by the president's story. BCC was prospering. It had received over two million dollars in state and federal funds, and had secured many private gifts for student financial aid, including one large private trust. The college had become a resource that enabled poor people in this rural community to break out of the poverty cycle.

So why had the president called us? We soon learned our mission. He provided us with a succinct statement of purpose—to help improve the quality of individualized instruction offered to developmental studies students. We were to develop strategies for better teaching of students who had never been successful in school. This seemed a fair enough task—following through to promote the success of his new programs.

Together we approached the board of trustees to present our proposal and receive approval of our contract. The board consisted of twelve people; four were intimately tied to the traditional power structure. One was an executive vice-president of the town bank, one a large landowner heavily in debt to the bank, another a local drug store owner also in debt to the bank, and the fourth a local political party leader who brought out the vote to insure that old interests would be protected. Two other board members were independent businessmen. An uneasy balance between forces for tradition and forces for change had existed for some time as reflected by a five-against-five voting pattern on the board. (The chair could not vote, one board member was gravely ill, and no provision for proxy existed.) The meeting seemed to go well. We were approved.

Our next step was to acquaint ourselves with the power structure within BCC and to involve members in carrying out our purpose. The president's cabinet consisted of five people, only three of whom reported directly to him. They represented student support services, business, and academic programs. This cabinet structure was unusual. The dean of instruction brought along with him his academic and vocational/technical deans, making up the five in the cabinet. This larger group of administrators responsible only for instruction made balanced dialogue difficult.

To implement effective changes consultants need to work through the existing authority structure. The structure of this cabinet was our first hint of trouble ahead. Achieving consensus of purpose or unity in an organization is at best difficult. It can usually be accomplished when:

- Power is equally distributed.

- The group reaches consensus on goals, and group members are committed to those goals.
- More than twelve hours have been devoted to team development to build contractual trust.

After first contact with the cabinet we began to organize workshops to promote individualized instruction. This kind of instruction is based upon the open systems approach to learning, which includes responsiveness to student needs and skill levels, written learning objectives handed to students at the beginning of the course, self-paced learning, immediate and accurate feedback on student achievements, and criterion-referenced testing to reflect stated objectives. The group of developmental studies instructors with whom we worked were intelligent and involved. They were excited by these ideas for improving the learning of their students. But something more critical emerged. They revealed that the developmental program—teachers and students—was struggling against discrimination by the dean of instruction and his subordinates. Encouraged by our support, instructors began to openly complain about the lack of support and actual resistance they felt. This situation pointed to a lack of common purpose within the institution.

The president himself had hired the director of the developmental studies program to work with the people who were high school force-outs and losers in the society. He hoped that BCC could be a place to reeducate them. This program had immediately become the target of the dean of instruction. He was an elitist educator. Philosophically he cared about minority groups, but he had no patience with anyone with academic deficiencies. His attitude automatically excluded any offer to help blacks, two tribes of American Indians in the college area, and those with backgrounds of failure in school. Members of the developmental studies staff did not have status in the college and the dean of instruction seemed to look down on the director of developmental programs as well as his staff. Morale was low. There was high turnover among program instructors.

The director of this program was our sponsor and his federal dollars paid our fee, but our real client was the whole college. The lack of consensus on goals and strategies for achieving them was the root of contention between the academic dean and the director of developmental studies. The academic dean was aligned with the dean of instruction, while the developmental studies director had the backing of the president. The conflict between the two groups was chronic.

We backed up a bit. Instead of focusing on one group of innovative instructors, we began to organize workshops designed to introduce the organization development process to the *whole* institution. These training sessions aimed to:

- Open the organization to more participation and involvement at *all* levels in rational problem solving
- Improve skills of participating in a democratic process
- Increase participation in decision making
- Improve teamwork
- Increase productivity
- Reduce instructor turnover and absenteeism from campus
- Achieve consensus on common goals and commitment to them

Our first strategy was to build unity through team building within BCC. The object of team building is to develop cohesion and trust among people involved with each other daily so that they can work together comfortably and effectively. Trustees, faculty, administrators, and students were invited to participate in these workshops to identify problems at BCC, learn skills to solve them, give specific recommendations, and take part in their resolution. Widespread enthusiasm was generated by the workshops, and specific task forces were set up to deal with problem areas that were identified.

Because of the lack of support for the developmental studies program at the higher administrative level, we also held retreats for the president's cabinet members. In isolated settings we worked on developing the cabinet into a team with common goals. Here we began to sense another problem. The dean of instruction, the academic dean, and, to a lesser extent, the dean of vocational/technical studies all acted as if they did not really have to participate. They seemed to show no commitment to developing a working team. These people were agreeable when we were all present in a group. However, they would speak against our efforts to others in private. They also complained about the burden of administrative responsibility for task groups formed at school workshops, the cost of workshops and consultants, and the implications of changing traditional methods of operating.

With the growing resistance of the dean of instruction and his followers and the academic dean's lack of support of the president's programs and apparent dereliction in most of his management duties, the president decided to take action. After weighing various steps with the consultants, he decided to remove the academic dean from his position but keep him as an instructor in his previous job. He informed the academic dean that he would not receive an administrative contract for the following year. The dean of instruction responded by going directly to a few board members without the knowledge or consent of the president, in direct violation of board policy. The academic dean hired a lawyer and requested a hearing before the board of trustees.

Now another pertinent fact came to light that would have changed our initial intervention strategies had we known. Four years earlier, after a nearly disastrous episode revolving around the firing of two faculty members, the chair and two members of the board had asked the dean of instruction to report directly to them any difficulties he might encounter which seemed detrimental to the college. This directive was later reported to the full board and the president, who acquiesced but apparently did not acquaint any other college personnel with it. This is why, after the firing and appeal of his academic dean, the dean of instruction met with the executive council of the board in his capacity as a special informant.

Now we understood why our efforts failed. There was not one seat of power at BCC, but two. The board members were divided in their support between the president and his subordinate. Under such conditions, unity could not occur. The board's decision to assign so much power to the dean of instruction had weakened the president's effectiveness and reduced the efficiency of the college. This arrangement had been initiated by one particularly powerful board member who reportedly had severe management problems in his own organization.

BCC had become a catalyst for change in a community which had successfully resisted change for nearly one hundred years. Its instructional programs and community development work had provided hope and opportunity for democratic participation of the many as opposed to the few. At the same time, it had become a threat to the very roots of the old power structure.

While the trustees had appeared to be unified in supporting the efforts of the president to build a good institution, differing political and economic positions were working to divide the board. The situation was brought to a crisis when the board learned that the dean of student development, a loyal supporter of the president, had collaborated with new businessmen in town to form a new bank. If there had been resistance and disapproval by some board members earlier, they now had concrete reasons to feel threatened by the shifting power in their community. They lashed out at the college president.

When we realized that the problem was one of power, we began mobilizing power support so that the board could not immediately fire the president. An independent state investigative agency was brought in to examine the situation before any drastic measures were taken. The attack upon the president took the surface form of charges of petty financial mismanagement meant to discredit his character. The real issue, however, was the political and economic power split between conservative (antebellum) and liberal (industrial) elements.

At the final board meeting, the chair's term of office ended, and he resigned to be replaced by a liberal member of the committee. Instead of a deadlock five-to-five vote, sides now were split six to four, and conservative board members were the majority. Despite a report by the independent investigative committee exonerating the president of all charges, he was asked to resign. This report was not released to the public.

All those involved in the college's renewal and growth and committed to high quality instruction and innovative leadership left within the next year. The eight people comprising an action research group resigned.

What did we learn from the BCC fiasco? First, we made a small but critical error at the outset. We assumed that the board's tacit approval was tantamount to unanimous support of individualized instruction and the developmental studies program—goals stated by the president. In fact, this power group was seriously divided. The initial meeting with the highest power level in an organization is an important time to begin gathering data. It is a crucial time for agreement on goals. We encouraged the board to talk while we listened, to describe to us what it was they thought they were getting. However, we had been only marginally successful in engaging them in planning, so we could not be certain about what they really wanted.

Second, the consultant must identify the actual client. This was an issue for us. We had been hired by the president, paid by the director of developmental studies, and asked to provide services to a large number of instructors. With such a confused definition of "client," how were we to be evaluated and by whom? Who was to provide support? Who was to lead in setting goals and planning?

Third, the importance of team development cannot be overemphasized. Unless all team members move to a new level of functioning, members will tend to return to the functioning level of the least effective member when the team goes back to the work environment. If the other team members choose not to operate on a less effective level, the least effective member will be isolated. In either case, a fully functioning team does not develop.

Most important is agreement on the overall mission or purpose. Even the best strategies and efforts to help people develop truth and trust will fail if upper level management is divided on mission or goals. It is possible that team building could have resolved the problem of unity had we been invited to work with the board. If top managers do not agree on goals, it is virtually impossible to resolve conflicts among subordinates with the usual organizational development methods. The foundation of a renewed organization is a solid commitment of all power elements and constituents to a common purpose.

PART III

Action Steps

5

INTRODUCING THE APPROACHES
AND PLAYERS

IN MOVING TOWARD an open organization, the first step to be considered is introducing a professional-technical change specialist into the organization. Managers who want to create institutional renewal and increase the effectiveness of planning and decision making should consider this step seriously. While use of a change specialist is not the only vehicle of change, we believe it is the main hope for management-sponsored change within the institution. Institutional costs and risks are less than those of other options, and can result in major organization improvement. This chapter will characterize approaches to change, describe the roles of the change specialist and manager, indicate functions performed by a change specialist to facilitate organization improvement, and summarize the steps of introducing a change specialist into an organization. A case study will illustrate how change specialists work with client groups.

Approaches to Organization Change

Literature on science-based organization change describes two major approaches to planned change: applied behavioral science (including organization development), and management science (including management engineering). These two approaches are evolving rapidly, overlapping and complementing each other. Some writers on organization development (OD) see this approach as the master concept (Beckhard, 1969). They define organization development as planned change or include many elements of management science in their OD approaches. However, the two approaches are distinctly different in their knowledge base and assertions about directions of change, the professional change agent's role, and management's role.

APPLIED BEHAVIORAL SCIENCE AND ORGANIZATION DEVELOPMENT

Organization development is based primarily on psychology, social psychology, sociology, anthropology, and political science—the behavioral sciences. OD, sometimes called the human or "soft" approach, emphasizes team development, intergroup relations, organization climate, and communication processes. This approach usually relies on training, data feedback, interventions by change specialists, and process consultation. The manager aids intervention by participating in planning, organizing, implementing, controlling, and evaluating the change process, using his or her power when appropriate. The change specialist generates options from which the manager elects a primary intervention strategy and alternative tactics. Organization health is defined by an open, problem-solving atmosphere, trust, participation, self-control, self-direction, and ability to deal with psychological and sociological resistances to change.

Many leaders in applied behavioral science and OD have been trained in the laboratory approach. Although OD is no longer synonymous with human relations training, it continues to emphasize effective collaboration and interpersonal relations. Recently OD writers have become concerned with developing techniques to resolve power and conflict issues (Bennis, Benne, and Chin, 1969).

MANAGEMENT SCIENCE

Unlike organization development, management science is based primarily on economics, engineering, financial auditing, and reward procedures. Management science is less likely to try to introduce trust and participation into the organizational system. Rather, it focuses on structural changes— facilities, positions, management control procedures. This approach is sometimes referred to as "hard" because the concern is about productivity rather than about employee satisfaction or organization climate. Management science embraces new inventions and techniques such as computerized management information systems, program planning and budgeting systems (PPBS), and systems analysis. Such control and information systems aid management in decision making, planning, and budgetary control. Institutional research focused on information flow and control structure is part of management science.

This approach does not concern itself with organization health as such, but with the efficiency of individuals and systems. In setting standards of efficiency, employee input is minimal. For example, a time and motion analyst will set a production standard for an electronic beam welding machine by using a stop watch and demonstration film. He will probably not ask the welder for information about work flow and pace.

When the management science approach is chosen, a change specialist may not be consulted. The analyst produces a standard of efficiency and the supervisor implements it. The manager's role is primarily to use the standard to determine incentives and pay. He does not participate in setting the standard he enforces.

The structural and technological emphasis of management science is indicated by the specialties of consulting firms using this approach: fund raising, facilities development, planning, and computer consultation. A full list of disciplines and specialties would also include environmental forecasting, design and decision systems, project management, and operations research. (Some refer to management science as "operations research," for example, Beckhard, 1969.)

THE OPEN ORGANIZATION PERSPECTIVE

Organization development and management science have many important features in common. Both rely heavily on empirical science and systems theory. Both approaches are capable of being holistic in acknowledging the interdependence among parts of an organization. They emphasize the importance of diagnosing the needs of a client's system, the intervention of a professionally trained consultant or technical advisor, and managerial sponsorship of change (Beckhard, 1969). Further, both approaches may use planned change, and have several functions in common, such as use of case studies, the Delphi technique, environmental assessment, management by objectives, and participatory governance. (See table 6.) In fact, these approaches address two fundamental aspects of every organization: sociopolitical dimensions, and technical-structural dimensions. To be effective, they must be treated as complementary rather than competitive approaches.

As indicated earlier, an organization is a sociotechnical system characterized by an interdependence of human and technical aspects. Therefore, total renewal necessarily involves content (structural) and process (sociopolitical) changes. Interventions of both kinds are needed, although one may be emphasized more than the other in a given situation. The general principle is to select interventions which will use present assets for planned development of both aspects of organizations.

The open organization perspective also rejects the notion that a particular type or size of organization is inherently more rigid than other types, and is therefore not amenable to interventions of either an OD or technical nature. For example, literature on higher education organizations points out features resistant to OD change, such as guild-like loyalties, weak leadership structure, traditions, and reactionary boards of trustees (Evans and Leppman, 1968; Gardner, 1964; Gross, 1963; Kerr and Miller, 1968; Rudolph, 1962; and Sanford, 1962). It can also be argued that management science interventions will

TABLE 6

Functions of Organization Development and Management Science

Functions	Applied Behavioral Science and Organization Development	Management Science
Action research methods	X	
Salary administration		X
Auditing		X
Conflict management	X	
Change analysis	X	
Community analysis	X	X
Community development	X	
Creative risk taking	X	
Change agent training	X	
Case studies	X	X
Cost benefit analysis		X
Computer modeling		X
Cost accounting		X
Delphi techniques	X	X
Environment assessment	X	X
Force field analysis	X	
Facility development		X
Fund raising		X
Group or team development	X	
Human factors	X	X
Inter-group negotiation	X	
Individual career planning	X	
Innovation	X	X
Instructional unit analysis		X
Job enlargement		X
Management by objectives	X	X
Management training		X
Market analysis		X
Media research		X
Mutual goal setting	X	
Organizational mirroring	X	
Organizational sensing	X	
Participative governance	X	X
Performance testing		X
PERT		X
PPBS		X
Personnel evaluation		X
Quantitative analysis		X
Role playing	X	
Scheduling systems		X
Sensitivity training	X	
Simulation	X	
Social research	X	
Survey feedback	X	
Task group therapy	X	
Time and motion studies		X

probably not be effective in an institution where decision making is diffused, the product is intangible, professional staff do not act like "workers," and leaders are not called "managers." Yet higher education as an institution can be improved by a comprehensive approach that includes both new management information and accounting systems and the development of consensus about professional roles, values, and goals (Etzioni, 1961). In this kind of organization, the developmental focus may be on sociopolitical rather than technical dimensions, but both need to be addressed.

Certainly, professionalism, complexity, massive size, and cost pressures are not unique to nonprofit institutions like universities. These traits also characterize certain industries which have made extensive and effective use of planned change interventions. For example, Sheldon Davis (Bennis, Benne, and Chin, 1969) described TRW Systems, a company which develops innovative technological products. TRW has resolved several problems similar to those of some universities and colleges. It has about 12,500 employees and includes a large number of professional engineers and people with advanced degrees. The company uses a complex matrix system of organizing work which requires of employees high skill in communicating, problem solving, and relating:

> There are project offices and functional areas of technical capabilities such as structures, dynamics, guidance and control. A project office, to perform its task, must call upon capabilities and people throughout the organization....No one can really get his job done in this kind of a system without working with others. (p. 360)

When the open organization model is applied, the focus is not on properties precluding change, but on how these properties can be assets for planned change. If we work with, not against, such complexities, the proactive managerial role can be strengthened.

The Roles of Managers and Change Specialists

The complementary roles of managers and consultant change specialists are analogous to the traditional distinction between line and staff roles. Like a staff person, the professional OD specialist is oriented to knowledge and to a cosmopolitan professional community based on common knowledge or technology. By contrast, the manager's line role is oriented to authority and administrative coordination within a given organization. In the broadest sense, *staff functions* have to do with expertise, while *line* or *operating functions* have to do with legal and economic authority and "rulership," with supervision of personnel, and with decision-making responsibilities. The key differences between the role of the change specialist and that of the manager are the style of operation and the basis for influence. The following descriptions will show what is involved in each of these roles, and how they complement each other.

THE MANAGER ROLE

The effective executive gets things done through mechanisms and systems (Likert, 1961; Barnard, 1962). Senior line officers, administrators, or executives in large, complex organizations have little time and are exposed to continuing crises and pressures. They are the major delegates of legal, economic, and even moral authority from the institution to individuals.

In planning change, the manager's most appropriate role is that of an indirect change agent. Managers create and support development mechanisms and can decide when to introduce changes into the main structure of the organization. If they try to be knowledge-based change agents, they suffer at least five disadvantages:

- Their authority and role can create resistance, miscommunication, or overcommitment.
- They tend to be out of date on emerging knowledge and change techniques.
- They tend to overplay a specific idea or approach.
- They lack time for following through.
- They must maintain the organization's balance between stability and change.

The limitations of managers as direct change agents emerge when they have had wide discretion in creating new and experimental organizations. Overselling a specific idea and too much ego-investment have been common. Since managers spend much time being busy day-to-day administrators, and since they lack a full technical grasp, many of their innovations are based on conjecture, training, reading, and experience. Hazard (1969) describes the role conflicts which limit managers in the change process. He notes several basic barriers to change, such as absence of an explicit change agent identity and a weak knowledge base. He concludes that managers should take responsibility for building planned change mechanisms into the organization rather than attempting personally to play the change agent role. (See also Lazarsfield, 1963; Meeth, 1971.)

THE EXTERNAL CHANGE SPECIALIST

The change specialist role has been related to staff as opposed to line functions. However, the change specialist's role goes beyond that of the usual technician or assistant. The change specialist is capable not only of tabulation and narrative reporting, but also of technically competent data collection. He or she must be skilled in conducting comprehensive diagnostic analysis and strategic study of an entire system.

While a manager uses authority to bring about structural changes, a change specialist influences the organization's future through knowledge and process skills. In a discussion about conflict resolution through the use of a *third party* (outsider mediating between two parties in conflict), Walton (1969) has described attributes generally characteristic of a change specialist:

1) high professional expertise regarding social processes;
2) low power over fate of principals;
3) high control over confrontation setting and processes;
4) moderate knowledge about principles, issues, and background factors;
5) neutrality or balance with respect to substantive outcome, personal relationships, and conflict resolution methodology. (p. 150)

Literature on management consultants points out main characteristics of the professional-technical role in OD (Vollmer and Mills, 1966). As described by sociologists, the consultant role is highly professional. It requires great integrity and self-discipline, outstanding knowledge and skill, strong commitment to the client's fate, and high status, credentials, and autonomy (Bennis, 1969).

The external consultant comes closest to the ideal of a knowledge-based change specialist. The external consultant works by *mandate*, commitment by the organization's officers to use his or her professional skills fully in key areas. The consultant has high *expertise*—broad, deep knowledge and experience necessary for major interventions. This expertise is reflected in credentials, accomplishments, and an up-to-date grasp of the array of change strategies, disciplines, and specialties. Finally, the consultant has *autonomous status* based upon the respect of the organization's officers for his or her professional judgment about choice of techniques and implementation strategies.

An external consultant is required whenever an organization is faced with the necessity of *second-order* change—change which influences the entire course of an organization. Such a consultant can offer a wider experiential base than an insider in understanding an organization's dynamics and solving its problems. Often, what is a unique crisis to a particular organization is a well-known problem which a consultant has helped resolve on previous occasions. Most importantly, the external consultant is not bound by group norms and conceptual biases of the client organization, and is much more likely to diagnose problems correctly and to discover solutions that transcend group-bound thinking. Insiders alone cannot, by the theory of logical types, achieve change in the direction of the whole organization. This theory states that "whatever involves *all* of a collection must not be one of the collection" (Watzlawick, Weakland, and Fisch, 1974, p. 6).

The external consultant should be a peer of senior officers of the organization in prestige, expertise, and trust. By training and background, the change specialist may well aspire to a national career in planned change and have advanced training in applied behavioral science and consultant skills. The role probably does not require managerial experience, however. The specialist's reference group is likely to be people in similar roles in other organizations. He or she does not have ambitions to become a manager, but sees the change specialist role as comparable in status and importance and as a better use of professional talents. The change specialist's influence is used, not to dilute managerial authority, but to strengthen the ability of senior officers to manage an organization's future. At the same time, the external consultant introduces greater flexibility into the system through interrelations among parts.

THE INTERNAL CHANGE SPECIALIST

The internal professional-technical change specialist monitors vast technical resources and facilitates their introduction into the organization. He or she has skills in consultation, organization diagnosis, and training; knowledge of social and organizational functioning; and a high level of self-awareness. (Bennis, 1969). The internal consultant works best when teamed with an external consultant (Beckard, 1969; Bennis, 1969; Lippitt, 1969; Lippitt, Watson, and Westley, 1958). As an insider, the internal consultant achieves in-depth understanding of the organization, but pays a commensurate price in the loss of system-wide perspective. However, the blend of the internal consultant's deeper view with the external consultant's broader view overcomes the limitations of each and creates the best leverage for diagnosis and planned change. Once a second-order change has been initiated, the internal consultant can provide the continuity and steady effort needed to sustain and extend that change. Most authorities, available data, and our consulting experience confirm the value of collaboration between internal and external consultants to achieve changes in organization climate and direction (Friedlander and Brown, 1974; Lippitt, 1969; and Taylor and Bowers, 1972).

The internal change specialist is most likely to be employed by organizations facing rapid environmental change. If the organization's leaders are acutely aware of major incentives for planned change and see the applicability of OD and management science in other areas of society, they are likely to make the change specialist role an internal part of the organization. Often, such leadership consists of sophisticated managers who foster such ideas as team building, delegation of responsibility, and increased competence in interpersonal relations.

Figure 11 presents a general model of the ideal internal consultant role. The model includes three core professional attributes of a management consultant prototype. It also includes external supports necessary to enable an internal consultant to function effectively. One of these is access to a senior external consultant, who is used to diagnose and plan the best internal role model, and later to serve as a resource person after an internal consultant is hired.

The external consultant works with top administration to define and redefine the internal consultant's functions. These will vary from organization to organization, and from one phase of development to another. Role definition should be based upon professional analysis of an institution's particular needs. Size, complexity of the organization, governance, operating pro-

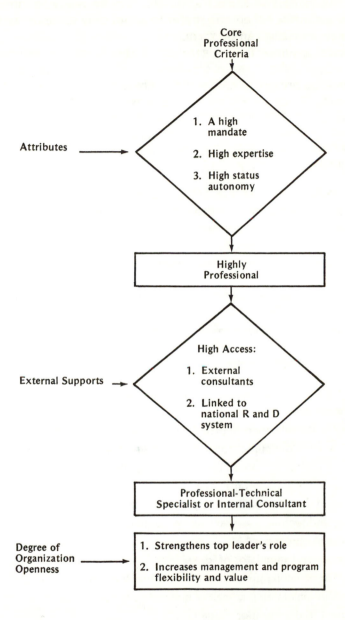

Figure 11. The Professional-technical Internal Role

cedures, and level of involvement desired by top administration must be weighed. The leaders of some institutions may be ready to introduce the entire concept, while others will prefer to adopt only some of the functions that a change specialist can perform.

This model assumes that, regardless of the functions performed by a change specialist, the three professional attributes and the two external supports must be present to ensure the internal consultant's ability to achieve desired results. Those results are two: strengthening the top leaders' role, and increasing administrative and program flexibility. The organization may choose levels of involvement for the internal consultant. However, if essential elements of the model are missing, the consultant's ability to effect planned change will be lessened seriously.

FUNCTIONS OF CHANGE SPECIALISTS

The functions performed by the external or internal consultant are manifold; they may include the following:

Internal catalyst for change

Link to national technologies, innovations, and research and development systems

Resource to those engaged in the organization's planning and decision making

Stimulator of continuous research to improve planning and decision making

Sensitivity barometer to changing demands in the organization's environment

Guide to professional literature and data sources for monitoring new developments

Center for identification of promising alternatives to current practice

Resource and communication link to senior administrators

Resource to those responsible for clarifying goals

Monitor of progress toward goals

Assistant in deriving measurable objectives for the organization

Training and technical assistant for management development

Mediator in conflicts

Questioner and stimulator of ideas

Initiator in developing management information systems

Assistant in maintaining a healthy internal communication network

Participant in organization research

Supporter of knowledge utilization in decision making

Member of a long-range planning committee or team

Resource to various task groups and other ad hoc groups

Disseminator of internal innovations

Creator of appropriate organization renewal mechanisms

Introducing the Change Specialist Role

The first step in undertaking a planned change is to assess an organization's readiness for such an undertaking. Careful assessment can save time, money, and energy. Senior officers must perceive a clear need for change and must want to apply new knowledge and professional skills to bring about that change. (See chapter 6 for a discussion of diagnosis.)

It may be wise to engage an external consultant to make a system diagnosis before committing resources to implementing any plan. A diagnosis can pinpoint organization issues and potential pitfalls. Based on the diagnosis, consultants and managers can prepare a plan describing change objectives and strategies, and the activities and roles of the external or internal change specialist. Management should approve this as a typical development plan, making sure that organization members understand the change objectives and the key concepts behind them.

A change specialist is selected to carry out the plan. An internal specialist may require time for pre-service training to provide a range of knowledge and skills, especially in the applied behavioral sciences. The specialist should be introduced formally with clear approval and support of upper-level management.

Initial diagnosis and implementation of the plan also require building four kinds of support groups: the chief executive officer and senior staff, external and internal change specialists, a staff resource team to work with the consultant, and an informal communication network among staff to support the change effort. Planning and evaluation roles must be assigned and clarified with appropriate people.

The first major intervention should be made in an area of visible need which is amenable to change with existing resources and able to yield measurable, visible success. Further interventions are planned collaboratively by management, consultant, and resource team based on results of the first intervention.

In our view, consulting, teaching, and counseling are virtually identical activities. The model the facilitator follows in each case in much the same. When a change specialist initiates activities which invite adults to grow personally, socially, and organizationally, attention to certain steps will bring greater benefit to the client. Briefly, the steps include entry, contract formulation and establishment of a helping relationship, problem identification and diagnosis, setting goals and planning action, taking action and cycling feedback, and contract completion (Lippitt and Lippitt, 1978 b, pp. 8–9). The following case study illustrates a successful intervention undertaken in order to share our consulting skills with people working as internal change specialists in a state social service agency. The study presents a typical training intervention often sought by managers to solve organization problems. It illustrates the kind of impact change specialists can have, and provides practical suggestions for a successful training event.

Case Study. Consulting with Consultants: An In-house Training Group*

Because of her attendance at one of our previous workshops on consulting skills, an administrator of an in-house training group in a human services government agency called on us for similar training for about forty people working in her branch. These were resource people with change specialist roles. They were organized into four divisions. The information, evaluation, and research division evaluated delivery of services in the field. The management training division trained new agency managers. The curriculum development division provided materials for in-service training and promotion of agency services. And the external resources division developed and used new knowledge in subject areas. Their clients were other agency members involved in delivering services to clients in the field. We were fortunate that our initial contact had seen the connection between the consultation skills we taught and the work done by these in-house professionals. Convinced that a similar workshop for the in-house training group would be appropriate, she influenced the chief of this group to invite us to a meeting to discuss contracting our services. Because of her introduction, our entry involved less selling and more negotiation about what they wanted and what we could do. The complete contract negotiation took three meetings between high administrators and us. When completed, we had a written statement of what we would do; when, where, and with whom we would do it; and how much we would be paid.

First, we held individual interviews with all potential workshop participants in their offices at hours of their choice. Our strategy was to find answers to such questions as:

- What is your job like now?
- How would you like it to be?
- What would help you move toward your ideal?
- What hinders your achieving your ideal?
- What do you want from the training?
- What are the ways you learn best?

This was the first time anybody had interviewed these people in advance of a workshop. The process drew a good response. It also encouraged them to vent views about job conditions and problems.

The interviews allowed us to meet the people we would be working with. On the first day of the workshop we were able to call people by first names; we had group rapport from the beginning. We also were prepared to call upon some of the participants' strengths which we had spotted in interviews. Two participants had already done private consulting, and another had studied with a widely known authority on consulting. We stroked these people for their strengths ("Carol has already done some work in this area.") and rewarded them for their uniqueness. This strategy helps prevent a transactional analysis game called NIGYYSOB ("Now I've got you,

*Case study written by Ann Linquist

you son of a bitch."). By acknowledging individual strengths early in workshop activities, we could include participants in the teaching process by inviting them to share their special knowledge or experience in the subject. Otherwise, they might wait until the last day of the workshop to say something like, "Well, when *I* did my training in that area...." This one-upmanship can be avoided by building an alliance instead of permitting a competitive spirit to develop. We were able to eliminate further entry problems in the workshops by orienting participants to our approach during the interviews. We explained our distinctions between an internal and an external consultant and the six phases of consulting.

Interviewing also allowed us to set contracts for learning before the workshop days. When working with adults, the leader does not pressure them to learn. Adults participate because they have identified needs, and the leader facilitates their satisfying those needs. By meeting everyone beforehand, we were able to find out what they wanted and tailor our workshop to fit their needs. Specificity in contracting is important. People tend to say that anything you give them will be all right, but they don't really mean that. It is important to watch for signs of what is going to excite them and what is going to disappoint them.

By asking *how* they preferred to learn, we were able to select learning formats wisely. In this case we learned that many participants enjoyed getting reading material to prepare themselves for the workshop, so we supplied workshop materials in advance. We also ascertained how they would prefer the workshop be taught. Some groups will not sit still for a lecture, and other groups will rebel if asked to break into small group work. It helps to know how a group prefers to work.

Interviewing and contracting for learning had an added bonus. They helped clarify not only personal needs, but organizational needs. They encouraged integrative thinking and broader perspectives as workers were invited to view themselves as part of a larger whole working toward shared goals.

Group learning can take many forms, but it is good to remember certain attributes of adult learners. (1) They learn best by doing (being actively involved). (2) They learn best through problem solving. (3) They want to know how they are doing. (4) They prefer an informal learning environment. We structure our consulting skills workshops so that learning experiences will take these attributes into account.

For example, our first exercise with the group was to do role playing. We asked them to divide into groups of three with one person being an interviewer, one an interviewee, and one an observer and analyst. The interviewer was to act as a consultant probing for problem areas felt by the interviewee (client). The consultant interviewer was to identify areas for improving competence the client wanted to work on and to find out what resources, special skills, and experiences the client was willing to offer the group as a whole. The analyst observed the diagnostic interview to collect data which would be used to help client, consultant, and observer improve the process and quality of information.

Roles were rotated and results of the diagnostic data collection were recorded on newsprint and posted. Here we called a coffee break. This pause allowed the group to share observations about similarities and differences of roles, interests, and needs of participants. The exercise combined building skills with gathering information and helped focus the trainers' and participants' attention on concerns common to the group.

We followed this activity with a more common teaching method, the lecture. We presented the group with our concept of consulting, outlining the place of the consultant in planning change, the power available to the internal consultant, and reasons a consultant can be an important resource to a work group. Our lecture combined talking and soliciting discussion from the group. Pure lecture allows for the presentation of much information fairly quickly, but when comments are solicited from the group, they become more involved in the activity. This balance can be slanted according to the needs of the group at any given time. We decide whether we should tell what we know or ask participants to think for themselves, so that we may organize their comments.

We also asked each participant to write down a situation in which he or she had been helpful to another person within the past week. After each identified an experience, we asked them to describe the action taken and decide whether their help was accepted or rejected. Then they were asked to diagnose reasons for this acceptance or rejection. After completing this activity individually in writing, the group compiled a master list of helpful and unhelpful behavior. This process was followed by a short discussion on the nature of giving effective feedback, emphasizing the effectiveness of telling the truth in a caring way.

We were particularly fortunate that our initial contact had prior knowledge of our methods. She aided us in preliminary customizing of workshop materials by rewriting two case studies, changing the situations from descriptions of industrial problems to the kinds of problems faced by a human services government agency. By using the case studies, we were able to create role-playing situations which involved an internal consultant in group problem solving. The case studies focused attention on such issues as the role of consultants, their dependence upon the people paying or inviting them to participate, their ability to diagnose the problem, their ability to help others see the problem, and their ability to aid problem solving. The following are the case study briefing sheets we used in the group.

DEPARTMENT OF HUMAN SERVICES
Briefing Sheet
THE COMMISSIONER'S ROLE

You are a strong commissioner of a successful state agency. You have been with the agency for five years, and have been in similar positions with the state for twenty-five years.

You believe in modern management methods and have kept the agency up to date with new practices.

You also believe in the importance of communication between various areas of the agency, particularly at the top, and you want to be well informed about activities of all areas of the agency.

One of your management practices is to hold a weekly two-hour staff meeting attended by your immediate subordinates: assistant commissioner, assistant commissioner for program, assistant commissioner for management and budget, assistant commissioner for medical services, and assistant commissioner for data systems. At this meeting, you bring the group up to date on recent policy development, discuss long-range planning, and review current operations. Each area head presents a report on matters in his or her area that should be brought to the group's attention. This information is discussed, and action is taken when appropriate.

You feel that in recent months the staff meeting has been getting out of hand. Some reports have dealt with trivia unnecessary at such a meeting. There has been too much discussion and too little action on many agenda items. You have frequently been forced to make decisions for the group to get action.

You have talked about this with your director of staff development who is supposed to be an expert in group relations. You have invited her to your next executive meeting. She suggested that the whole staff discuss the problem.

You have decided to limit the agenda of today's staff meeting to one subject: "How can we improve the effectiveness of our weekly staff meetings?" You have had your secretary notify the staff that this will be the agenda for today.

DEPARTMENT OF PUBLIC WELFARE
Briefing Sheet
AGENCY STAFF ROLES

The commissioner's weekly two-hour executive meeting has deteriorated steadily in effectiveness and become virtually useless for communication.

The bulk of the meeting is taken up with reports of executive action that you have heard about previously, and with an analysis of the past week's program problems and discussion of corrective actions.

Each of you is expected to give a report of activities in your area and to discuss current operational problems.

It has been the practice, based on bitter experience, not to bring up anything controversial or of a complex nature at these meetings, because the commissioner tends to make quick judgments and decisions that put you on the spot. He also tends to use staff meetings to criticize the performance of an individual, to the discomfort of all present; so you have avoided getting into that position.

Most of you feel that the commissioner wants to keep close control of all operations, and he wants to be involved in decisions on all important matters. Therefore, you tend to get his help on these matters in private meetings with him rather than at these executive meetings.

You are responsible executives, and you are concerned with what you feel is wasted time at these meetings. But you know the commissioner believes strongly in the weekly meeting as a communication device, and you have been reluctant to bring up this subject with him.

Last week he mentioned that he was getting concerned that perhaps the meetings were not as effective as they should be, to which you all agreed. His secretary notified you that the current meeting will deal with the single agenda item: "How can we improve the effectiveness of my weekly executive meetings?" She also informs you that the commissioner has asked the director of staff development to come to the meeting to serve as an in-house consultant on this problem.

STAFF MEMBERS

Assistant commissioner (with agency twenty years)
Assistant commissioner for program (with agency four years)
Assistant commissioner for management and budget (with agency two years)
Assistant commissioner for medical services (with agency five years)
Assistant commissioner for data systems (with agency for two years)

Participants were asked to form groups of threes or fours so that one person could take on a particular role in the case study situation and others could coach him or her in that part. Then the role players came to the center of the group (fish-bowling) and began to act the part of an in-house consultant meeting with the group who wanted to change ineffective ways of operating.

The observers had checklists to assess the performance of both the consultant and the consultee. Three different checklists were distributed among them: one for the consultant's actions, one for the consultees' actions, and one for the dynamics of the situation itself. Discussion helped determine some pitfalls and strengths observed by the group.

A three-day workshop can be a grinding ordeal or an exhilarating learning experience. Participants must be attentive and sharp, since they have the major role in learning. We like to intersperse learning activities with exercises which make people feel good, raise the energy in the room, and promote sharing among members. With this group we did what we call "success bombardment." We invited each member to share with the group a successful experience he or she had had during the last month. Finally, we asked them each to share a successful experience of the last week. The group gained a tremendous rush of good feeling, appreciation for others and self, and eagerness to learn more.

Another method we used to build a positive spirit was to invite each person to pick a partner and share one thing which he or she likes about himself or herself—mental, physical, emotional, or spiritual. These pairs then formed groups of four, introduced their partners, and shared what they liked about themselves. The activity built group cohesion and helped participants appreciate each other as individuals.

Like all workshops that take several days, this event had periods of highs and lows. The initially high energy reflected the participants' expectations for the workshop ("This is going to be really good. . . . I am going to get what I want."). After the first day the energy level dropped somewhat ("This is not exactly what I had in mind."). Such a drop is inevitable since no workshop can meet the exact expectations of each participant. By customizing this workshop through interviewing and preparation of supplementary materials, we minimized this drop in energy. Nonetheless, the drop is something trainers need to expect and cope with. Participants may even drop out from dissatisfaction ("This is no good; they are not meeting my needs."). In this workshop we had no drop-outs. Instead participants made the adjustment to what they could get out of the workshop ("Perhaps my expectations were a little high."). By the end of training, their energy had gone back up again ("This experience has been valuable to me.").

To stay current with the group's reactions to our training, we used a short evaluation form at the end of each day's activities. The form consisted of a quick impressions list of twenty-one descriptive adjective pairs, such as "clear–confusing." The participants marked a seven-point scale for each pair of opposites. This kind of evaluation is formative—it lets the leader adjust his or her strategies to meet participants' needs more exactly. (For a discussion of the merits of the semantic differential in formative evaluation, see chapter 11.)

For our final evaluation, we asked participants to write answers to the following questions:

- How do you feel about the workshop's achieving its stated objectives?
- How do you feel about the mix and balance of learning activities?
- How do you feel about the pace and level of learning experience?
- How successful were we in building a learning community?
- How could staff have helped more?
- How could participants have helped more?
- What would you recommend be done differently in the next workshop?
- Additional comments you would like to make.

The final evaluation let us know what the participants felt worked well and what did not. It also provided an assessment that we gave to the administrator responsible for our performance. Through the final evaluation she could tell if the group had gotten its money's worth.

6

DIAGNOSTIC REVIEW

ORGANIZATIONS AND PEOPLE have many characteristics in common. One characteristic shared by successful, creative persons and organizations is the consistent use of a fact-founded approach to problem solving (Steiner, 1965). They separate source from content when evaluating information. They follow a problem wherever it leads. Developing a capacity for data-based feedback and problem solving is essential if a person or an organization is to be internally responsive, adaptable—"intelligent" in the words of Piaget (1950). And internal adaptability is prerequisite to an organization's ability to respond to the external environment effectively.

When confronted with a problem or a challenge to grow, an open organization may obtain data-processing assistance from two sources: collaborative relationships with outside specialists, and internal feedback mechanisms. If a situation requires second-order change (a change affecting the organization as a whole), an external consultant can be particularly helpful. One method used by external consultants is *survey feedback*, participatory data collected from members of the organization, analyzed in summary fashion, and fed back to organization members with extensive group discussion (Friedlander and Brown, 1974). The diagnostic review described in this chapter is a survey feedback process that diagnoses organization strengths, weaknesses, and growth potential in terms of the open organization model. It is a system-wide self-study process especially appropriate at major turning points in the life of an organization.

Internal feedback mechanisms are essential to maintain growth accomplished through second-order change and to make full, efficient use of organization resources. Internal mechanisms may include the use of internal specialists to facilitate planned change, and action research teams to conduct ongoing data collection and problem solving. Chapter 9 will describe how an action research team functions and what it can accomplish.

Data-Based Change

Professional diagnosis of organizations is not a cure-all or a sure-fire methodology. The potential of outside and in-house consultants and formal renewal programs for organizations has only begun to be tapped. The state of the art of organization renewal is analogous to that of psychotherapy for individuals and medical treatment for health problems. As scientific knowledge about organizations becomes more accurate, change strategies will become less one-sided, more comprehensive. Their potential will be immeasurable. An accurate model of an organization and its potential can make a difference of millions of dollars with a very small investment in consulting time.

FORMAL RENEWAL PROGRAMS

The advantage of formal renewal programs as opposed to low-key, informal efforts is that organizations work largely by making changes explicit and institutionalized. The question is not *whether* to institutionalize change processes. It is rather what kind of improvement to seek and which order of change, first or second. Any method which can institutionalize system-wide diagnosis and ongoing release of organization potential will contribute to organization health. All rubrics under which such organization change takes place today—research and development programs, organizational renewal programs, staff development, organization development, management development, planning, planning groups, long-range planning programs, development plans, self-studies—increase the chance for organization growth and development by being explicit. The danger in their becoming explicit is that they may favor a narrow diagnostic model, arbitrarily choose techniques of intervention, and become preoccupied with first-order change.

Even with the present state of the art, four factors are known to promote the release of organization potential and enable second-order change:

1. DEVELOPING AND WORKING THROUGH A STRONG FORMAL LEADERSHIP TEAM (POWER AND STRUCTURE). The leadership team must consist of a partnership between the chief executive, other top staff officers, and board representation. If the organization is nonprofit, top volunteer policy makers should be included as well.

2. IN-HOUSE AND OUTSIDE CONSULTANTS (EXPERIENCE AND SKILL). Only professional organization diagnosticians are suitable. Internal consultants may combine organization development skills with technical specialties; however, their OD role must be primary.

3. A FORMAL CHANGE PROGRAM (ENERGY AND PURPOSE). A formally legitimized program is usually conducted for at least a year under some rubric such as self-study, long-range planning, reorganizational study, research and development, or organization development. The diagnostic review is designed to initiate such a program.

4. AN ADEQUATE CONCEPTUAL FRAMEWORK (A MODEL). A comprehensive framework enables leaders and consultants to be open-minded and visionary while making concrete plans and mastering practical details. The open organization model is the underlying framework for the diagnostic review as a change program.

THE VALUE OF SURVEY FEEDBACK

Survey feedback is an important method of initiating a formal change program. It involves much collaboration between inside authorities and outside consultants. The collaboration may include designing questions, sampling decisions, analysis and interpretation, conducting feedback sessions with organization units, and planning change to increase benefits and reduce dysfunctions.

From the early work of Peak (1955), later expanded by Gross and Grambsch (1968), Peterson (1970b), and Bowers and Franklin (1972), such feedback has taken on clear organization development or guidance purposes. These researchers have shown that discrepancies between "is" and "should be" (real and ideal) responses to critical questions will generate motivation for change. Appel and Mink (1977) have developed a useful four-sector scatter diagram for determining priorities of change goals using, in part, the real–ideal discrepancy format. In chapter 7 we discuss this method.

Many studies of small groups have demonstrated the impact of feedback upon group process and outcome. Detroit Edison studies found that in groups experiencing intense feedback sessions, a more positive attitude change occurred than in groups with less intense feedback sessions (Baumgartel, 1959). Other studies have shown: (1) participants are more receptive to feedback after meetings, (2) face-to-face feedback sessions are more effective than written reports, and (3) the quality of interaction of participants improves after a feedback session (Friedlander and Brown, 1974).

In a landmark study contrasting OD methods, Bowers (1973) presented data on 14,000 respondents in twenty-three organizations. Four different methods were contrasted—survey feedback, interpersonal consultation, task process consultation, and laboratory training—in organizations receiving data feedback influencing these results. Survey feedback appeared the only method significantly associated with this variable. Of the other methods, only interpersonal process consultation was associated with improvement on more than half of sixteen indices measured.

Problems often arise in developing a data-based feedback system because of individual and organization complexity, ego investment in diverse viewpoints, and communication errors. These reflect human and social realities. But there is hope in building upon what has worked in the past. The concept of *data convergence* promises to increase the validity and utility of data feedback. When diverse groups are surveyed to gather opinions, diagnose problems, and derive plans, the first results are sometimes quite disparate. When, however, the data are summarized and fed back to groups with explanations for the positions taken by each group, a second round of gathering data often reveals a convergence of the groups toward a common agreement. Thus, dialogue between those providing data and feedback results in a convergence of diagnostic interpretation (Bowers and Franklin, 1972; Hauser, Pecorella, and Wissler, 1975; and Heller, 1969). Convergence of data from different sources on the same event can increase the validity of perceptions (Friedlander and Brown, 1974; Taylor and Bowers, 1972). Temporal convergence can be obtained by examining patterns over time (Bass, 1976; Friedlander and Brown, 1974; Golembiewski, Billingsley, and Yeager, 1976; Lippitt, 1969; and Taylor and Bowers, 1972).

Survey feedback, then, is a powerful data-based intervention. Like other methods, such as action research teams, it rests on several assumptions: Sharing data can be valuable, especially when it has not been shared previously and has influenced or is influencing organization process. Sharing data increases potential for responsiveness and adaptability. Data presented in an "is" and "should be" format can generate energy for change, and provide the basis for action plans. Participating in decisions can lead to increased commitment (Friedlander and Brown, 1974). And confronting and working through differences among people who work together can enhance collaboration. The uses of data in a change effort are shown in figure 12.

USING SURVEY FEEDBACK

The use of survey feedback is fairly common in current OD practice. In business and industry, the survey may be referred to as *sensing*. Sensing may be conducted within a work group, horizontally across work groups, or vertically through hierarchical levels of the organization. In fields like education, the survey is a common method used by researchers. The survey research method may be abused when it is directed at a narrow, predefined problem area. For example, a small manufacturing plant may hire a consultant to help "improve communication." The consultant will probably take a vertical-slice sensing of communication problems. However, if the problem area was not accurately identified by the company, the results are likely to be too narrow, out of context, and possibly even misleading.

Much so-called organization intervention is the application of a fixed set of answers or techniques—usually first-order, like team building—to a predetermined problem. Organization leaders are sometimes so hungry for action and change that they jump into buying one of the prepackaged answers and methods on the current advice market. For example, who helps an organization decide whether it needs fund raising or improved fiscal management of funds already available? Who helps an organization decide whether it needs an architect to plan a new building or a program planner to structure a program less dependent on buildings? Such choices of technical services and utilities are. crucial. The mere fact that an organization announces a desired change, such as a new building, and calls on widely known technical experts, say, in architecture and construction, does not mean a new building will actually improve organization health. The outcome of a change depends on whether the initial organization diagnosis and the choice of strategy were accurate. If a church, hospital, or college does not need a building, then the best architect will probably be of little help. A technical expert has a specific knowledge for sale, and the organization usually confronts the technical expert with a given set of parameters. In this case the directive is, "Build."

Clarifying values is a key component of rational decision making, practicality, and realism. Asking which technical expert is appropriate or what intervention is needed are questions of value. What are the organization's purposes? What are its strengths and weaknesses? What are its priorities? What is its current stage of development? Conscious exploration of these questions

1. Data help a manager define the problem.

2. Data enable a manager to see a need for change.

3. Data help a manager identify appropriate solutions.

4. Data provide a basis for a manager to measure results of a change effort.

5. Data assist a manager in dealing with complex problems without over-simplification.

6. Data permit a manager to avoid relying on authority figures.

7. Data enable a staff person to take an experimental-minded attitude without relying heavily upon pressure, persuasion, or prayer.

8. Data enable a staff person to get some indication of the results of change efforts he or she has stimulated.

Figure 12. Why Data Are Powerful

Adapted from "Diagnostic studies and surveys: powerful tools for the training director" by W. R. Mahler. Paper presented to the National Conference of the American Society for Training and Development, Anaheim, 1970. Reproduced by permission of the author will uncover ambiguities in values. While not a cure-all, value clarification can unquestionably reduce the unconscious avoidance of key questions. Perhaps the failure to clarify values and then in turn to define problems accurately are the two key factors which keep organizations from developing effectively. It takes much less effort to select one of many available first-order solutions—the kind that works on building a team out of the crew of the Titanic while the ship is about to smash into an iceberg. This has been the fate of many organizations.

The diagnostic review is a data-based change program which uses an open organization approach to diagnosing the whole organization and its parts. Survey feedback instruments are designed to identify system malfunctions within and between various levels of the organization in terms of three variables: unity, internal responsiveness, and external responsiveness. For example, improvement of a manufacturer's marketing (an external responsiveness variable) may require diagnosing problems in the relationships among materials management, accounting, data processing, and product assembly functions (internal responsiveness variables). The diagnostic review takes a holistic, clinical, highly intuitive approach to the identification of problems and growth areas.

A Diagnostic Review Consultation

The diagnostic review is a process for in-depth organization self-study. It provides more comprehensive and intensive analysis than most planning or goal-setting processes. An external consultant facilitates it with broad participation by organization leaders who must set aside time and energy. A diagnostic review may be precipitated by a crisis—a deficit or an unresolved leadership struggle. The crisis is used as an impetus to open up a concentrated and comprehensive review of the organization's situation and future possibilities. Although a diagnostic review may be brought about by outside groups, such as a regional office for a local government agency, an accrediting body for a hospital, or a corporate headquarters for a field operation, the client organization must have a strong sense of internal ownership and responsibility.

The subject of a diagnostic review is shown in figure 13. It includes clarification of the organization's mission, environment, and internal operations with increased unity growing out of mission review.

Working with staff members, consultants set up an ongoing process that will help the organization's leaders answer at any time basic questions:

- Where are we now? (current situation)
- Where do we want to go? (goals and objectives)
- How do we expect to get there? (strategies, tactics, and policies)
- What organization structures are needed? (matrix, task force, or single leader)
- Who is going to pay? (source of funds)
- How will we know when we've arrived? (evaluation plan)

The diagnostic review and self-study provides a concentrated, comprehensive, professional analysis demanding full staff involvement, written diagnosis and recommendations, and development of the organizational skills of managers. The review favors use of open systems theory as a framework to define the organization's problems and indicate the direction of desired change.

The diagnostic review draws on management models and techniques, many of which were developed in profit organizations. It also takes into account the peculiar dynamics of voluntary nonprofit organizations which need to maintain high involvement, consent, and sense of purpose while integrating these with the business realities of the enterprise.

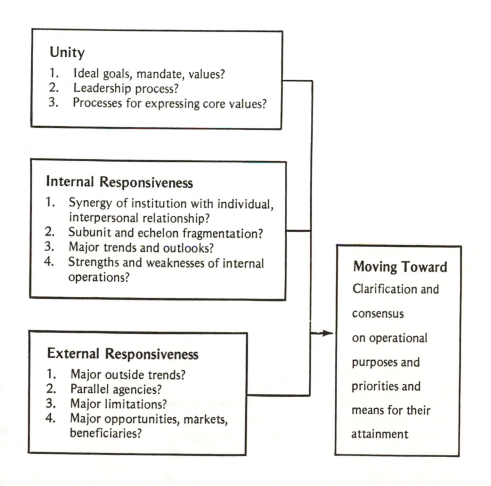

Figure 13. Aspects of the Diagnostic Review

When designed for organizations engaged in community action, religious, educational, health care, charitable, welfare, and youth work organizations, the review tries to establish a broad data base. It often involves membership or marketing surveys. The diagnostic approach may yield information applicable to neighborhood, metropolitan, regional, and national units, ranging from large urban or national organizations to relatively small churches, agencies, neighborhood organizations, community colleges, and industries.

GOALS

Depending on the situation, symptoms, and motives of each organization, the diagnostic process will be an open review without reservations. The review presents a picture of the present dynamics of an organization or a subunit. It enables more open than normal sharing among leaders and staff. It aims to increase communication and common agreement about future directions. During the review process, a clearer perception of the organization's direction emerges. Individuals and groups make data-based plans and begin to implement them.

Information is only one part of organization renewal. Many studies are discarded because results run counter to opinions and feelings. The diagnostic review attempts to integrate sophisticated data collection with an involvement process that results in action. The review process blends knowledge, research, joint problem solving, clinical insights, and highly intuitive diagnosis with the development of appropriate action plans.

WHEN TO CONDUCT

The diagnostic review is appropriate only at critical periods or adaptable moments in the life of an organization. It is tailored to supply quick, comprehensive knowledge at major turning points or periods of organizational soul-searching. The diagnostic review is indicated when leaders have a sense of urgency precipitated by:

- Transition from one stage of growth to another
- Sense of unrealized potential
- Mounting deficits, fiscal insolvency, profit decline
- Conflicts in the organization about its future direction
- Increasing dissatisfaction with drift and inaction
- Low staff morale, high turnover
- Major changes in the organization's environment
- Declining appeal of standard services or products
- Retooling to meet new problems or opportunities
- New leaders desiring to take new approaches

The analysis may take from one to several months to complete from the time the external consultant is engaged until the summary report is presented. The period should be timed to ensure no loss of momentum and timeliness of the recommendations. The depth and breadth of the diagnostic review make its application unsuitable more often than every three to four years, though brief annual updating may be desirable.

STAGES

The diagnostic review corresponds to the six phases in the consulting process as identified by Lippitt and Lippitt (1978b).

1.   INITIAL ENTRY. The external consultant confers with the manager to develop a consensus about ways in which a diagnostic study may help satisfy organization needs. A joint analysis of the possibilities results in a tentative plan for diagnostic review (or both parties agree to discontinue the relationship).

2.   CONTRACT FORMULATION AND ESTABLISHING A HELPING RELATIONSHIP. A brief working agreement is prepared which defines diagnostic activities to be performed, the consulting relationship, specific objectives for the diagnostic study identifiable at this point, the time period of the consultation, and the cost for services described in the agreement.

3.   PROBLEM IDENTIFICATION, DIAGNOSTIC ANALYSIS, AND RECOMMENDATIONS. A survey is conducted which consists of individual structured interviews of top and middle managers and of other key people in the organization. Within each unit and administrative level, information is collected, organized, and analyzed in terms of the open organization model. The diagnosis is summarized in a written report which identifies areas of strength and weakness, and discrepancies between present actualities and desired goals. The report also presents various options for action and recommends specific actions.

4.   GOAL SETTING AND PLANNING. The consultant presents the review summary to the client organization for discussion and planning. At this point, the consulting relationship may be terminated. Or, the consultant may be asked to facilitate a jointly determined action plan based upon the findings of the diagnostic review. The plan and the consultant's role in its implementation are described in the final working agreement, which serves as the contract for consulting. Whatever the specific terms of the agreement, the consultant's objective is to foster the client–consultant relationship through joint agreement on needs and goals, joint evaluation and revision of plans, and open communication between consultant and client.

5.   TAKING ACTION AND CYCLING FEEDBACK. The action plan provides a blueprint for choosing, orchestrating, and carefully monitoring change steps. In general, activities will include:

- Continuing development of alternatives and possible solutions to specific problems
- Developing skills to enable people to take necessary action
- Establishing procedures to elicit feedback about progress
- Promoting operational flexibility to deal with unexpected problems
- Using feedback to reexamine goals and strategies

6. CONTRACT COMPLETION: CONTINUITY, SUPPORT, AND TERMI-NATION. The external consultant is phased out when immediate goals for improvement are achieved, and independent leadership and data-based feedback processes have become established. Often, the skills of internal consultants are upgraded to manage first-order change in newly established directions. Trained action research teams are another important means of continuing the process of data-based action planning and implementation.

ROLES

Consistent with the open organization model, the diagnostic review encourages responsible, informed participation of leaders, constituents, and members of the organization. It is tailored to help leaders lead. People are interviewed in depth; reports and recommendations are prepared in consultation with leaders. These reports accurately present the ideas and opinions of all relevant groups. Follow-up activities take place within full and open discussion. The approach recognizes each organization as having an innate intelligence (adaptability) which, when aided, will identify its own needs and discover the best ways to fulfill them.

The review process calls for wide prestudy planning and follow-up consultation after the study is made. When working with local units of national organizations, it is often desirable for a knowledgeable staff member to join the external consultant in conducting the study. In-house members implement all action plans. If they need training in processes like team building, the consultant does the training. Under no conditions does the consultant upstage existing leadership structures or replace leaders.

Experiences of consultants in using data to aid development warrant a few notes of caution. First, top leaders tend to abdicate thoughtful, decisive leadership once sophisticated data are collected. They should remember that no amount of data substitutes for hard intellectual discipline, decision making, human relations, and other leadership qualities. Second, data collection by consultants can lead to unwarranted dependency upon them. Their conclusions may be accepted without a thorough critique based on a leader's own experience. No scientific study or consultation aid can replace a manager's personal experience in an organization.

The consultant's role in a diagnostic review differs from that of a consulting firm brought in to provide expert answers. Outside expertise may, of course, aid a diagnostic review, but much of the review focuses upon helping to crystallize and apply the latent wisdom of the organization. The outside consultant often works with an in-house colleague. He or she gives professional guidance for analyzing, planning, and decision making. He or she encourages openness in this process in both scope and time perspective. The consultant can ensure thoroughness in reviewing purposes and internal and external factors independently of daily operations.

The part played by managers in survey feedback is critical. In a study by Roueche and Boggs (1968), the president of a community college was found to be the key to a general "willingness to use data and act on it" (p. 53). Some studies have shown that managers (power brokers) critically influence the perceptions and behavior of those around them. Baumgartel (1959) found perceptions of supervisory behavior changed as a consequence of increased communication and confrontation between hierarchical lines as a direct result of feedback. Chase (1968) showed that feedback tends to equalize a sense of power among various people in hierarchical positions. Klein, Kraut, and Wolfson (1971) and Hauser, Pecorella, and Wissler (1975) report that the use of supervisors in the feedback process results in greater satisfaction and greater perceived use of the data. Antagonistic supervisors can also undermine the process. Alderfer and Ferris (1972) and Hauser et al. (1975) suggest that managers meet in peer groups to prepare feedback or review results and strategies before meeting with subordinates. This "waterfall" process encourages involvement and commitment to the process and follow-up planning.

RESULTS

Written diagnosis and recommendations. Careful in-depth interviews with members of groups crucial to the organization's well-being (staff, governing board, clients, or consumers) bring a detailed description of its problems and potential as viewed by key participants. The diagnosis gives leaders a quick and impartial assessment of where the organization is, compared to where it wants to be.

A written report is no panacea. But it is highly valuable when it summarizes in-depth discussions, interviews, site visits, community consultations, observations of meetings and events, and surveys of records and documents. Besides the consultant's view, data from people inside and outside the organization can be reported (usually anonymously) in detail. If appropriate, an appendix to the report may add any of the following organization and human resource development activities:

- Long-range planning
- New program priorities
- New location and facilities
- Fiscal management systems and actions
- Personnel changes and staff reorganization
- Criterion-referenced or competency-based training programs
- Approaches to new constituencies
- Public relations and promotional activities
- Fund-raising methods and targets
- Market and community surveys
- Mergers and interagency links

In rare but appropriate instances the diagnostic review might recommend that no action be taken or even that the organization consider ending its very existence.

Action start-up. As indicated earlier, the review process is more than a method of gathering data. It is also an intervention that begins change. The review creates a sense of participation and responsibility by members, leaders, and clients or customers of the organization developing the diagnosis. It mobilizes energy for change and provides a blueprint for achieving it. Problems often may be resolved as they are identified. A somewhat arbitrary line divides diagnostic review from intervention phases. That is, the process of participatory diagnosis itself often produces desirable changes as a by-product of new perspectives, relationships, and skills. An accurate problem definition can bring quick remedial action.

When appropriate, the diagnostic review can include experience-based workshops and seminars for managers as part of the process of sharing data and developing leadership skills. In special workshops or informal meetings they may acquire skills and knowledge in such areas as matrix management, team development, budgeting, information systems, supervision and management styles, performance appraisal, conflict management, career planning, job enrichment, time management, in-house consulting, and affirmative action planning.

Resolution of chronic problems or crises. In addition to improved communication and a more widely shared perception of the state of the organization, the diagnostic review often resolves difficult problems. Typical outcomes of this kind are:

- Crystallizing the merger of two national organizations after years of discussion about increasing overlap and competition
- Stabilizing a chronic power struggle among trustees of a community college
- Converting a nearly bankrupt private college into a state-supported institution
- Balancing the budget of a metropolitan agency through city-wide integration
- Avoiding an outside take-over bid of an association by clarifying and strengthening its fund-raising and service program
- Integrating two factories turning out duplicate products in one location

Diagnostic Instruments

OPEN ORGANIZATION VARIABLES

All diagnostic instruments—management surveys, homespun instruments, and structured interview forms—may be designed or reformulated around the key dimensions of the open organization model: unity, internal responsiveness, and external responsiveness.

For example, Goldman (1977) has reorganized the *Institutional Goals Inventory (IGI)* produced by Educational Testing Service into clusters to reflect these three variables. The *IGI* will be described in greater detail in chapter 7.

Snow and Mink (1977) have also restructured the *Survey of Organizations* to fit the three open organization dimensions. A common instrument in continuous development since 1966, the *Survey of Organizations* was used in Bowers's Inter-Company Longitudinal Study (ICLS) to provide systematic information on organization variables (Taylor and Bowers, 1972). The most recent edition (Taylor and Bowers, 1974) has been revised several times to improve format and questions. Revisions were based on Bowers's and Seashore's (1966) grounded four-factor theory of leadership and the meta-theory of Rensis Likert (1967), which integrates a large array of empirical findings. Copies of the instrument are provided in the test manual (Taylor and Bowers, 1972). A manual for consultants is also available (Hauser, Pecorella, and Wissler, 1975).

The *Open Organization Managerial Profile*, described in detail in chapter 10 and shown in part IV (pp. 252–265), is a self-evaluation instrument designed to assess managers' competencies in terms of the open organization model. The instrument consists of a nine-cell grid formed by the three open organization variables on one axis and three levels of the organization on the other axis. The manager may rate his or her general skill level or achievement of specific competencies within each cell on the grid. Taken together, the ratings yield a general picture of strengths and weaknesses in the system functioning of the manager.

Some Characteristics of Unhealthy (Closed) and Healthy (Open) Organizations, located in part IV (pp. 213–217), is a twenty-three item instrument based upon the characteristics of open and closed organizations identified by Fordyce and Weil (1971). The items examine attitudes and norms related to problem solving, handling conflict, collaboration, decision making, and feedback. For each item, you mark a nine-point scale according to the way you perceive your organization. Higher scores indicate greater openness. This instrument is an excellent teaching, as well as diagnostic, tool.

FORCE FIELD ANALYSIS

We have found force field analysis, developed by Lewin (1946), to be one of the most useful open-ended frameworks for the development and analysis of tailored data. Force field analysis looks upon a phase of organization behavior not as a static condition, but as a quasi-stationary state maintained by dynamic balance of opposing forces within an institution and its environment. Factors that facilitate change are *driving forces*. Factors which inhibit change are *restraining forces*. These forces can originate inside the organization, in the environment, or in the behavior of the manager or consultant. In figure 14, the length of the arrow of each force represents its relative strength as do vectors in geometry.

An organization is in dynamic equilibrium when forces tending to change the status of a situation (driving forces) are matched in strength by those tending to prevent any change (restraining forces). The manager must assess the change potential and resistances and try to alter the balance of forces. He or she can add to driving forces. This choice is usually less desirable since it may mobilize more opposing forces and increase tension. The manager can remove or reduce restraining forces. This alternative is more desirable, though less obvious. It minimizes the danger of overlooking or working against forces fostering change. Finally, the manager can add to driving forces and trim or eliminate restraining forces. This is probably the most effective strategy.

Once an imbalance of forces unfreezes the status quo, allowing a change to occur, it is vitally important to refreeze; that is, to stabilize forces at a new level in order to avoid backsliding and maintain change. Most change efforts ignore driving forces, which may include individuals, groups, traditions, policies, laws, and occupations.

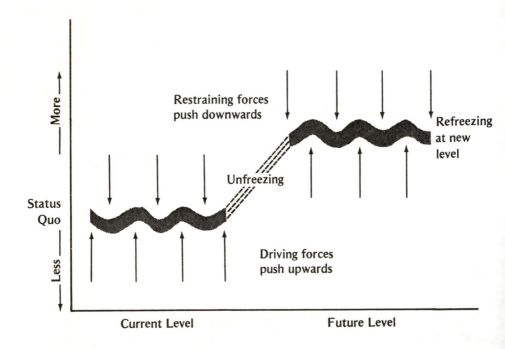

Figure 14. Force Field Analysis

We have devised diagnostic interview forms using a force field analysis based on our three variables of open organizations. The structured interview form is designed to yield data for an institution-wide force field analysis leading to an action plan in the direction of a more open organization. The *Individual Manager Needs* instrument, described in chapter 10 and presented in part IV (pp. 249–250), is an example of a structured interview instrument based upon force field analysis.

There are three values of force field analysis. First, it is open-ended about the kinds of individual and organizational factors which can be included as driving and restraining forces. Second, it avoids univariable analysis by using a brainstorming technique which encourages people to view their situation as a field of mutual, interacting causal factors. Third, although open-ended, it encourages movement from the theoretical to the practical, from diagnosing to selecting specific strategies and tactics of intervention. It encourages clarity, specificity, and thoroughness, and it aids communication. It is especially useful in diagnosing small units and their everyday problems. It can also be used for large change efforts for the whole organization.

The stages and methods of the diagnostic review process are illustrated by the following case study, "Recreating the Whole: Buckingham YMCA." The study describes a diagnostic review which led to the successful reorganization of a large metropolitan YMCA faced with reduced membership, weak leadership, and financial crisis.

Case Study. Recreating the Whole: Buckingham YMCA*

The Buckingham YMCA is a large metropolitan community agency serving youth and families in a city with a population of two million people. At the time we became involved, the Buckingham Y included ten branches, each with its own building: six within city limits, and four in suburbs. The organization was highly decentralized, with each of the ten branches having its own board of directors and a strong sense of identity with its neighborhood. The director of each branch reported directly to a metropolitan chief executive who reported to a city-wide board of directors. Four years before we became involved, the Buckingham Y had raised three million dollars to finance a building campaign. This capital improvement project had targeted corporations for donations, but a large portion of the annual operating budget came from the United Fund. In spite of the massive building campaign, membership failed to grow in proportion to the capacity of new facilities. United Fund support was also diminishing. As a result, there was a growing deficit—$40,000 one year, and $70,000 the next. A sense of financial crisis and worry over weak leadership resulted in the board of directors calling in a consultant from the YMCA regional offices. The regional consultant asked us to work with him on a diagnostic review of the Buckingham YMCA.

A year before our involvement, the chief executive, Mr. Burbank, had retired after many years in the top leadership position. His assistant, Mr. West, who had given many years of dedicated service, was promoted to the position without a thorough selection process. After one year in office, Mr. West was pressured by board members to initiate more innovative program services and find solutions to the financial difficulties. These urgent issues provided the impetus for our being hired to do a diagnostic review.

The procedures of this diagnostic review followed the six stages of consultation described previously.

Phase 1: Initial Entry. As the first step in the diagnostic review, the external consultant conferred with leaders of the Buckingham Y to develop a consensus about the scope of his task. This meeting consisted of the director of each YMCA branch, the metropolitan chief executive, and a representative from the board of directors. During a thorough discussion of the Buckingham Y, the consultant asked questions about three primary areas: the management's efforts to provide a sense of unity in the organization, the responsiveness of various branches to the central organization, and the relationship between various branches and their constituencies. These areas correspond to the three core variables: unity, internal responsiveness, and external responsiveness.

The discussion indicated a need to take a comprehensive look at the Buckingham YMCA's missions and goals, management structure, relationship among branches, and relationship between branches and the central office. A representative task force of ten people was appointed to assist the outside and regional consultants in carrying out a complete diagnosis of the organization. The diagnostic

*Case study written by Ann Linquist

report was to include a series of recommendations on possible corrective courses of action.

Phase 2: Formulating a Contract and Establishing a Helping Relationship. The working agreement formulated in this instance was an understanding that consultants would be involved in completing a diagnostic review and presenting findings and recommendations to the board and administrators. The specific objectives for diagnosis were:

- Carry out structured interviews with thirty key YMCA personnel and thirty civic leaders to determine their perceptions of the YMCA's purpose, effectiveness of administrative practices, adequacy of coordination between branches and the central office, and specific strengths and weaknesses in the organization
- Perform an extensive study of programming activities of components of the Buckingham Y, and assess the productivity of program offerings compared to those of similar agencies in other metropolitan areas
- Assess current levels of utilization of physical facilities and compare these with facility use of other agencies
- Examine financial records to determine relative costs of operation for the components and compare them with the costs of other agencies

We agreed that this review would be completed within ninety days. The estimated time necessary to complete work by the outside consultant was twenty days.

Phase 3: Problem Identification, Analysis, and Recommendations. In this phase, activities outlined in phase 2 were completed, including synthesis and analysis of the interview and other data, and writing a final report with recommendations for corrective action. These results were reported to and discussed with the board and the task force. Some highlights of the joint analysis follow.

One of the first issues apparent from interviewing was a strong tendency for the new chief executive to be used as a scapegoat. It was easier to avoid issues than to engage in real problem solving. The data clearly indicated that Mr. West had inherited such a negative organizational momentum that it was impossible to make a clear evaluation of his performance. We attempted to call attention to overall organizational issues and to minimize this scapegoating.

Perhaps the most serious problem revealed by the diagnostic review was the independent functioning of the ten branches. They were run in a secretive way that attempted to preserve their autonomy even at high cost to the whole organization. While legally the Y was a single corporation, much initiative and power fell to the branches. The central metropolitan leaders had abdicated their responsibility for the whole organization by pacifying and bargaining with individual units. There was no strong centralized planning and quality control.

High overhead resulted from the self-sufficiency of the units; each maintained most of the essential management functions and support staff. The executive head of each branch attempted to be an expert in many areas rather than taking advantage of the larger organization to create greater efficiency. There was little attempt to franchise their services. This decentralization resulted in heavy personnel costs.

Another factor increasing personnel costs and adding to organizational overhead was what might be called a tenure system of staffing. The YMCA was an old organization which had drawn lifelong career people at lower salaries much as in church vocations. The classical Y leader was respected mainly for his dedication, and often lay people were too loyal to confront him with issues of performance. Particularly as staff size leveled off in the 1960s, people were almost automatically continued in their positions. When they neared retirement, they were allowed to work the last four or five years even if their productivity was low or their training out of date. Once appointed, a person was secure until retirement, barring major conflicts. This practice, combined with branch fragmentation, meant that one could have a kind of empire, with a building and specialty such as camping, physical education, or urban action). With lack of staff turnover, the YMCA became ingrown. In some cases there was tension between young and old staff. Often there was consensus about noticeable job incompetence, yet such people were continued. The combined cost of such positions (charity for the staff, not the client) was nearly a third of personnel costs. These salaries were the primary expense in the budget, resulting in unduly high operating costs.

Part of the energy resulting in a desire for change at the YMCA was generated by their sense of crisis, conflict, and urgency. They were faced with several pressing issues, such as personnel problems and high deficits. However, as outside consultants, one of our most important functions was to help these people relate immediate symptoms to deeper and more long-term issues. Many symptomatic problems reflected their loss of unity and subsequent fragmentation.

Underlying the financial crisis was the problem of relative decline in membership. There was widespread disappointment that the building and renovation program did not in itself produce a proportionate growth in membership. In interviews some people expressed ambivalence over the YMCA's traditional mainstay, gym-and-swim. They wondered if the Y was responsive to key developments of the last fifteen years such as the civil rights movement, riots, urban coalitions, and the new focus on jobs and self-help programs rather than charity. There had been little unified action in response to the challenge of moving from a predominantly white to a mixed racial constituency. The YMCA as an organization lacked credibility because of its slow, reluctant identification with black progress and integration. Lay people, while polite toward the Y, expressed reservations about how important it was and how much it really did for the community.

This confusion was partly the accumulation of many years of sentimental and traditional acceptance of the Y program. ("We know it's good; let's construct a building for it." "We know that recreation builds character.") These assumptions about programming, combined with pressures for high cost efficiency in programs, lessened program quality, particularly the kind of special impact that makes people want to give donations.

Finally, the YMCA's heavy facilities orientation demanded sophisticated fiscal management tools. Heavy emphasis on branch autonomy meant complicated and confusing bookkeeping. The Buckingham YMCA lacked comprehensive financial data that could have helped in assessing current programs and their impact. Questions such as How many people do we serve for each $100 subsidy; How much are we spending on salaries for branch executives? How much money will we need to raise?—demanded rapid, accurate data to set and enforce policies and coordinate complex operations. Interviews indicated that for years it had been difficult for board members to get data necessary for effective decision making. Financial reports were unclear, incomplete, or clouded by complex organizational maneuvers. Lay people could not get answers to basic questions:

- How many assets do we have?
- How are we using them?
- What are we getting for our money?
- How much money do we owe and to whom?
- What is our endowment?
- How much are the buildings worth?
- Which of our activities are in financial trouble and which are successful?

Lay and staff leaders needed training to cope with an increasingly complex organization and a changing environment. Up to that time there had been tolerance for "business as usual" and delegating as much as possible to branches. Board members often acted on oversimplified assumptions. To save time and trouble, they avoided problems involving conflicts and overlaid with complex social and value issues. There was a sense of frustration and inability to make changes even when the need was apparent. The limited time of lay leaders in the YMCA meant that professionals were needed to do the actual managing of the voluntary organization within guidelines set by the board. The chief executive should be a a professional manager.

The interviews also showed doubt and confusion about where the YMCA should be heading and how important it really was. The 1960s polarized many issues which were never resolved: Are we a charity or a sales-supported business? Shall we remain in the city or go out to the suburbs? Are we white, black, or both? Are we centered in buildings or in outreach? Are we involved in physical education or group work? The Buckingham Y lacked a strong picture of itself as an essential part of the community in the 1970s.

This diagnosis was supported by the fact that branches had become islands to themselves. While they demanded autonomy, they drew heavily on the central organization's financial resources and undermined its public relations. Without a unified identity there could be no concerted metropolitan effort to respond to changes in society, such as affirmative action. Internal responsiveness was lacking between branches as well as between the organization's center and its parts. To compound these problems, any basic moves toward unity, internal responsiveness, and external responsiveness had to be combined with increased cost containment because of two years of large deficits.

One of our most effective interventions was to help the task force compare its YMCA with similar agencies in comparable environments. They needed to view their organization as a whole and develop a stronger sense of unity of purpose and operation. The comparison study helped them gain this focus. It revealed that they were falling behind other cities in terms of their membership, operating income, contribution income, property indebtedness, and deficits.

Throughout the diagnostic review and comparison study, we tried to avoid focusing too heavily on problems or weaknesses and to keep underlining the strong potential and excellent past record of the organization. Focusing only on problems can undermine an organization's creativity.

There was general agreement with the analysis and recommended action. This opened the door for succeeding action steps.

Phase 4: Goal Setting and Planning. In the case of the Buckingham Y, the initial working agreement remained relatively intact throughout the consultation. Initial goals and action steps remained appropriate.

Phase 5: Taking Action and Cycling Feedback. A number of problems were identified by the diagnostic review. Once these problems were revealed to board members, they were able to weigh alternative courses of action. The board ultimately decided to initiate a highly participatory metropolitan planning process involving all ten branches in key issues identified by the diagnostic review. As a result of this planning the board made changes in budgeting, staffing, programming, and capital improvement.

The board renewed the chief executive's contract for another year on recommendation of the task force. The board decided to merge two overlapping branches left from the days of segregation. Several smaller branches were grouped and put under the leadership of a single chief executive. This reorganization resulted in saving several thousand dollars in payroll costs. Fiscal management functions were centralized in the metropolitan office.

The board also began working on more complicated long-term issues. The lay governance structure was changed from a wide variety of committees, many of which were inoperative, to four working committees. Several nonworking members of the board resigned, and new members were appointed representing previously unrepresented groups. The board sought ways to increase program innovations, raise contribution income, and reach the black constituency.

Board meetings emphasized team building and confrontation to bring issues out into the open and deal with people's feelings as well as ideas. As actions were implemented, all were apprised of the progress. Previously, board meetings tended to be perfunctory with long agendas of detailed items. Now meetings changed to focus in depth on one or two major issues or policy decisions. Detailed operational decisions were left to the chief executive or one of his immediate assistants.

The chief executive did his best to adjust to a newly sophisticated and active board of directors. A year later, he resigned to take a different position. After a careful national search, the board chose a new executive qualified to pursue the priorities developed from the diagnostic review and long-range planning.

Phase 6: Contract Completion: Continuity, Support, and Termination. As the outside consultant's tasks neared completion, increased attention was given to the Buckingham Y's use of internal resources to maintain or extend renewal efforts. The most important result was the board's decision to authorize the ad hoc task force to continue operations for an additional year. The task force was asked to prepare a five-year development plan outlining organization goals, target constituency, and program priorities. It had specific tasks.

1. Prepare a revised statement of the YMCA's business (develop a charter), overcoming usual dichotomies of membership and outreach, charity and sales, and physical education and community action.

2. Identify major trends in the environment and specify assumptions that the Y was making about its environment.
3. Analyze constituency by types of people, location, needs, attitudes, preferences, and life styles to improve planning for programs, financial development, and facilities. Set membership and participation targets.
4. Test all present program concepts and reconceptualize in terms of contemporary community needs.
5. Pick one major metropolitan program goal and undertake special promotion and service delivery for all units.
6. Compare actual to potential service coverage. Plan for covering broader areas.
7. Explore collaboration among agencies and ways to cooperate with other community organizations in taking on problems too big for any single organization, such as jobs for youth, crime, and drugs.
8. Plan for more joint branch programs (like camping) to transcend barriers which separate people.
9. Describe in detail what each branch does, whom it reaches and in what way, and how much it costs.
10. Develop a plan for reaching blacks using a task force made up of black leaders.

Throughout, we emphasized unifying purpose and goals of the whole organization. This emphasis on superordinate goals allowed Y leaders to resolve controversial issues through open discussion. The resulting collaboration among coworkers reduced competition between units and allowed the organization as a whole to prosper. Four years later, the Buckingham YMCA had improved its comparative position from being one of the weakest of its type of association to being one of the strongest. In particular, it gained success in attracting financial support from both private and government sources.

7

SETTING GOALS*

AN ORGANIZATION'S GOALS are shared understandings about why it exists and what it seeks to accomplish. Goals give direction, channel energy, and set limits. Careful attention to specifying goals enhances an organization's capacity to plan meaningful action. When decision makers are united by commitment to particular goals, they are better able to resolve conflicts within an organization. Goals also serve as standards by which to evaluate an organization's progress and productivity.

The central importance of organization goals is generally recognized. Almost everyone would agree, "If you're not sure where you're going, you're liable to end up someplace else" (Mager, 1976, p. v). In recent years Mager (1976), Lee (1972), Ross (1977), and others have offered precise methods of formulating operational, measurable goal statements. Despite access to increasingly sophisticated methods of formulating goals, many organizations experience difficulty obtaining clearly articulated goals and operating on the basis of them. One source of difficulty is the perennial drift of organizations away from goals formed at their origin, and failure to revise them. Other difficulties stem from the increased complexity, rate of change, and diversity of values in today's society.

The open organization model provides an approach to goal setting that attempts to overcome some of these difficulties. The model makes three assumptions about organizational goal setting. First, goals are the heart of a healthy organization—the basis for its unity, its efficiency of operation (internal responsiveness), and its effectiveness in carrying out its purpose

*Written by Victor H. Appel, Ph.D., Associate Professor, Department of Educational Psychology, The University of Texas, Austin, Texas

(external responsiveness). They are the most important determinant of its decisions and actions. Therefore, organizations must devote energy and attention to setting clear, explicit goals. Second, organizations exist within a changing rather than stable context. They must be prepared to respond adaptively to those changing conditions that impinge upon their purpose. To do so, organizations must periodically reexamine and revise goals in response to evolving circumstances. Finally, all constituent groups must participate in formulating an organization's goals and prioritizing them. Involving internal groups increases members' understanding of goals and their motivation to carry out goals effectively. Involving outside groups provides a way to test goals for relevancy and timeliness and increases the likelihood that the goals selected will be accepted by diverse groups.

If goal setting is to become a continuing process that encourages participation, organizations must develop structures and methodologies for formulating alternative goals, selecting among them, and deciding upon their relative importance. Exploration of collaborative goal-setting methods has barely begun. Nevertheless, strategies have been developed which may serve as models for organizations wishing to develop their own goal-setting methods.

This chapter distinguishes several kinds of goals and describes their functions in an organization. It examines current goal-setting problems that indicate the need for reviewing goals periodically and involving constituent groups in their selection. The chapter concludes with a sequence of recommended goal-setting strategies: designing a goal assessment instrument for a particular type of organization, identifying goals most in need of revision, and building group consensus through systematic feedback.

The Nature of Organization Goals

Goals are shared conceptions of the intentions, purposes, or aims of an organization. They may be stated in bylaws, charters, policy statements, and similar documents, or they may remain implicit. Stated goals vary in the degree of their explicitness. Often organization goals are stated very broadly and loosely. These may be termed *mission, purpose,* or *aim* to indicate the function of the organization in society. These statements answer the question, "Why does the organization exist?" Broad statements may be termed *results* or *wants,* to indicate what the organization is seeking to accomplish. They answer the question, "What is the organization trying to do?" When stated with greater precision or in operational terms, goals are likely to be labeled *objectives* or even more specifically, *behavioral objectives* (Mager, 1976). In common usage, the terms are often used interchangeably. We will use the word *objective* to mean a specific, operational statement related to a broader goal. To illustrate these differences, let us apply the terms to a hypothetical organization, Greystone Industries, which manufactures heavy equipment for the oil and coal extraction industries.

Greystone Industries, a long established, large producer, might state as its mission "to maintain market leadership in the development, production, and distribution of heavy equipment for the extraction industries." To achieve this mission, it would specify a number of more limited goals, such as "to maintain or enhance the organization's share of the market in the sale of oil rigging equipment." Stated as a behavioral objective, the organization might plan "to increase by six percent the organization's share of the market in the sale of oil rigging equipment by January 1, 1980." Note how each formulation is successively more specific and the attainment of the goal more easily verifiable.

As might be expected with so broad a term as *goal,* many have found it useful to distinguish among various types of goals. Here we will make two major distinctions: *process* versus *outcome goals,* and *actual* versus *ideal goals.*

PROCESS AND OUTCOME GOALS

Outcome goals specify what the desired accomplishments are for an organization, and *process goals* specify how these are to be achieved. For example, an outcome goal of Greystone Industries may be to increase production. A related process goal would be to achieve maximum efficiency of operation through continuous monitoring of production and use of accountability procedures and cost-benefit analyses.

Process goals are of particular interest because they are often given less attention than outcome goals, or are omitted altogether. Yet often there is less agreement about process goals than outcome goals. Organization members may agree about what they want to accomplish but disagree about how to go about achieving the desired outcome. For example, Greystone Industries may achieve high consensus about the need to increase sales. But the firm may have difficulty deciding whether to achieve this outcome through increased incentives for sales personnel, more active advertising, or improving equipment design.

ACTUAL AND IDEAL GOALS

Actual goals are the de facto, current goals an organization's leaders are striving to achieve. By contrast, an *ideal goal* is the view of a particular person or group about what an organization should be striving toward. Peterson (1971) has termed these "is" and "should be" goals. For example, a research and development engineer within Greystone Industries may believe that because coal will become a more important energy resource, the company should allocate greater resources toward improving the design of coal extracting equipment. However, the company may, in fact, decide to give higher priority to increased sales of current equipment models.

In a more traditional, closed organization where goal setting is the purview of a select few, there is a higher probability that those not included in goal setting will have discrepant views about what the organization should be trying to accomplish. Moreover, discrepancies between "is" and "should be" goals are likely to increase when an organization does not revise its stated outcome goals periodically.

Effective Goal Setting

Two conclusions have emerged from our study of organizations from an open systems perspective: goal revision must be continuous, and it must involve an organization's constituent groups. This section will review some problems of organizations in setting goals effectively and outline an open organization approach to overcoming these problems.

PERIODIC REVIEW OF GOALS

Virtually all organizations are concerned with determining goals at the time of their founding. However, many organizations tend to give insufficient attention to these goals thereafter. The goals no longer serve as the frame of reference for decision making. With different leaders and other personnel, new markets, or other contextual considerations, goals which were appropriate initially may no longer be so. Without periodic review of the relationship between actual and ideal goals, significant discrepancies can develop between what an organization is actually seeking to accomplish and what some personnel think it ought to. Thus, periodic reevaluation of goals is necessary to revitalize organizations, particularly during rapid social change.

Organizations may be faced with loss of credibility and even obsolescence if they fail to develop periodic goal review mechanisms accountable to external constituencies. Public colleges and universities offer a special case in point. Peterson (1970a, 1971, 1973) has discussed at length what he calls the "crisis of purpose" facing higher education. He argues that colleges and universities can no longer continue to serve as "firehouses on the corner," responsive to all calls for help. He contends that these institutions have failed to set adequate priorities among a number of desirable goals. Without clear priorities, universities have not been able to evaluate adequately the appropriateness or effectiveness of their activities (Richman and Farmer, 1974). Peterson sees these institutions on a collision course between increasing demands for service and shrinking financial resources. How could such a situation develop?

Modeled on European institutions, the first colleges and universities in the United States had a few fairly well-defined goals:

- To prepare lettered people through exposure to a classical curriculum including literature, Latin, Greek, philosophy, and ancient history.
- To prepare people of high potential for medicine, law, and the ministry.
- To prepare scholars of promise to teach and expand the range of knowledge within scientific and humanistic fields such as physics, chemistry, biology, philosophy, and literature.

Over time, however, higher education has expanded the range and scope of its goals. In a large-scale comparative study, Gross and Grambsch (1968) identified forty-seven goals of higher education. These include preparation of students for scholarship, research, and a wide range of useful careers. Other goals include the conduct of both pure and applied research, community cultural leadership, and consultation services to other organizations. At the same time, higher education institutions must protect academic freedom and find continued financial support.

This proliferation of goals has not been accompanied typically by careful review and selection. As highly valued organizations with high credibility, college and universities have perhaps felt that it is not necessary to specify goals (Richman and Farmer, 1974). They have supposed that legislatures, alumni, and students would be willing to support whatever these institutions were doing in the belief that it must be worthwhile. As service rather than product-producing organizations, they may also have balked at the difficult task of specifying goal outcomes less tangible than those of industry. The governance structure of colleges and universities has usually shared decision making between administrators and faculty with attendant difficulties in reaching consensus about goals. Whatever the reasons, higher education institutions have tended to avoid goal specification. The result has been characterized by Appel and Mink (1977) as a state of "benign ambiguity" in which organizational goals have been so broadly and vaguely stated that faculty could be free to pursue personal goals while remaining under the institutional goal umbrella. Now these institutions must learn not only to channel energies selectively, but also to demonstrate that they have carried out selected goals in order to justify continued financial support.

Colleges and universities are not alone in facing a need for goal redefinition. Other nonprofit organizations, such as churches, PTAs, Girl Scout troops, YMCAs, and similar service organizations, have often failed to reexamine goals. More than any other institutions in our society, service organizations depend upon the voluntary acceptance and involvement of outside groups for their very existence. They are particularly vulnerable to loss of support when they fail to modify goals to meet changing community needs and expectations.

Because of an assured source of income through taxation, government organizations have generally been lax about reassessing goals and evaluating performance. In the vacuum created by this passivity, special interest groups have often been able to promote their goals at the expense of the general welfare through lobbying and informal alliances with government agencies. The result has been increasing public disenchantment with government as a vehicle for supporting and enhancing society. Mounting public demands for government accountability are reflected in the emergence of citizens' lobbies, consumer interest groups, single-issue elections, efforts to open government activities to public scrutiny, and referenda to reduce taxes. In response to these pressures, government and community organizations are increasingly adopting management by objectives and similar practices developed in the private sector, and are seeking new methods of collaborative goal setting.

In contrast to nonprofit and government organizations, business and industry have been more attentive to goals and have spent much time and money formulating them and assessing progress toward their attainment. There are a number of reasons for the development of more effective goal-setting methods in profit organizations. Goals are more tangible for organizations producing or distributing products than for service organizations. The traditional hierarchical structure of profit organizations has placed the main responsibility for goal attainment upon designated individuals—top management. Managers have been accountable to boards and stockholders who tend to interpret ultimate success in terms of profit and loss. Further, competitive markets have necessitated careful goal setting to produce more desirable products less expensively.

Despite these advantages, however, goal setting in business and industry is becoming more complicated because of increasing pressures from diverse internal and external constituent groups. Women and minorities are seeking increased employment opportunities. Environmentalists are raising issues about the impact of technology. Stockholders may object to bank investments in South Africa. Federal regulations are imposed or withdrawn for different business activities. As business networks become international, individual organizations become vulnerable to changes in politics around the world. On the horizon are very difficult issues, as energy supplies and raw materials become scarce and world-wide inflation raises costs. The concept of accountability is expanding to include not only increasingly complex issues of profit and loss but also broader social responsibility.

INVOLVING CONSTITUENT GROUPS

In traditional closed organizations goal setting has been an exclusive management function. While managers have generally been clear about their goals, this knowledge has not always been available to others. Sometimes those not in leadership roles have had to infer the actual goals on the basis of current activities, decisions, and allocation of resources. At other times, actual goals might be clearly specified but widely discrepant from the ideal goals of people not included in goal setting.

As organizations of all kinds are being held increasingly accountable by diverse groups for the kinds of goals they set and the way they go about accomplishing them, the goal-setting process must be modified to include all constituencies. *Constituencies* are the various groups who affect and are affected by the organization. Returning to our hypothetical firm, Greystone Industries, a list of constituencies might include:

- Stockholders
- The board of directors
- Management personnel

- Other employees
- Customers to whom equipment, parts, or services are provided
- Labor unions to which personnel belong
- Government regulatory agency personnel concerned with the extraction industry
- Representatives of communities in which Greystone Industries' plants are located

Among nonprofit organizations equivalent groups exist. A United Fund agency might list the following constituents:

- The board of directors
- The agency's advisory council
- Management personnel
- Other employees
- Clients
- United Fund governing board, which allocates money
- Citizens of the community in which the agency is located, whose contributions help finance the agency, and who may become its clients

Seen from the perspective of Kurt Lewin's field theory (Hall and Lindzey, 1957), all these groups directly shape the well-being of an organization. As we noted earlier, an organization can be understood as a field of forces in equilibrium. Each constituent group constitutes one force exerted upon the organization. When the views of groups differ, forces are exerted in different directions. The progress of an organization toward its goals may be thought of as the result of the combined energy of all divergent forces. Competing forces within an organization will impede progress in a particular direction. When principal constituencies strongly support antagonistic aims, the organization may be destroyed. Thus, progress toward goals depends upon achieving at least near consensus about organizational goals.

Building consensus is a critical requirement. Institutions tend to be more efficient and productive when general agreement exists about the appropriateness of goals and goal priorities. The health of an organization depends largely upon the degree to which its goals are clearly defined and accepted (Kessel and Mink, 1971).

SETTING GOALS IN OPEN ORGANIZATIONS

In organizations moving toward the model we have presented, managers recognize the importance of setting process goals through collaborative methods. For example, Greystone Industry managers are concerned that expensive high-speed welding machines are being operated far below capacity. The result is a serious slowdown in the production schedule. They decide to involve welding machine operators in identifying the problems, selecting solutions, and setting process goals toward increased operator productivity. One manager is assigned to spend some time in the welding area talking with operators and working with them. He learns that operating a high-speed precision machine to perform repetitive tasks creates boredom and eventual loss of morale. Joint efforts to improve the work environment and provide greater task diversity result in a substantial improvement of operator efficiency. A problem has been solved by combining the system-wide perspective of managers with workers' awareness of specific problems. Open organizations create management structures through which problems may be solved regularly in this way. Process goals are best developed within team settings, as described in chapters 8 and 9.

In an open organization, managers also devote careful attention to periodic revision of outcome goals, with input from all constituent groups. Goal setting is made more complicated and difficult by including many people. In addition to skillful use of power and influence, managers need more sophisticated methods. First, they need a classification system by which to generate a comprehensive list of possible goals. After asking constituents to identify which goals they prefer, managers will need a relatively simple, precise method of determining the nature and extent of goal discrepancies—between actual and ideal goals, and between the goal orientations of various groups. The results of the organization goal assessment must then be translated into a manageable number of high priority goal issues. Finally, there must be some means of reaching group consensus about the selected goal issues. The following section presents some strategies which may serve as models for developing an organization's goal revision process.

Goal-Setting Tools

DEVELOPING AN ASSESSMENT INSTRUMENT

The design of goal assessment instruments is relatively new. To our knowledge, the *Institutional Goals Inventory* published by the Educational Testing Service (Peterson and Uhl, 1972) is the best attempt to develop a comprehensive instrument that may be used by a specific type of organization to assess the goal orientations of its constituents. The *IGI* is a standardized instrument developed for use by collegiate institutions. Using its methodology, comparable instruments can be devised for other types of organizations. For this reason, a description of the instrument and the methodology employed in its construction will prove helpful (Peterson, 1973).

The *IGI* was developed after collecting samples of goals from a broad spectrum of colleges and universities. The sample included public universities, independent colleges, church-affiliated institutions, and community colleges. Key groups within each institution were asked to submit lists of actual or desired goals they saw as most appropriate for their institution. To assure an adequate universe of goals, both outcome and process goals were sought. The collected samples were carefully culled to eliminate duplication and to select a representative pool of goals. The lists were used to construct two preliminary versions of the instrument. The two instruments were pilot tested, using respondents at several institutions. Based on field research, a final version of the instrument was constructed (Uhl, 1971; and Peterson and Uhl, 1972).

The resulting *IGI* consists of ninety goal statements. There are twenty goal areas, each represented by four statements, and a miscellaneous category containing ten statements. Thirteen of the goal areas describe various possible outcomes:

- Academic, vocational, personal, and religious development of students
- Promotion of certain values: self-directed learning, concern for the welfare of humanity, and cultural and aesthetic awareness
- Opportunities for advanced training and research
- Meeting other societal needs—continuing education for adults, cultural events for the local community, public service to government agencies, evolving interests of minority groups and women, and promotion of social change

The remaining seven goal areas describe possible processes:

- Maintaining academic freedom and democratic governance
- Fostering a learning climate—open communication, intellectual and aesthetic richness, and innovation
- Providing opportunities for off-campus learning
- Evaluating accountability and efficiency in relation to stated goals

The instrument provides space to add optional goal statements generated by the local institution.

The respondent indicates the relative importance of each goal statement by rating it on a five-point scale ranging from "of no importance" (a rating of one) to "of extremely high importance" (a rating of five). Each statement is rated twice: for how important it *is* at the present time, and for how important it *should be* in the judgment of the respondent. From these ratings the importance of each of the twenty goal areas can be calculated.

The respondent is identified as a member of a group: faculty, students, administrators, governing board, alumni, or off-campus community group. By pooling the ratings of respondents within each constituency, it is possible to determine the general level of importance each group tends to assign each goal area, both for actual and ideal goals. One can then examine discrepancies among ratings of various groups and between each group's "is" and "should be" ratings for a goal area. Figure 15 illustrates the kind of information which can be derived from the *IGI*. The left column lists the goal areas being assessed. The two line profiles represent the combined ratings of the faculty and administration of Community College 3. The solid line indicates relative importance of "is" goals and the broken line the relative importance of "should be" goals. The distance between the two lines indicates the degree of "is" and "should be" discrepancy for various goal areas.

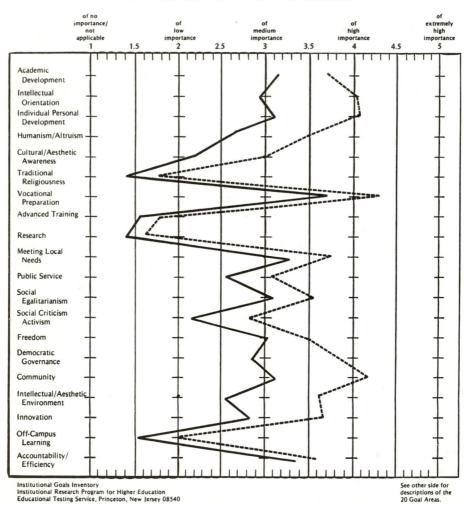

IS _____

SHOULD BE - - - - - - - - - - - - - - - -

PROFILE FOR   Community College 3   (Total scores, Faculty and Administration)

INSTITUTIONAL GOALS INVENTORY PROFILE CHART

Institutional Goals Inventory
Institutional Research Program for Higher Education
Educational Testing Service, Princeton, New Jersey 08540

See other side for
descriptions of the
20 Goal Areas.

Figure 15.   *IGI* Results for Community College 3

SELECTING GOALS FOR REVISION

While the *IGI* profile sheet is helpful in assessing relative importance and discrepancies among goals, it does not provide a clear basis for determining which goals most need current reconsideration. Drawing upon *IGI* data, we have developed a more systematic procedure to pinpoint target areas for goal revision in the locus for focus model (Appel and Mink, 1977). The procedure can be used by any organization. It draws upon two sets of scores derived from an *IGI* type of instrument: (1) the rated importance of "should be" goals, and (2) the discrepancy between "is" and "should be" ratings.

By examining the "should be" goal ratings, we can determine which ideal goals are valued most highly, and therefore are most likely to generate strong commitment. The degree of discrepancy between an actual and ideal goal can be viewed as an index of tension: the greater the discrepancy, the greater the pressure for reconciliation of the two ratings.

To determine the most appropriate goals for revision at Community College 3, a scatter diagram was constructed, as shown in figure 16. The horizontal axis represents "should be" ratings from one to five. The vertical axis represents discrepancy scores expressed as the arithmetical difference between "is" and "should be" ratings. The two measures for each goal area were plotted on the diagram. The resulting points were numbered to correspond to the twenty goal areas. The diagram was then bisected at the mean point on each axis to form four quadrants or sectors. These sectors are characterized as follows:

SECTOR 1.   HIGH DISCREPANCY/LOW IMPORTANCE. Given the relatively low importance assigned such goals, the high degree of discrepancy may be overlooked for the present, but will eventually require attention.

SECTOR 2.   HIGH DISCREPANCY/HIGH IMPORTANCE. Given the fact that these goals are both high in importance and discrepancy, they represent the most pressing of the organization's goal target areas. Goal revision is most urgently needed in this sector.

SECTOR 3.   LOW DISCREPANCY/HIGH IMPORTANCE. A generally satisfactory situation exists. The organization can congratulate itself on nearly attaining valued goals.

SECTOR 4.   LOW DISCREPANCY/LOW IMPORTANCE. The organization can safely ignore these less consequential goals about which there is relatively little concern.

Three of the sectors show a lower degree of pressure for goal revision. Sector 2 goals are those having the greatest tension as well as importance, so they are the most important targets for goal revision. Only eight of the initial twenty goals fall in sector 2, for Community College 3. Thus the model identifies a more manageable number of goals with which to work in facilitating fruitful change.

Although sector 2 is clearly the most important, a manager or change specialist may want to consider beginning goal modification in sector 3 to ensure that a goal-revision program begins with success. According to Hauser, Pecorella, and Wissler (1975), the most motivating discrepancy may not always be the largest.

> A moderate discrepancy may be most motivating. A moderate discrepancy often indicates a problem area which needs a significant amount of work, but which is not such a sizable problem that it could not be solved within a reasonable time period and with available or obtainable resources. (p. 15)

Success with goal revision in sector 3 can provide the motivation to tackle more difficult problems in sector 2.

The model illustrated in figure 16 identifies goals which might be targeted for revision, but it does not indicate how closely respondents agree in rating individual goals. The scatter diagram shows only mean ratings which mask the actual variation in respondents' ratings. The range or spread of individual ratings of a particular goal can be determined by calculating the standard deviation of each mean score. (The *standard deviation* is a numerical index of the spread of a set of scores around a mean score.) The smaller the standard deviation, the greater the degree of agreement among raters.

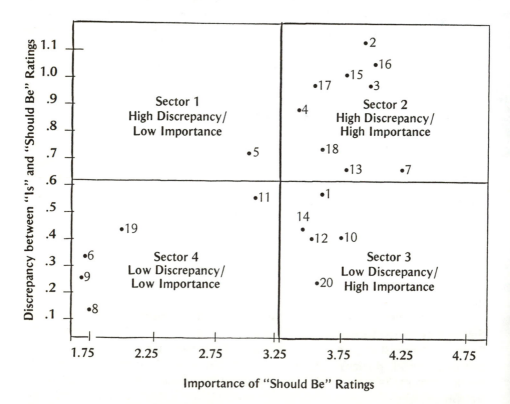

Figure 16. A Scatter Diagram Showing Relative Goal Priorities at Community College 3

BUILDING CONSENSUS

As we have seen, when a set of organization goals is rated by members, there will likely be differences in emphasis among and within constituent groups. These differences may be particularly apparent with respect to ideal goals. Two strategies have been developed to narrow such differences and to promote organizational goal consensus: the Delphi technique (Uhl, 1971) and participative structuring (Baker, 1973). These procedures are applicable to any organization once a list of potential organizational goals has been generated. Both approaches use systematic feedback about the ratings of others as a method of promoting consensus.

The Delphi technique was developed in 1962 by the Rand Corporation, when it was experimenting with methods of bringing government consultants into closer agreement on recommendations without requiring face-to-face communication. The strategy was modified for use with higher education goals by Norman Uhl of the National Laboratory for Higher Education. Uhl (1971) asked respondents to examine an array of potential goal statements and to give each an "is" and "should be" rating on a five-point scale. After results were tabulated, each respondent received a summary showing his or her individual ratings and the group (modal) ratings for each goal statement. Respondents were asked to rate the goal statements again, this time providing a justification for each rating. Again, respondents received a comparative summary of ratings along with a summary of both majority (modal) and minority rationales for ratings. Respondents were asked to make a third rating after examining the materials given them. Uhl found that significant movement toward consensus had occurred.

Baker (1973) reasoned that if movement toward consensus was possible simply as a result of knowing the views of others and the reasons for them, even greater movement should result from extended face-to-face discussion of goal ratings. He developed a consensus game for community colleges. Each respondent selected goal statements from a pool and assigned them to priority positions on a game board according to their perceived importance. After initial independent ratings, participants were assigned to groups of multiple constituencies. The groups of four discussed and defended their priority ratings. They then sought to achieve consensus on ratings through a series of discussions and arbitrations. Baker found that this strategy was capable of achieving marked movement toward agreement.

An organization wanting to adapt the Delphi or Baker procedures for its purposes must first develop a pool of goals and construct instruments specific to its setting. Appel (1978) has identified alternative procedures for formulating instruments appropriate to individual organizations. Organizations which have previously made virtually no attempt at collaborative goal specification will have different needs than organizations which can draw upon goal statements already formulated.

8

DEVELOPING TEAMS

TYPICALLY, MANAGERS AND OTHERS in work groups come to know each other by accident rather than plan. However, the leader who wishes to develop organization openness at the group level will not leave such an important matter to accident or chance. As indicated in chapter 3, a group's potential for growth is not determined by chance, but by the structure of the work environment and such social phenomena as role expectations.

Today, many organizations are also making use of the ad hoc or temporary team, cutting across established work units to accomplish objectives which require high trust. All too often, however, leaders do not take the time and make the effort necessary to develop these groups as functioning teams. Experience consistently shows that it takes twelve to fourteen hours of fairly intensive interaction to develop the contractual trust necessary for giving appropriate mutual feedback and solving individual problems. These stages must precede the stage of group problem solving.

Much has been written recently on team building. *Team building* is defined as an activity directed toward getting team members to know each other better so that team goals can be achieved more effectively, and members can satisfy needs for inclusion, support, power, and achievement (Seashore, 1977). Besides building trust, team development includes increasing information about what resources members have, what their personal needs and goals are, and what kind of environment is needed to work creatively. It also includes setting norms about how decisions will be made, who will lead, and who will assume other role assignments. This chapter presents some team-building methods and goals useful in developing group cohesion, improving work performance, and identifying conflict and agreement problems accurately.

Building Group Cohesion

The first step of team building is the development of a group identity and a supportive environment with clear behavior norms within which individual members can communicate and solve problems effectively. Two methods of building cohesion in groups are developing friendship pairs and establishing open communication norms.

FRIENDSHIP PAIRS

If group members are to develop confidence in their team, a series of friendships between two people is prerequisite. The leader should encourage individuals to make at least one friend with whom they have a warm, helping relationship. However, group members must not be allowed to dabble in amateur psychiatry: no mind probing or "mind reading."

Most leaders can build interpersonal attraction simply by applying everything they have ever learned about making friends. The essentials are simple honesty, consistency, caring, and responsibility. The humanistic psychology movement has produced hundreds of structured exercises which help people make friends. Such exercises are useful to experienced leaders but are not essential for a helpful group experience.

The leader must, however, set positive norms for friendship. He can do so partly by using sincere compliments, provided that they are concrete and specific. For example, "I like your blue scarf" is a specific statement drawn from observation and more believable than "I think you're beautiful." This second statement can be construed as thoughtless flattery by a person who sees himself or herself as a failure and does not feel beautiful. He or she does not feel deserving of compliments. A few carelessly stated compliments could undermine the leader's credibility with such a person.

OPEN COMMUNICATION NORMS

After each person has at least one friend, trust and attraction exist in sufficient degree to permit further group development. Within the initial climate of trust, the leader can aid cohesion through a carefully negotiated social contract that permits relevant feedback as part of a general openness agreement between group members. To be effective, feedback must be specific, descriptive, and behaviorally oriented. It must present constructive, feasible alternatives to the perceived negative behavior. Feedback sessions have two foci: problem definition and problem solution. They can deal with both work objectives and personal development within the supportive context of ongoing relationships.

Internalized behavior change will probably occur only when a person trusts those who are giving him feedback about problem behavior. Confrontation without trust will lead to conformity if the group leader has power, or to fight or flight behavior if the group leader has no power. Both are undesirable outcomes. Trust without confrontation usually leads to friendship but not necessarily to internalized change (Smith, 1976).

Used properly, confrontation helps group members become aware of and change personal behavior that creates distrust. For example, the development of friendships is often difficult for someone lacking self-confidence. He is afraid that he will not be liked. He suspects that his inner feelings are socially unattractive, so he suppresses them when talking. Verbal communication often does not match physical demeanor, facial expressions, or even voice timbre. He sends double messages, saying one thing while feeling something else. Repeated exchanges of double messages discourage trust (contractual and disclosure), jeopardize a possible friendship, and further undermine self-confidence. Such a person can be helped to make his outer expressions congruent with his inner feelings so that he appears honest and sincere.

Communication occurs through many methods and media. Most people use body language—posture, position, muscle tone, voice tone, dress, and eye contact. They send messages out and receive them from many separate sources, interpreting them in a myriad of combinations. Mismatched messages are verbal or nonverbal. When people notice distortion in dialogue, it usually means that the words indicate one thing and the body another. The challenge of a learning group is to create the psychological situation in which people will communicate honestly, so that inner feelings and outer expressions coincide. Under such conditions, the energy available for the learning becomes enormous compared to situations in which people feel conflicted by double messages. The manager must convince group members that honest self-disclosure and keeping simple agreements will discourage double messages and prepare for contractual trust and friendship. Helpful communication is honest, open expression which avoids double messages.

Schiff (1975) has identified two types of nonrelevant response called *faulting* and *redefining*. For example, if someone were to say, "John, will you have lunch with me?" you could reply "Yes," "No," or "Maybe Tuesday." However, if you replied, "Well, I've really been busy lately," you would be faulting. If you responded, "Do you like tomato soup?" you would be redefining to avoid the question. These avoidance responses generally add to the deterioration of trust.

Another dishonest communication pattern identified by Eric Berne (1964) is the *game*. People who are convinced they cannot get positive payoffs through intimacy and friendship will resort to playing games with others in order to get negative payoffs. At times, all of us avoid the "here and now," honesty, intimacy, spontaneity, and autonomy, and resort to playing games with ourselves and our closest associates. Berne, who popularized the standard and common approaches to games, believed that people are very inventive in avoiding intimate friendships and regularly add to the standard repertoire of games. To establish positive conditions for making friends, a work group leader should help individuals avoid games by being honest with each other, by focusing on the "here and now." Any group will be effective only to the extent that the leader can replace old learnings—games, habits, and failure patterns—with an open and honest form of communication.

GROUP BEHAVIOR NORMS

Managers should apply the authority of their role. They must control and lead teamwork, channel communication, and limit disruptive behavior such as individual domination, resistance, and violation of group mores. Yet the manager need not assume full responsibility for successful work group operation. Each group member should help maintain teamwork. Often the team as a whole will have the most impact on members' behavior; peers can better provide the reinforcements, motives, and support crucial to behavioral change and work output, while the manager supervises the process.

Although one's management philosophy will determine many guidelines for the team process, several conditions appear universal and requisite for building positive human relations. Managers may find it useful to discuss these requisites with the team. Certainly, team members must show a sincere and personal interest in one another. Honest expression is essential; outward expression should be congruent with inner feelings. From honest interchanges will grow respect and understanding of differing values.

While encouraging and guiding this atmosphere of disclosure trust, leaders must be wary of the pitfalls of leadership. They cannot hide their feelings for tactical purposes, or become maudlin or manipulative, lest they damage the group and lose credibility. They must consider the effect of individual behavior on the group's welfare in determining when to curb and when to permit radical behavior. They must know when to tighten reins and when to loosen them, so the group becomes neither rigid nor anarchic. This balance between firmness and flexibility should be free of guile and arrogance, and leaders should be willing to discuss their method of leadership if questioned.

Good team members participate actively in problem-solving discussions. They adhere to group mores; avoid monopolizing the group; and support, accept, and confront deviant team members. They assume responsibility for their own behavior, accept group controls, pursue responsible goals for personal growth and work, and obey ground rules. The ground rules may vary, but they usually require regular attendance and active commitment to team goals.

The initial basis for team membership may be no more than employment in the same organization. However, if the team is to be effective, it must become a reference group in which members base critical decisions on team expectations and reactions as well as on personal inclinations. As Seashore (1977) describes, transformation into a cohesive reference group occurs as members move toward deeper involvement. The transitions between levels are marked by disclosing feelings like anger or despair, and by resolving conflicts. Curiously, involvement with the leader is similar to that with group members, measured by the frequency and intensity of transitions as well as the number of successful plans.

Interpersonal Contracting

Contracts made in the team setting are a primary vehicle for team development. Contracts can be made for several purposes:

- To clarify expectations about standards of task and job performance
- To clarify team roles and relationships
- To set work objectives for a specified period
- To assist group members in changing ineffective behavior

Contract agreements vary from general to specific. When they describe personal dynamics and desired general traits, they seem less useful. The more they state decisions and specific actions, the more effective they become.

CONTRACTS TO CLARIFY STANDARDS AND ROLES

It is important early in the coaching relationship that managers and subordinates clarify expectations by asking questions like, "What do you want to achieve?" "What are you wanting from our relationship?" "What do you want from performance reviews?" "What do you want from our target-setting and coaching sessions in management-by-objectives format?" Any question comfortable for managers could obtain meaningful responses from individuals with whom they work. These questions may seem simple, but most people in a supervisor–subordinate relationship will probably not have formed specific responses to them. The purpose of this discussion is to clarify the expectations of leaders and team members about what they want and expect from team relationships, to agree on what each person is to achieve, and to set criteria for evaluating performance.

CONTRACTS TO CHANGE BEHAVIOR

Once a basis of trust and rapport has been established with team members, the team leader can assist individuals in setting behavioral problem-solving contracts. But first it may be helpful to identify the assumptions or beliefs underlying someone's behavior. These assumptions have been called "personal constructs" by Kelly (1955) and "private psychological logic" by Dreikurs (1957). In the language of transactional analysis, people have systematic ways of gaining "payoffs" which can either be beneficial and rewarding or hurtful and punishing. Helping people focus on their operating assumptions is difficult since it can involve discovery of the painful payoffs they are experiencing as a result of past decisions. People must also learn that they can change behavior for better payoffs. A series of self-study questions can assist in this process. The following are questions found to be useful by practitioners of transactional analysis:*

1. What kind of person are you?
2. What experiences in life led you to be the person that you are?
3. From these experiences, what decisions about your life did you make?
4. Which of these decisions led to the difficulties you are experiencing?
5. To be the kind of person you want to be, which decision must you change?
6. Which decision will you change?
7. How will you and I know that you've made these changes? (Express in simple behavioral terms.)

An alternative approach to uncovering the private psychological logic is to use the sequence:†

I am (example: afraid) _____
(your worst feeling)

that if I (example: trust you) _____ ,

I will (example: be abandoned) _____

instead of (example: loved) _____ ,

so I will (example: take care of your fear so that you can take care of me and love me) _____ .

Self-evaluation requires skill, patience, thought, and caution, but may be necessary as a preliminary to behavioral contracting.

ELEMENTS OF A CONTRACT

The following are three definitions of interpersonal contracts useful for understanding the contracting process:

A contract is a set of expectations or orientations, written or oral, setting the conditions of an agreement that can be formalized, and usually having some statement about sanctions against violations.

---

*Questions by William H. Holloway, M.D., Garden Grove, California. Used by permission of the author.

†Reprinted with permission from "A 'think structure' for feeling fine faster" by Pamela Levin, *Transactional analysis journal*, 1973, 3 (3), 38–39. Copyright© January 1973 by the International Transactional Analysis Association, Inc.

Contracts are the initial phase of any work arrangement, and may be viewed as the mutual, two-sided arrangement made between person A and person B and beneficial to both.

Contracts involve:

- Mutual consent of both persons
- Valid considerations (the worker gets paid and the employer gets anything agreed upon)
- Competency—employer and employee are both competent to consummate the contract (not intoxicated, and so on)
- The pursuit of work has a lawful object (no contracts to rob a store)

If the contract is to be meaningful to both persons, each must agree to plans that reflect his or her wants and needs, and that are likely to be followed. The ability to make and keep contracts depends upon achievement of modest growth toward being a healthy person with a functional integration of both intra- and interpersonal processes. Failure to keep a contract, when followed by constructive confrontation and recontracting, is an opportunity for the person to grow toward greater awareness of self and others. Figure 17 depicts the contracting process.

A and B stand for individuals *or* groups. A verbalizes what he wants from B and B verbalizes what he wants from A in interpersonal terms. A and B also form contracts in terms of what they want *from themselves* while in their relationships to one another.

Figure 17.   Interpersonal Contracting

CONTRACTING EFFECTIVELY—SOME TRAINING TOOLS

Located in part IV (pp. 221–227) is *Contracting,* a packet of training exercises and materials which may be used to develop contractual trust and contracting skills in teams. They include:

- An outline for a brief lecture on contracting.
- Contract exercises in team building, with instructions for group leaders. This guide is helpful in sessions involving a group larger than a single team.
- Contract exercise form with space for three individual contracts.
- Contract questions useful in identifying participants' needs, goals, and strategies. The questions may be used between pairs during the exercises.
- Contract criteria checklist for evaluating the contracts made during the exercises.

Coaching Relationships

Coaching is the relationship between supervisor or team leader and subordinate or team member as they progress toward agreed-upon targets or objectives. Coaching may be the most neglected part of management by objectives as applied in most organizations. Once a target-setting contract has been developed, it is often felt that the subordinate can carry out tasks without additional psychological, material, or other support from the leader. This is not the case. Coaching is particularly important when workers are not continually involved with their group leader. Volumes have been written on dimensions of relationships between two persons, although little directly concerns coaching. We have found three sources particularly helpful in identifying elements of the coaching relationship: Carl Rogers, William Glasser, and Eric Berne. (Pertinent works by these authors are cited in the references.)

There are a great many differences in approach to coaching. The approach selected is largely determined by the nature of the organization within which one is working and the assumptions one is willing to make about others. Figure 18 compares the philosophical assumptions and methods of traditional hierarchical and open organization approaches to coaching.

The hierarchical coaching process is highly directive and controlling because it assumes that workers are inherently weak and incapable of developing constructively from their inner resources. By contrast, the open organization approach assumes that people are capable of being responsible for their own behavior and decisions, and that they will become self-determining if allowed to practice problem-solving skills. In this view, coaching is aimed at helping workers identify and solve their own problems. In our experience, the open coaching style works better in a team setting where the leader wants to increase performance of individual workers and enjoy the advantages of the extra problem-solving ability that comes from developing synergy in a group. In addition, as both workers and managers experience increasing control over payoffs in their work environment, the quality of life improves, and beneficial changes occur in personnel selection, development, performance review, and evaluation methods.

Dimensions of the Coaching Relationship	Hierarchical Model (Subordinates are Other-determined)	Open Organizations Model (Subordinates are Self-determining)
1. Individual capacity	Subordinates cannot overcome their own bias in viewing themselves.	Within people there are great forces for growth which enable them to adjust to the environment.
2. Purpose of coaching	Guide and direct subordinates into channels of thought so that eventually they can go on their own.	Create atmosphere in which colleagues are encouraged to explore and solve their own problems.
3. Nature of problem solving	Intellectual problem-solving attitude is required.	Feelings and intuitions are resources for solving problems.
4. Predictability of process	Poorly defined developmental steps.	Seems to be a definite pattern followed by most recorded experiences.
5. Training necessary for coach	Development over an extended period of time.	Useful to colleagues within a few months.
6. Information on individual felt to be necessary	All that is available or attainable is necessary to gain an intimate understanding of the individual.	Present condition most important; records may hamper coaching process.
7. Amount of interpretation	Necessary that coach be skilled in interpretation and judgment making	Minimal to avoid possible misinterpretation or premature interpretation by subordinates.
8. Advice and suggestion	Colleagues must be brought to understand the basis of choice making. Help them to eliminate irrational factors.	Professional and personal growth hampered if advice, suggestions, and directions are consistently given.

Figure 18. Coaching: a Comparison of Traditional and Open Organization Approaches

Managing Agreement

Probably, most organization problems perceived as conflicts with others are not conflicts in reality. Rather, they are situations in which existing agreement has not surfaced because people do not trust and communicate with each other. Jerry Harvey (1974) believes that the failure to disclose and confront others with one's honest feelings results from the fear of being dispensable. In short, people feel that unless they continually agree with others in a group, the group will decide they are not team players and will take steps to get rid of them.

When people don't level, they are forced to second-guess each other and may come to a false consensus which in reality no one wants. Harvey named this situation the Abilene paradox after a personal experience—a failure to confront others which took him on a "trip to Abilene." Harvey's father-in-law proposed that the family drive eighty miles to Abilene, Texas, in a dust storm to eat at a greasy spoon. Others, thinking he was serious, reinforced the idea. Finally, all decided to go, although nobody really wanted to. After returning home, the father-in-law revealed what had happened. Others confessed they had not wanted to go, and a family fight ensued.

In a discussion of myths held by consultants, Harvey (1975) maintained that

> confrontation does *not* inevitably involve conflict. Confrontation is simply the process of discovering the nature of the underlying reality of organizational situations. . . . I also find that most organization members know what the nature of that reality is, but frequently hesitate to state it or assume that they share it with others. (p. 4)

Trips to Abilene can be a way of getting nowhere in an organization. Harvey points out how critical it is for a manager or consultant to distinguish between real and phony conflict. The task of the group leader is to cut through surface agreement and test to see what the real agreement is before proceeding to planning or problem solution. Honest confrontation can lead to better group process, improved productivity, increased problem-solving skills, and resolution of chronic ills.

There are two instruments by Harvey in part IV (pp. 228–229) which can be used to diagnose the nature of a problem in a work group: *Organization Problem Analysis* and *Organization Diagnostic Survey*. They are designed to be completed in sequence by each group member. After tallying responses on the survey, the leader checks to see which conditions are seen as characteristic of the problem. Items 1 and 2 indicate the presence of a genuine conflict whereas items 3 through 7 indicate a phony agreement, a trip to Abilene characterized by blaming, fragmented cliques, and avoidance of disclosure at organization meetings.

9

ACTION RESEARCH TEAMS*

IN CHAPTER 6 we emphasized the importance of data-based feedback and problem solving to the adaptability of an organization. The diagnostic review was presented as a program for initiating second-order change or organization renewal. The diagnostic review is a method of getting people to talk with each other about common organization problems, growth areas, and goals. It raises awareness of discrepancies between the present situation and what people want their organization to become. It clarifies values, renews purpose, sets goal priorities, and motivates change toward a more open organization. However, without internal feedback mechanisms that enable people to digest second-order change and deal successfully with both old and new concerns, the momentum begun through an organization's self-study may be quickly lost.

Chapter 8 noted the importance of the team as a locus within which organization openness is practiced in daily operations. The action research team is a special type of team designed to build feedback and problem solving into organization structures. By addressing emerging problems of the whole organization, the action research team becomes a vehicle for self-propelled change from inside. The team assists in resolving problems in the whole system as well as those specific to particular units or combinations of units. Organization members themselves become agents of change through diagnosis, planning, implementation, and evaluation.

Establishing an action research team directly addresses a problem common to many modern organizations: perceived lack of responsiveness to goals, energies, capabilities, and needs of employees. Such a lack of responsiveness is not a conscious effort of leaders to deny employees self-fulfillment. It is a by-product of modern society and of organization customs and culture. Use

*Written with the assistance of V. N. Comstock, a doctoral student in educational administration at The University of Texas at Austin, Austin, Texas

of an action research team begins to provide for individual needs, particularly the need to understand and adjust to change throughout an organization.

The Practice of Action Research

A DEFINITION

The definitions of action research are almost as numerous as those who have studied or practiced it. They do, however, reduce to a single pattern. Action research is perhaps best described as a process, although it is also described by many as an approach to problem solving. As a process it consists of systematically collecting data relative to a problem, feeding the data back into the system, taking action, and evaluating the results of actions by collecting more data. By nature, action research is cyclic: the evaluation of each action yields data for planning the next action.

The action research team provides a mechanism for weighing emerging concerns and problems in the organization. It can generate alternatives for solutions to problems and determine the best changes and strategies for coping with these concerns, all in a collaborative framework within the organization structure.

When an action research team is functioning, the chances that change will be accepted are increased. First, those who will be most affected by the change have been involved in planning for it. They are much more likely to understand and act upon changes when they helped collect data, identify pressing problems, and work through options for resolving those problems. Second, human resources will be used in interesting, new, and challenging ways. Skills lying dormant will be called upon. New skills may need to be learned. Team members learn new group processes while working on real problems. Thus, the two kinds of change become synergistic.

An effective action research team is built upon certain assumptions. One is that there is a recognized need for change. A second is that there will be systematic data collection to diagnose causes of problems and dissatisfaction, and to set goals. Still another is that it is possible to devise group action to achieve goals. It is assumed that new ideas will come from the interplay of research and action, once new and better data are collected and analyzed.

Successful use of action research teams results in several valuable outcomes:

- Implementation of system-wide change programs
- Progressive resolution of chronic operational problems
- Identification of emerging concerns
- Confronting and working through differences
- Increased worker involvement in change
- Increased worker skills in group processes and problem solving

The following case study illustrates perhaps better than any description how an action research team can function in an organization.

A Case Study. Rational Change on the Inside: The Action Research Team*

A multiplant division of a heavy machinery company nestled in the hills of Appalachia employed more than six thousand people. A vice-president, who was born nearby and who had come up through the ranks, headed the division. He had seen this division through repeated three-year cycles of long, costly strikes and contract renegotiations. Beyond its strike history, this division had hardly ever known a steady production rate. It would fall short of output goals in the first two months of a quarter. Speeding up during the third month to meet quotas meant overtime and double-time. Workers increasingly resisted adapting their life styles to this ebb and flow. Younger employees particularly resented working eight or more hours a day, seven days a week. They blamed management for poor planning.

In the past few years the company had mushroomed. Where there had been one plant there were now four. The vice-president developed a new office of industrial relations (OIR) to cope with increasingly critical labor relations problems and prevent strikes. But his vision was broader than this. He knew how important it was to call on workers' expertise and draw on real experience for management decisions. So he created three new positions, headed by a manager of human resource development (HRD).

The HRD manager set the goal of creating an organization in which people work together for greater productivity, as opposed to one split by antagonism. She began by tackling the problem of worker and management apathy. She and the vice-president felt that most production problems could be solved and working conditions improved were it not for poor communication among work groups, from line workers to top managers. People's abilities for problem solving were just not being tapped. So the vice-president and the HRD manager made plans to restructure the information flow.

The HRD manager hired us to help her. We first suggested a team to come up with appropriate solutions and begin adopting them. We called it an *action research team* (ART). It would define the problems, collect up-to-date information on them, digest the data, and take action according to the data. Evaluation of the team's actions would make possible the modification of new procedures to provide some solutions satisfactory to all.

The action research team was made up of the vice-president, new HRD manager, head of industrial relations, and three managers. The vice-president stated their purpose:

> People make things go. The greatest waste of resources here is the waste of human brain power, enthusiasm, and the creative ability of workers who know more about their jobs and how to improve them than they're given credit for. We hope to weld technology, human resources, and managerial skills into one effective unit by being conscious of goals of the company and goals of the workers which incidentally, are not always the same. As a result we hope everyone—company, workers, community, customers, and in a larger sense, the country—will benefit.

---

*Case study written by Ann Linquist

As its first activity, the ART forged a group identity by drawing up a list of skills and resources each person was willing to share with the group. We, as external consultants, led the group in preliminary team-building exercises to develop a working model of honesty and trust. Everyone understood honesty as sharing relevant facts for problem solving, and trust as each person's fulfilling the commitments made to the group and anyone else. Our goals were improved group process, higher productivity, and good morale. We knew there would have to be improved communication and more rational problem solving first.

For one of its initial studies the ART chose the division's data-processing group because that group could generate the data necessary for improved management. Much irrelevant information was being generated and needed data was going unprocessed. Diagnostic interviews were held with all data-processing personnel. The ART sought facts about their job functions, ideas about how their work could be better, fantasies about new endeavors, problems in actualizing their ideals, and skills and resources each was willing to share with the whole division. Structured interviews were conducted. The format of the open organization model served as a guide. (See figure 19.) A force field analysis was completed around each section of the model. Results formed a basis for restructuring the group as a true center for processing information.

	Unity	Internal Responsiveness	External Responsiveness
Individual			Who helps? Who hinders? Morale?
Work Group	What is it like to work here? Personality of the group?	Conflicts, work group problems? Who helps whom?	How well do you sense other work groups?
Manufacturing Division	How does management help?	How is your work group perceived by other units in the organization?	

Figure 19. Applying the Open Organization Model to Work Group Diagnosis

Organizations tend to follow the same kinds of neurotic patterns individuals do. Here we found a large manufacturing operation with the same handicap as many American males—a drive to be strong and an injunction against being close. In daily operations these imperatives led to overwork ("Do everything perfectly and on time.") and isolation of work units ("Never share what you know or rely on anyone else's help."). Rational decision making based on actual human and material concerns was missing. In this operation bosses behaved like parents and workers like children. Management handed down production quotas (parent saying, "Here's what should be done."), while line workers reacted to the reward and punishment system (child responding, "I will do only what I must to get what I want or avoid punishment.").

How could we break up this tyrannical system? First we elaborated on the vice-president's vision of worker satisfaction and productivity by stressing the role of data-based decision making. We hoped that strengthening the flow of reliable and pertinent facts from the top down and from the bottom up would break down these parent and child roles, replacing them with identities of reasoning adults willing to contribute valuable, needed skills and knowledge to common goals.

Borrowing terms from transactional analysis, we hypothesized that the division was like a person experiencing *contamination* or clouding of the *adult* ego state (rational computing) by *parent* (oughts, shoulds, antiquated policies and procedures) and *child* (conformity, compliance) as pictured in figure 20 (Berne, 1961). Shaded areas show the contamination of the rational management process (steady production, effective planning, organizing, implementing, controlling). The result is that the rational adult state (or computer) is not permitted to function but is used merely as a weapon in bickering between the parent/boss and the child/worker. If the contamination were removed, the reasoning adult (whether worker or boss) could lend expertise and knowledge to problem solving. He or she would bring out the parent ego state only for self-protection ("I should not work so hard that I make myself sick.") and the child ego state for creativity and enjoyment ("I did good.") (Dusay, 1977).

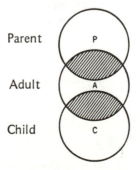

Parent

Adult

Child

Figure 20. The Contaminated Adult Ego State

Adapted from *Transactional analysis in psychotherapy: a systematic individual and social psychiatry* by E. Berne. New York: Ballantine Books, 1961

The ART devised and initiated a new management system based on monthly one-to-one meetings of each supervisor with employees to report expectations and set realistic goals. Workers met with foremen and foremen with section heads. In these contracting sessions some pertinent problems surfaced around a variety of issues ranging from workers' comfort and safety to assembly-line bottlenecks, from personality clashes to workload inequities. Relevant data were sent to the data-processing group which began to monitor the information flow. The ART also began to tap this source of information to assess the new management system.

As a result of monitoring, the ART initiated another intervention. They asked us for management-training aid. We answered by sponsoring workshops for top and middle managers in transactional analysis, team building, rational problem solving, conflict resolution, and communication skills. Our aim was to strengthen their capacities as reasoning adults by sharing knowledge and values, and to discourage the use of strong-arm, parental influence. Rather than saying, "You'll do this because I'm your boss," we encouraged the attitude, "Let's see what we can work out together." Then we followed up by building skills to make these attitudes functional.

We encouraged the ART's interventions. We also emphasized the importance of assessing and reassessing the effectiveness of their strategies. When there were no results, we encouraged the team to try another tack. Not only does this data-based approach keep actions relevant, but it also sharpens evaluation tools and monitoring systems.

Today the data-processing group and the ART are working together on a strategy to compare standard production hours with actual clock hours as a measure of present and potential productivity. Other measures of productivity, efficiency, and employee satisfaction are being devised and tested. Meanwhile, workers are experiencing improved job conditions. Serious strikes have been avoided for over three years. Participation in solving problems of production and work environment has increased as employees' talents have been recognized. Workers have had the satisfaction of seeing good suggestions acted upon and positive results shared throughout the organization. Once the division was a parental influence invading the private lives of workers with demands for overtime and overwork. Now it has become a source of worker pride and an integral part of the community.

HISTORIC DEVELOPMENT

The paradigm for inquiry as well as the scientific method underlying the action research model was introduced by John Dewey, who listed five phases of reflective thinking: suggestion, intellectualization, hypothesizing, reasoning, and testing the hypothesis by action (French and Bell, 1973). The first use of the term *action research*, however, was made by John Collier, a commissioner of

Indian affairs in the thirties, who had to struggle with race relations and make recommendations. He discovered he could succeed only with the advice of a scientist, an administrator, and a layman; that is, a researcher, a practitioner, and a client. He hailed research as an indisputably necessary tool for action. He demanded that practitioner and client contribute to the work of the researcher (French and Bell, 1973).

As a formal approach, however, action research was pioneered in the late 1940s by Kurt Lewin (1946), a social scientist interested in the development of data-based feedback. He recognized that problems were being tackled before progress standards had been set for measuring results. He is said to have stated that the only good theory is a practical theory, and that action research bridges the gap. He deplored time wasted in futile efforts that were tossed aside without any attempt by innovators to learn from what they achieved or failed to achieve. They were failing to test whether their actions were leading them in the right direction. To develop a better methodology, Lewin conducted action research projects in areas ranging from intergroup relations to eating habits. He stressed collaboration between scientists and people of action, hence "action research" (French and Bell, 1973). Lewin examined action in two steps: (1) investigation of laws contributing to theory and practice, and (2) diagnosis of a situation leading to solving a particular problem. A later scholar, R. A. Jenks, divided action research into four aspects: diagnostic, participant, empirical, and experimental (Lippitt and Lippitt, 1978b, pp. 89–90).

In recent years, action research has become almost synonymous with organization development in the minds of some practitioners. The close association of the two terms appears to result from the work that took place in several Exxon refineries in the late 1950s. Originally the term *organization development* was applied to the development of work teams through the use of action research. Later the term was extended to refer to all teams within the organization, regardless of the activities or methods of team development.

Other practitioners, however, disagree vehemently with this view, seeing action research as a separate and distinct approach not necessarily tied to OD. At any rate, those who differentiate between the two are also quick to point out that any sound organization development program includes action research.

A MODEL

Earlier, action research was described as a problem-solving process. It is more precisely defined as

> the process of systematically collecting research data about an ongoing system relative to some objective, goal, or need of that system; feeding these data back into the system; taking actions by altering selected variables within the system based both on the data and on hypotheses; and evaluating the result of actions by collecting more data. (French and Bell, 1973, pp. 84–85)

Gordon and Ronald Lippitts' action research model (1978b) seen in figure 21 shows in more detail how action research is carried out by a team within an organization setting. The action research team plays the role of an internal consultant (3 in the figure). Their client (1) may be a work unit, a larger unit such as a division, or the entire organization, depending upon the problem being addressed. The ART may call upon an external consultant (2) to provide training in problem solving and group process skills, but the responsibility for action planning and implementation rests with the team.

The ART collects data from the client system, processes it, and feeds it back to the client for joint analysis and diagnosis (4, 5, 6). Next the ART devises and initiates an action plan (7), completing one cycle of the action research process. Note how collaboration between team and client tends to break down the traditional distance between research and action. As Lippitt points out, action research allows the researcher and the subject to exchange roles, so that subjects become researchers, and researchers participate in some of the action steps.

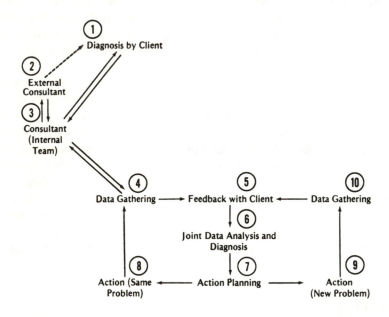

Figure 21.   The Action Research Model in Consulting

Adapted from *The consulting process in action* by G. Lippitt and R. Lippitt, p. 88. Figure by Mary Roberts. Copyright© 1978 by University Associates, La Jolla, California. Reproduced by permission of Mary Roberts

The ART monitors implementation of the action plan, collecting data to see how well it is working. If the problem is not satisfactorily resolved, the data are used as the basis for another cycle of action research which results in a revised action plan (8, 4, 5, 6, 7). When the data indicate a new problem, the team initiates a new cycle of research (9, 10, 5, 6, 7).

Perhaps the most important feature of the action research process is the provision for recycling problems through four steps: data gathering, feedback, action, and assessment. The recycling aspect of action research is particularly well emphasized in the model shown in figure 22. According to H. A. Shepard (1960):

> In front of intelligent human action there should be an objective, be it ever so fuzzy or distorted. And in advance of human action there should be planning, although knowledge of paths to the objective is always inadequate. Action itself should be taken a step at a time, and after each step it is well to do some fact-finding.... Through fact-finding, the present situation can be assessed, and this information, together with information about the objective, can be used in planning the second step. Movement toward an objective consists of a series of such cycles of planning—acting—fact-finding—planning. (pp. 31–35)

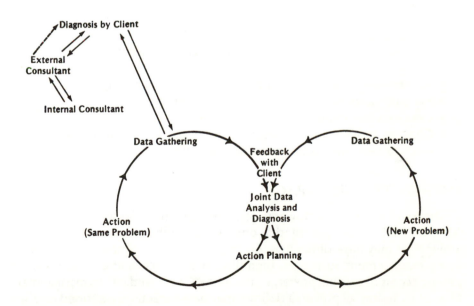

Figure 22. The Action Research Model: Recycling Features

Adapted from *The consulting process in action* by G. Lippitt and R. Lippitt, p. 88. Figure by Mary Roberts. Copyright© 1978 by University Associates, La Jolla, California. Reproduced by permission of Mary Roberts

Through recycling, the ART strives to continuously improve the everyday operations and the environment of the organization. If this process is to work effectively, certain features must be present: client and consultant collaboration, internal resource development, the interplay of research and action, and continuous monitoring and evaluation (Frohman, Saskin, and Kavanagh, 1976).

The Action Research Team

The action research team has a number of characteristics which, taken together, distinguish it from other kinds of teams and committees within an organization. By nature, the ART:

- Uses a form of calculated data collection to define and analyze a problem. It does not accept any diagnosis already made, and it uses its own to plan further action.
- Examines its own functioning as a group to solve problems or get work done. It provides for mutual influence among group members, develops trust within the group, promotes individual involvement, analyzes meetings, and explores its leadership through freedom and participation.
- Has a basic philosophy of collaboration among members and other groups regarding change strategies.
- Becomes involved in implementing collaborative change, not just giving recommendations.
- Accepts learning and relationships of members as important.
- Evaluates and modifies its internal functioning.
- Uses external consultants.
- Chooses freely areas for work. It needs autonomy to function, which leads to task ownership, commitment, and high investment of energy.

AUTHORITY AND IMPACT

The ART has no formal power unless management chooses to give it power. When an ART is self-appointed, it enjoys high member interest and energy. However, it may have difficulty acquiring resources of time and space, countering management suspicion, blending in with prevailing structures, and gaining access to existing power. When an ART is created by top management, it has a link to formal power, a definite mandate for action, a defined role, and a ready framework for achieving change. But it may be viewed as a tool of management, greeted by employees with suspicion and hostility, and hampered by too little commitment of members to the task. One must weigh the advantages and disadvantages of appointed and volunteer teams in relation to the organization's particular situation.

MEMBERSHIP SELECTION

The team works best with members who have a real interest in serving, an aptitude for working in groups, a high trust level already established within the organization, an investment in the organization, a healthy personality, good communication skills, and established membership in an informal communication network. In choosing members who will provide high energy and involvement, interest in serving is a more important criterion than special characteristics that ensure a representative group.

Ideally, however, an action research team should have representatives from all organization areas affected by a change. For system-wide change, a team should have representatives from all constituents. In a corporation, a team would include a top executive, middle managers, and workers. A team in a small college would include a dean, department chairperson, and faculty. However, for change primarily affecting an individual work unit, the team could be composed of representatives of management, work teams in the unit, and perhaps key groups which interface with the work unit. In a small department, each person might be a member, and action research would be used as one of several methods to get work done. The nature of the task, available technology, goals, and the kind of change (first- or second-order) all influence the composition of the action research team.

THE CONSULTANT'S ROLE

The aid of an external consultant can be valuable, though not necessary. Such a person does not bring any vested interests in the status quo, and may provide skill training that can speed the progress of the team. The consultant can be particularly helpful in coaching the team in the action research process. He or she may aid team members in collecting data and making a tentative diagnosis of the particular problem area. Collecting data may involve various instruments on task, environment, or attitude; or may involve training in data collection skills and procedures.

Feedback to the client should be quick, to the point, and specific enough to help in an analysis and discussion of the problem. It should be given in an open, supportive climate without value judgments, and be relevant to the desired goals of the client (Lippitt and Lippitt, 1978b).

Planning should include all people who will be affected by the action, and it should also be relevant to the client's goals. It should involve close collaboration among consultants, managers, and team members. It should be feasible within the system and be based on implications of the data.

As the action is implemented there should be built-in standards for measuring results and progress. The action should lead to collecting more data and making further changes if results show they are needed to meet goals. Once begun, the process should be continuously monitored and based on further research.

Starting an Action Research Team

The process of setting up an action research team and working through an initial problem involves four phases: entry, start-up, action interventions, and evaluation. Each organization will want to design its own problem resolution scheme to suit particular needs and resources. An effective problem resolution design includes provisions for official recognition of the action research team, resources to facilitate effective team work, sufficient time to succeed in a change, and a predetermined point at which responsibility for change is transferred from the action research team.

The following is a description of a plan for establishing an action research team to address system-wide problems in one organization:

PHASE 1. ENTRY

Top managers have decided to introduce an action research team into the organization as an ongoing mechanism for change. They identify an issue of concern and announce it through an official vehicle of the organization. They assign responsibility to the office of human resource development for establishing the ART to address the issue. Next, vice-presidents (or executives one authority level below the chief executive) present the ART's concept to their managerial subordinates. This process is followed down the authority structure until every employee has received information about the ART. These actions sanction and legitimize the ART as a function of the organization.

Finally, the chief executive and key staff develop team selection criteria.

PHASE 2. START-UP

TEAM SELECTION. The office of human resource development announces the creation of the ART and solicits voluntary membership through a newsletter and announcements on bulletin boards. A date is mentioned for an informational meeting. The meeting includes a brief orientation lecture and a question and answer period for those considering membership. Members are selected from applications based upon previously developed criteria. New members are notified of the first meeting time.

TEAM DEVELOPMENT. Team building is an ongoing process that begins with the first meeting. Between twelve and sixteen hours of team building time are scheduled, preferably in one or two large time blocks, to develop group identity, trust, shared values and norms, and mechanisms for group maintenance and renewal. This initial step is crucial to ensure team cohesion when working with others to solve problems. The ART may want training in communication skills, interpersonal contracting, group problem solving and decision making, conflict resolution, management of agreement, developing trust, goal setting and clarification, and problem definition. The ART may request assistance from a trainer from the office of human resource development or from an external consultant, or may rely upon a team member with group process skills to facilitate team-building meetings.

TEAM TRAINING. Training is also an ongoing process that begins during the start-up phase. Members begin by getting to know one another's skills and areas of interest. They assess resources already available in the group and skills they want to acquire. They may request training in collecting data, analyzing problems, action planning, and designing evaluations.

PROBLEM DEFINITION. The issue was initially stated by top management, but the ART must define the problem and its ramifications, and establish ownership through its own analysis. It will review historical documents and other pertinent data and will develop a definition which is subject to change as more information becomes available.

SUMMATIVE EVALUATION PLAN. The ART develops a plan to evaluate the impact of its intervention at the conclusion of the change. The plan includes collection of base-line data before action interventions begin. If the ART has access to the necessary expertise, it may design an evaluation instrument instead of using a commercial one. Design meetings may be open to all or part of the organization, depending on the intensity and complexity of the activity, and on availability of resources.

PHASE 3. ACTION INTERVENTIONS

BASE-LINE DATA COLLECTION. The ART collects information about the problem situation it has identified. It may use interviews, surveys, observation, and questionnaires to gather information.

ANALYSIS AND FEEDBACK. The ART analyzes the data and prepares a report summarizing its conclusions. Depending upon the problem, it holds small or large group meetings to present conclusions and solicit questions and comments from others.

PROBLEM REDEFINITION. At this point the ART has gathered sufficient new and reinterpreted information to allow for either problem restatement or refinement. It *must* stop to check for congruency before going on to the next step.

ACTION PLANNING. In a meeting with the group receiving assistance, the ART sets goals and criteria for successful achievement. It generates alternative strategies for achieving the goals and selects the alternative that seems most promising. Then the ART designs an action plan which includes objectives, activities, evaluation criteria, and an evaluation method to judge whether the plan is working as intended.

IMPLEMENTATION. After the plan has had sufficient time to be tried, its implementation is evaluated. Based on collected data, the plan is continued, revised, or terminated. The plan may be reevaluated and revised at several checkpoints during the implementation step.

PHASE 4. EVALUATION

SUMMATIVE DATA COLLECTION. At this point the ART administers instruments to collect base-line data for a second time. This information will be compared with data collected in phase 1 to evaluate the impact of the ART's intervention.

ANALYSIS AND FEEDBACK. The ART analyzes data and prepares a comprehensive report. After meeting with the client group to present the findings and obtain questions and comments, the ART revises the action plan as needed.

TRANSFER OF RESPONSIBILITY. The ART plans for transfer of responsibility to the appropriate organizational structures. Now the team will leave this particular concern and move on to another.

If an action research team is to be successful it must have both the freedom and requisite skills to assume responsibility, as well as the freedom to choose its own goals. Freedom does not imply lack of direction, however. In order to carry out their roles, team members are instructed in planned change strategies through the assistance of skilled members or ART consultants, with the aid of the open systems model as a theoretical frame. With energy, power, and skillful use of the existing organization structure, the ART should have little difficulty contributing to the organization and to the individual growth of its members.

TRAINING ACTIVITIES

Chapter 8 presented some activities and instruments for developing teams. Four additional skill-building tools are located in part IV.

Confronting Organization Issues, on page 232, is a seven-question exercise designed to give group members permission to confront others on significant organization issues. Members think of current problems or situations in which they are personally involved that call for confrontation. Individual completion of the questionnaire can be followed by group discussion and role playing of selected situations.

Conflict Resolution: Strategy Questionnaire, on page 233, is a list of thirteen ways of responding in a conflict situation. Team members determine how often they use various strategies, how effective the strategies are, and how members feel when these strategies are used in response to them. The questionnaire provides an excellent point of departure for group discussion and role playing.

Task, Group-Building, and Maintenance Functions (pp. 234–236) is a self-assessment scale of twelve leader and member behaviors required to accomplish group tasks and to maintain the group as a working unit. After reading a brief description of each behavior, the members mark a five-point scale to indicate their degree of skill. After completing the instrument, they can identify areas in which they want to develop skills.

The team may also fill out the group profile sheet. The horizontal column of the profile lists twelve task and maintenance roles, and four antigroup roles. The members' names are written into the vertical columns. Each person places check marks in his or her column corresponding to roles he or she has played most often in the group. By comparing the group profile with individual assessments of strengths and weaknesses, the team can discover untapped resources and identify areas that need special attention and development.

Analysis of Skills in Groups (pp. 237–239) is a scale listing attitudes and abilities characteristic of an effective group member, such as "tolerance of opposing opinions" and "ability to present ideas forcefully and persuasively." For each item, members mark a seven-point scale with "P" at the point that represents present skills, and "F" at the point that represents aspirations for the future. After marking all scales, members identify three or four they would most like to change. This instrument may be used for motivational, diagnostic, and training purposes.

A follow-up activity should be designed to assist team members in developing skills they have chosen as most important. One method is to ask team members to form pairs. With the help of a partner, each person formulates plans to develop selected skills. The activity can be turned into a skill practice by asking pairs to match with other pairs. In each foursome, one pair works on developing an action plan while the other pair listens as process observer. After the plan has been evaluated, the pairs reverse roles. We have found that a pair of observers is more objective, accurate, and effective than the single observer commonly used in triad group exercises.

10

DEVELOPING MANAGERS

WE HAVE EXPLORED the foundations and potential of open organizations, and have presented some steps that enable an organization to develop flexibility and responsiveness. These steps include resolving value differences, developing cohesive teams, making appropriate use of power and authority, formulating goals that will elicit broad support among various constituencies, developing performance objectives and action plans compatible with these goals, and evaluating and modifying plans based upon continuous feedback. We have also emphasized the crucial roles played by the outside consultant, the in-house consultant, and the action research team. The most important role of all, however, is played by managers. Organization openness depends upon developing managers who have a vision of the potential of their organizations, and who possess both the commitment and the leadership skills to guide their organizations in a desired direction. Therefore, we include as a part of a diagnostic review an assessment of the strengths and growth needs of managers.

We use a variety of instruments to assess managerial competencies, and integrate the data within the open organization model. As part of the diagnostic review, managerial assessment has several purposes: to introduce the model to managers, to raise awareness of manager competencies required in an open organization, to identify system elements that hinder or aid the work of managers, and to provide the basis for a competency-based manager development program.

This chapter will introduce the assessment instruments we use, and describe our process of collecting, interpreting, and using assessment data. The instruments and process are not presented as a finished procedure, but as a stimulus for others who want to develop their own managerial assessment methods.

Collecting Information

SETTING AND APPROACH

Through personal, structured interviews and through a variety of instruments, data are gathered about the manager in these areas:

- Present and desired skill levels related to standard roles and functions of managers
- Areas in which the individual wants to develop
- Skills the individual feels are most needed for effective functioning of the organization as a whole
- Present and desired skill levels related to open organization variables of unity, internal responsiveness and external responsiveness, both for the individual and for the organization

Instruments will carry some distortion even when combined with personal interviews. The preferred measurement of manager skills would be by direct observation of different situations over time—an expanded notion of the assessment center. However, this process involves much time and expense. Most organizations are willing to accept the structured interview as an alternative to more costly behavioral observation and situational test methods.

It is important to give the manager the instruments in person, not by interoffice mail, and to explain their purpose and use. The distinction between evaluation and development should be made clear. Even if the instrument seems useful for evaluation, it should first be used for six months to a year as a development instrument to allow managers time to assess their own strengths and to formulate action plans. Beginning with an assessment and training phase also allows the development of local competency norms.

When assessment is being conducted for development rather than for performance evaluation purposes, data collection and interpretation should not be conducted by a person responsible for hiring and firing. A manager is more likely to share areas of weakness and to ask for assistance from someone in a coaching role. For those interested in a manager's getting feedback from peers and subordinates as well as immediate supervisors, a climate of trust and openness must first be developed. It is well to back up if necessary and structure interventions that will build the necessary trust and honesty.

Opportunities for managers to develop must be available. A manager's awareness of personal areas of weakness is not helpful in itself without opportunities to help remedy the deficiencies. If an organization is interested in having effective, caring managers, it supports them in their growth and development.

As part of the diagnostic review or as a separate review, the purpose of the managerial assessment is to obtain a comprehensive picture of individual and group areas of strength and weakness and to relate this profile to the dynamics and system issues of the organization. Therefore, we use a variety of instruments that include competency-based measures of both traditional and open organization skills, and open-ended, problem-oriented instruments. The instruments will be described under two categories: individual development needs and organization development needs. They are located in part IV.

ASSESSING INDIVIDUAL DEVELOPMENT NEEDS

We use two self-assessment instruments. The *Manager Role Checklist* (pp. 243–244) lists fourteen roles such as planner and team builder, each described in one or two sentences. Respondents answer "yes" or "no" to questions about whether they now perform the role, and whether they want to develop that role. *Manager Functions* (pp. 245–248) briefly describes thirty-three actions grouped under five categories: planning, organizing, staffing, directing, and controlling. For each function, respondents mark a seven-point scale to indicate their present level of skill and the level they want to achieve. These instruments are used together because some people relate better to role descriptions and others to functional descriptions. Interviewing with these structured instruments is a teaching opportunity for the development specialist to explore the potential of managers for operating in ways not usual for them.

We also use two open-ended problem identification instruments. *Individual Manager Needs* (pp. 249–250) consists of nine questions to help people focus on the kind of managers they want to become, and to make tentative action plans. The questions are based upon the force field model of problem solving (see chapter 9), with several advantages. First, managers are encouraged to fantasize the ideal, to sit back if only for a moment and remove themselves from daily routines to look at a broader picture. Second, managers are encouraged to do some problem solving around environmental forces within their control which they might strengthen or diminish, depending upon whether the forces are seen as helping or hindering movement in the ideal direction. Third, managers are helped to claim some ownership in the development plan instead of seeing development as something done to them. Question 8 is so worded that managers see the development specialist as aiding plans important to them. Question 9 requires managers to verbalize their criteria for successful development, and their way of measuring progress. This provision helps to prevent a common problem in training—feedback from participants at the conclusion of a training event that the experience is not what they wanted, expected, or needed. Thus, managers design their own development schemes, allowing the management development specialist to function as a facilitator. The responsibility for significant learning is clearly on the manager.

Getting a Problem Statement, on page 251, is a set of five open-ended questions based upon the synectics problem-solving model. It is a quick and effective way for people to identify concerns underlying their frustrations and to formulate goals based on those concerns.

Finally, we administer the *Open Organization Managerial Profile* (pp. 252–265), a thirty-six item list of competencies based upon the open organization model described in chapter 1. This instrument measures managerial skill in operating within and among subsystems of the organization. The items are grouped into nine categories which link the three roles of the manager (individual, team member, and organization member) with the three characteristics of an open organization (unity, internal responsiveness, external responsiveness). Figure 23 summarizes the structure of the managerial profile.

The instrument briefly describes manager behaviors in each category, as follows:

Section A is unity on the individual level, defined as the manager's sense of his own worth. He has a positive regard for himself. He is seen by others as being consistent. The manager possesses a set of qualities, values, and beliefs that define his uniqueness. He is seen by others as congruent, and as having self-esteem.

Section B is internal responsiveness on the individual level, defined as the self-awareness of the manager. This section investigates her awareness of her feelings, needs, motivations, and defenses. It also assesses her ability to acknowledge her feelings and frustrations rather than projecting them upon others. It indicates how free she is to allow others the freedom to be themselves.

Section C explores the external responsiveness of the individual manager. The effective manager listens to others actively and generates relevant responses. He is open to different people, experiences, and ideas. He sees himself as constantly interacting with his environment and has a plan for personal and professional growth.

Section D considers the manager's ability to promote unity within her own work group. She identifies team goals and builds cohesiveness by communicating these goals and relating each member's tasks to them. The manager involves work unit members in establishing and revising goals, and she focuses team production (energy) on established goals.

Section E deals with how well the manager uses the internal responsiveness of the work group in relation to achievement of a task. The effective manager balances concern for team members and concern for task achievements. He allows himself and others to perform group functions based on expertise rather than on position in the organization. He facilitates personal and professional growth of team members as an aid to better team functioning.

Section F considers the ability of the manager to promote external responsiveness of the team by serving as a link between the team and other subsystems of the organization. The effective manager gathers data concerning

	UNITY	INTERNAL RESPONSIVENESS	EXTERNAL RESPONSIVENESS
INDIVIDUAL	Identification of my basic beliefs; who I am; my uniqueness; self-concept, perceived self. Values: Am I open and other-oriented or closed and self-oriented? A	Awareness of myself, my feelings, my needs, my defenses; freedom to fulfill my wants and needs. B	Hearing and responding to others; active listening; openness to ideas, experiences, persons; love—ability to enter into and establish enduring relationships; interpersonal attraction and involvement. C
GROUP	Identification of team goals and objectives; building the team. Group achieves syntality (personality) and synergy (group output is greater than the sum of individual outputs). D	Interpersonal skills; facilitation of interaction among team members; process observation; sensitivity and coherence; interpersonal attraction or cohesiveness develops. E	Gathering and relating external information relevant to task of team; linkage with other individuals and groups; cooperation for achievement of common purpose with other systems. F
ORGANIZATION	Development of common goals of organization; management according to purpose and mission. G	Ways components within organization react to and impact each other; data sharing; organization development and human relations. Linkages between individuals and groups. H	Organization responsiveness to larger community; social relevance, profitability. I

Figure 23. Open Organization Behaviors

the team tasks from relevant sources and conveys them to team members as an aid to problem solving. She ensures that her unit's plans and decisions reflect all available organization data. She serves as a spokesperson for team decisions and shares team data with others.

Section G explores the manager's promotion of organization unity. The effective manager knows all organization goals and works to establish the organization's knowledge and commitment to those goals. He realizes the need for establishing an organization identity.

Section H assesses the manager's skill at maintaining internal responsiveness among the subsystems of the organization. The effective manager sees how all components of the organization function and relate to each other. She has a grasp of the total organization and can help make changes that result in smoother internal efficiency.

Section I considers the manager's skills relating to the external responsiveness of the organization. The effective manager is aware of the world outside of the organization. He is able to gather and use information on the impact of the organization on the larger social system, and that of the larger system on the organization.

Within each category, managers respond to several statements of competency by marking a seven-point scale to indicate their present skill level. For example, one of the competencies described under section E, team internal responsiveness, is as follows:

2. Assigns tasks without regard to who is best skilled to accomplish task.

Knows unique skills of each team member and uses each person's skills in team problem solving.

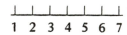

1 2 3 4 5 6 7

The instrument is best used if completed by several people in the organization. After managers complete forms on themselves, they then select several peers or subordinates to assess their skills by completing the instrument. Supervisors should also give their views. The value of such feedback is to overcome managers' blind spots about their behavior and how it affects others. (See the discussion on the Johari window, chapter 3.) Three scales are printed under each competency statement to permit feedback from supervisors and subordinates. They should assess the present skill level only, and not indicate a desired level. Only managers themselves can determine the desired level of achievement.

The *Open Systems Model of Manager Competencies*, on page 266, is a short version of the *Open Organization Managerial Profile* which describes each category briefly. Instead of responding to several items in each of nine categories, managers rate their overall current skill level for each category on a seven-point scale. They also indicate the desired skill level. The interviewer may wish to give this instrument first. If more information is wanted in a particular category, respondents complete the appropriate section of the managerial profile. Because of the one-page schematic format of the short version, it is also useful as a graphic aid during the structured interview, when pulling together and interpreting data to get comprehensive picture of strengths and weaknesses.

ASSESSING ORGANIZATION DEVELOPMENT NEEDS

The instruments described previously can yield information about organization as well as individual development areas. Respondents to the *Individual Manager Needs* instrument, for example, are asked to identify restraining and helping forces that have an impact on their accomplishment of desired goals. The instrument often identifies system blocks and strengths. The *Manager Functions* instrument asks respondents to identify functions for which there is a general training need. Individual needs indicated on the manager competency instruments can also be tallied to develop a profile of high and low priority organization development areas.

Needs of the Organization is a back-up for the above methods of determining training areas. It often reveals some information about general organization issues that do not surface when managers are asked to assess their competencies or to identify personal growth areas. It consists of five sentence completions which require managers to think beyond their current positions and to hypothesize about the needs of the organization. (See page 267.)

Organizing and Interpreting Information

INDIVIDUAL AND GROUP PROFILES

After managers complete the instruments described above, they meet with the interviewer to discuss the results and to develop individual profiles of strengths and development areas. Figure 24 shows the matrix format used to record the profiles. The matrix lists manager roles, functions, and open systems skill areas. Space is also provided to summarize growth areas identified through the open-ended instruments or the interview process. Copies of individual profiles are kept by respondent managers, management development specialists, and any other appropriate officers in the organization, such as supervisors or personnel officers.

MATRIX OF MANAGER COMPETENCIES

DATES

COMPETENCIES					COMMENTS
I. Roles					
A. Advocate					
B. Diagnoser					
C. Planner					
D. Problem solver					
E. Team builder					
F. Conflict manager					
G. Systems analyst					
H. Process observer					
I. Change process expert					
J. Information expert					
K. Individual developer					
L. Organization developer					
M. Interpersonal developer					
N. Skill builder					
II. Functions					
A. Planning					
B. Organizing					
C. Staffing					
D. Directing					
E. Controlling					
III. Open Systems Qualities					
A. Individual unity					
B. Individual internal responsiveness					
C. Individual external responsiveness					
D. Group unity					
E. Group internal responsiveness					
F. Group external responsiveness					
G. Organization unity					
H. Organization internal responsiveness					
I. Organization external responsiveness					
IV Additions					
A.					
B.					
C.					
D.					

General Comments:

KEY: **X** = Needs to develop
O = Possesses competency
® = Resource person (strength)
■ = Not applicable

Figure 24. Individual Growth Profile

This profile is used as a diagnostic rather than a job evaluation tool. Its purpose is to identify both the resources and deficits of managers. Interpretation of the profile begins by pointing out the strengths of the manager. Then, areas of development are discussed. The managerial profile instrument, in particular, serves as an excellent frame for assessing overall training needs. For example, if the manager is low in section C of the instrument, external responsiveness on an individual level, the person may be provided experiences designed to increase skills in active listening and basic communication. If he or she is low in section E, internal responsiveness on the team level, appropriate training may be provided in such areas as process observation, team development, and group theory. Thus, the management development profiles provide a good frame for assessing training needs and for judging the relevance of outside seminars and conferences to the development plans of individual managers.

From individual profiles, the person charged with monitoring manager development may compile a group skills summary sheet, as exemplified in figure 25. The group skills profile enables one to tell at a glance which managers to involve in particular development activities.

When resources for training are limited, it is important to set priorities for in-house training programs. Group training may be provided in areas of greatest need, and other opportunities may be arranged (self-study, outside events) for areas of lesser need. There are several ways of ranking training needs, such as the number of specific requests for a particular type of skill training, stated need on open-ended instruments, degree of discrepancy between current and desired skill levels on the competency instruments, and perceived importance of various skills. Assessing needs must take all these factors into account. Perceived importance and need should be checked for internal consistency. For example, figure 26 shows a summary profile of management development needs for an organization we shall call X. The profile for X was compiled from individual profiles. The numbers recorded for each competency represent the number of people who scored the desired skill level at six or seven on a seven-point scale. The summary indicates that team building and conflict management skills were perceived to be of highest *importance*. As indicated by open-ended instruments and by discrepancy scores, these skill areas were also perceived to be of greatest *need*. Discrepancies were measured by calculating the percentage of responses on each item which showed a two-point difference or more between "am now" and "would like to be" on a seven-point scale.

MATRIX OF MANAGER COMPETENCIES

NAMES

COMPETENCIES		COMMENTS
I Roles		
A. Advocate		
B. Diagnoser		
C. Planner		
D. Problem solver		
E. Team builder		
F. Conflict manager		
G. Systems analyst		
H. Process observer		
I. Change process expert		
J. Information expert		
K. Individual developer		
L. Organization developer		
M. Interpersonal developer		
N. Skill builder		
II. Functions		
A. Planning		
B. Organizing		
C Staffing		
D Directing		
E. Controlling		
III. Open Systems Qualities		
A. Individual unity		
B. Individual internal responsiveness		
C. Individual external responsiveness		
D. Group unity		
E. Group internal responsiveness		
F. Group external responsiveness		
G. Organization unity		
H. Organization internal responsiveness		
I. Organization external responsiveness		
IV. Additions		
A.		
B.		
C.		
D.		

General Comments:

KEY: X = Needs to Develop
O = Possesses Competency
® = Resource Person (strength)
▪ = Not Applicable

Figure 25. Group Skills Summary Sheet

COMPETENCIES	Undecided	Needs Training	Possesses Competency	Strength
I. Role				
A. Advocate		2	7	2
B. Diagnoser		9	2	3
C. Planner		9	5	3
D. Problem solver		8	7	
E. Team builder	1	20	1	
F. Conflict manager		17	4	1
G. Systems analyst		16	2	1
H. Process observer		6	6	
I. Change process expert	1	12	4	
J. Information expert	1	7	6	1
K. Individual developer	1	9	4	1
L. Organization developer	1	12	7	
M. Interpersonal developer		15	1	1
N. Skill builder		14	6	

II. Functions

Areas That Need Training

Planning #	Total	Organizing #	Total	Staffing #	Total	Directing #	Total	Controlling #	Total
1	1	11	2	14	3	20	4	27	4
2	6	12	11	15	4	21	10	28	8
3	3	13	10	16	6	22	7	29	11
4	2			17	8	23	9	30	8
5	3			18	4	24	9	31	0
6	3			19	3	25	5	32	7
7	5					26	0	33	4
8	2								
9	2								
10	3								

III. Open Systems

	Undecided	Needs Training	Possesses Competency	Strength
A. Individual unity				3
B. Individual internal responsiveness		4	1	1
C. Individual external responsiveness		4	2	1
D. Group unity		14	1	
E. Group internal responsiveness		9	2	
F. Group external responsiveness		10	2	
G. Organization unity		7	1	
H. Organization internal responsiveness		8	1	
I. Organization external responsiveness		10		

Figure 26.   Profile of Manager Development Needs of Organization X

ORGANIZATION PROFILES

The open organization model serves as a valuable frame for integrating management development data for the entire organization as well as for individuals and groups. The model allows training needs to be seen realistically within the context of system strengths and blocks, and it makes possible accurate diagnosis of needs. It can help to identify hidden needs that people do not express accurately, for one reason or another. For example, when scores compiled from organization X were compared and examined for internal consistency, one interesting contradiction emerged. On the open systems model, managers said that it was important to get cooperation from other organization components in order to fulfill unit objectives (section F, group external responsiveness). Their frustration with other units and the need for cooperative planning was evident in open-ended problem statements. Yet on the open systems instrument they indicated both low strength and low interest in understanding how the parts of their organization related, and in coordinating their efforts with other units (section H, organization internal responsiveness). The interviewer hypothesized that middle managers felt powerless to remedy the situation through communication with other individual units. They believed that cooperation between units would be achieved only after organization goals had been clarified and agreed to (unity), and after middle managers could have more effective input into top managers' decisions about organization procedures (internal responsiveness). In this case, the needs assessment report recommended not only team building for work units (the most strongly perceived need), but also the formation of vertical task forces (action research teams) to tackle problems of organization unity and internal responsiveness. Training would be provided to these task forces in the process of carrying out their assignments.

11

EVALUATING PROGRESS

EVALUATION IS AN ESSENTIAL of planned change. In the first stage of identifying problems and setting goals, evaluation pinpoints discrepancies in an organization: differences between what people say and what they do, and differences between what the organization is doing and what it aspires to do. Gathering and sharing data about discrepant behaviors helps generate the energy needed to change and define the direction the change should take. It permits forming clear goals by which later efforts can be evaluated. Without initial agreement on goals, the results of a change effort will have different meanings to different people. Evaluation is also important during implementation of organization goals. Especially when limited resources, retrenchment, and chronic change mark the times, evaluation mechanisms provide an organization with ongoing information about what is working well and what is not. Decision makers can continue some practices, modify others, and eliminate still others. Finally, evaluation is necessary to determine how well goals have been met.

In an open organization, members participate actively in evaluation, sharing information freely within and among subsystems, and using data collaboratively to make constructive changes in strategies and goals. They evaluate the achievement not only of substantive goals related to the organization's purpose, but also of the system's effectiveness.

Because evaluation is an integral part of change, elements of our evaluation approach have already been presented in the introduction; in chapter 6, "Diagnostic Review;" chapter 9, "Action Research Teams;" and chapter 10, "Developing Managers." This concluding chapter will integrate earlier discussions within the conceptual frame offered by the CIPP model, which describes the stages and elements of evaluation during change. The chapter also introduces instruments useful in measuring the impact and outcome of change.

The Evaluation Process

In chapter 1, we compared organization planning to preparing for a trip. Planning involves asking questions like the following:

- Where are we now? (present situation)
- Where do we want to go? (mission, goals, objectives, assumptions, potentials)
- How will we get there? (methods, strategies, tactics)
- Who will drive? (how to organize)
- Who will pay? (resources)
- How will we know when we have arrived? (evaluation criteria for product)

Questions like these provide the basis for later evaluation of success. When the answers are clearly formulated, they serve as a set of criteria for evaluating the process and outcome (product) of the "trip."

Evaluation is a process of asking questions and collecting information as a basis for making decisions. The evaluation process consists of eight steps:

1. SPECIFY GOALS AND ACHIEVEMENT CRITERIA. Define observable events and behaviors or measurable outcome which are seen as desirable (meeting stated goals).

2. DECIDE ON METHODS OF DATA COLLECTION. Given the above criteria, determine what methodology can describe the events or outcomes.

3. GATHER DATA.

4. ANALYZE DATA. Refine raw data. A rationale for analysis is needed.

5. INTERPRET DATA. Begin to isolate meaningful results of data analysis in terms of the criteria set.

6. DECIDE ON VALUE. Question whether what is found out is good or bad, and to what extent it is good or bad. Agree on criteria of goodness.

7. MAKE A DECISION. Make decisions to change or modify processes or events evaluated.

8. TAKE ACTION. Translate decision into action steps. Implement. Share (Harris, in press).

This process is repeated in cycles during the coures of change.

A change specialist makes use of a variety of methods of data collection. Basic forms of data collection include observation of behavior in meetings or on the job; reading written documents, such as speeches, letters, and reports; interviews and discussions with clients; tests of knowledge and skills; and survey questionnaires. The choice of data collection methods rests on such considerations as the amount of time and money available, available facilities, degree of cooperation, complexity of the problem, and the developmental stage of the consultant-client relationship.

During a consultation the change specialist is continuously evaluating the impact of his or her interventions. There are three areas which need to be monitored: these are the client-consultant relationship; events or significant interventions, such as training or survey feedback; and progress toward specific goals (Lippitt and Lippitt, 1978b).

Action research is our preferred method of evaluation throughout a change effort. *Action research* was previously defined as the process of collecting data relative to a problem area, feeding that data back into the system, taking action, and evaluating results of actions by collecting more data. This methodology is effective not only for in-house problem-solving teams, but also for changes involving external consultants. As a consultation method, action research ensures that implemented decisions involve the client in collecting data and making decisions related to the goals of the consultation process. The client should take an active role in all steps of evaluation. For a full discussion of action research methodology, refer to chapter 9.

The CIPP Model of Evaluation

In consultations with client organizations, the basic model we use to evaluate change is the CIPP model of evaluation originated by Daniel Stufflebeam (1971). A four-part model which can also be used in training, learning, or counseling situations, CIPP includes evaluation of the following:

- Context—needs assessment and problem identification
- Input—problem-solving resources
- Process—actions to solve problems and make changes
- Product—outcomes

These parts may be viewed as evaluation stages occurring sequentially during a change effort. They may also be viewed as levels of data collection during any given evaluation. The CIPP model is presented in figure 27.

Our approach combines the concepts of the CIPP model with the methodology of action research. Collection of data about context, input, process, and product will ensure sufficient information to diagnose problems and find solutions. Clients are involved in this process as much as possible. The information gathered is fed back to decision makers to generate new actions and decisions.

Let us look more closely at the parts of the CIPP model, both as evaluation stages and as types of information.

CONTEXT AND INPUT EVALUATION

Evaluation of context and input is the first stage of a change effort. Context evaluation aims at describing the major subsystems within the observed context, identifying needs, and delineating problems underlying these needs. Context evaluation also includes gathering data about actual and intended inputs and outputs of systems. Then the data are analyzed to identify possible causes of these discrepancies. Basic problem identification should be undertaken before any intervention, to provide data about areas in which intervention will be most potent. The diagnostic review described in chapter 6 is a context evaluation tool. Input evaluation identifies a system's available human and material resources, and strategies currently used to solve problems. Information can be gathered through questionnaires, observation, reading, and interviewing. The diagnostic review also includes input evaluation.

Context and input evaluation should lead to identifying specific, measurable goals. Participants must agree on the criteria of success. They must also agree about what results will be valued. After goals have been chosen, measures to quantify or describe the desired outcomes can be defined. Possible outcomes might include decreased costs, increased satisfaction of client or customer, and decreased employee turnover. At later stages of evaluation, participants may reconsider context and input as more data become available. The evaluation process is cumulative and cyclical.

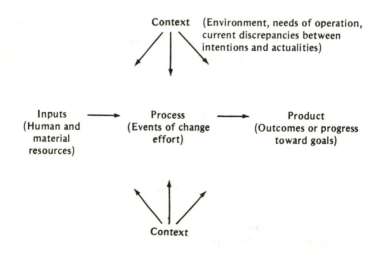

Figure 27. The CIPP Model of Evaluation

Adapted from "The relevance of the CIPP evaluation model for educational accountability" by D. L. Stufflebeam, *Journal of research and development in education*, 1971, 5 (1), 19–25. Reproduced by permission

PROCESS EVALUATION

It might seem simpler to evaluate only outcomes—did we accomplish our goal? Yet the defect of this approach becomes apparent as soon as the answer is "no." If only product evaluation is undertaken, there are no answers when the decision maker asks why an effort did not succeed. Process evaluation yields *formative* information, data that allows one to modify a process to bring about more effective results. It asks "What works or doesn't work?" and "Why does it work or not work?"

Process evaluation should be conducted in a way that ensures active client participation in the evaluation process. A collaborative consultant-client relationship helps to maintain commitment to change, and to take the sting out of judgments about how well processes are working. Developing in-house action research teams not only ensures a built-in structure for process evaluation, but also teaches useful skills to organization members. Action research teams are a natural context for consultants to provide training.

Evaluation of the change process can take many forms, and obviously must be tailored to the specific situation. Whatever the methods used, one must have a way to (1) obtain *feedback*, information about the impact of a particular intervention action, and (2) interpret the meaning of the information collected. Here we will present a useful feedback instrument, and a method of analyzing data to determine the causes of a particular outcome.

Getting feedback. *Quick Impressions* (pp. 271–273) is a feedback instrument using "semantic differential" items (Osgood, Suci, and Percy, 1957) to identify the quality and direction of participants' feelings toward a training event. It measures attitudes rather than content or skills learned through participation in the event. The instrument presents a list of dichotomized terms such as "impractical-practical" and "clear-confusing," situated at the poles of a seven-point scale. For each item, mark the scale at the point closest to your immediate impression of the training event. The trainer first tallies all responses, then groups total scores under four categories: potency, understandability, practicality, and evaluation. These categories reflect participants' attitudes in a general way. Based upon the interpretation of results, the program coordinator decides which elements of the event (presentation methods, content) to modify, and which to continue as they are.

The dichotomized terms in this instrument have been used in considerable research, and the scale has construct validity. The coordinator may thus feel confident in relying on results of this reaction form. The four constructs of potency, evaluation, understandability, and practicality, into which the thirteen dichotomized pairs are grouped, may be defined more specifically:

The *potency* construct allows the trainer to understand how the participants feel about his or her "character." Character refers to charisma, strength, effectiveness, and impact on the participants. Words like *powerful, strong,* and *moving* reflect strength of character and personal worth.

The *evaluation* construct directly relates to what actually takes place during the event. It refers to participants' attitudes toward the quality and methods of interaction, use of varied strategies, and styles of facilitation. Words like *outstanding, warm,* and *good* indicate that the environment created by the coordinator is seen as conducive to positive learning and sharing experiences.

The *understandability* construct focuses on content. Attitudes toward the subjects of discussion are reflected in these responses. Participants' comprehension of program content is revealed by words like *understandable, clear,* and *sharp.*

The *practicality* construct is quite useful to ascertain the perceived relevance of the event. Words like *useful, practical, realistic,* and *relevant* indicate that the program meets participant needs.

Branching analysis. Instruments like *Quick Impressions* are useful in identifying what intervention elements work or do not work, but they do not enable the change specialist to determine the causes of success or failure in a complex situation. Branching analysis integrates the data from input, process, and product components of evaluation to determine which factors contributed to the achievement of a desired outcome. In this way, informed decisions can be made about subsequent interventions.

Figure 28 represents a branching analysis evaluating the success of a training event. The figure shows how data are correlated from three evaluation levels. Context evaluation is not included in branching analysis, but is assumed to have taken place during initial definition of the problem area or need, and formulation of the goal of change. In this example, the desired outcome (product) was participants' eagerness to use techniques presented in the training event. The branching analysis indicates that the degree of eagerness was contingent upon participants' perception of the potency of the session (process data) and differed from older to newer employees (input data). Those who perceived training as powerful were more eager to use what they learned by a margin of four to one, while those who perceived the training as powerless were less eager to use the techniques, again with a four-to-one margin. Older employees, however, seemed able to benefit from the program despite their varying assessment of the power of the presentation, perhaps because they already possessed a framework into which they could integrate new information. If the eagerness and lack of eagerness of older employees had been equally split, the trainer would need to look at other factors to determine why only half the older employees benefited from the event. Other factors could include understandability or practicality.

In order to conduct a branching analysis, a change specialist may need additional data. Often data on input factors can be gathered through the addition of a few questions to a feedback questionnaire already in use. In this

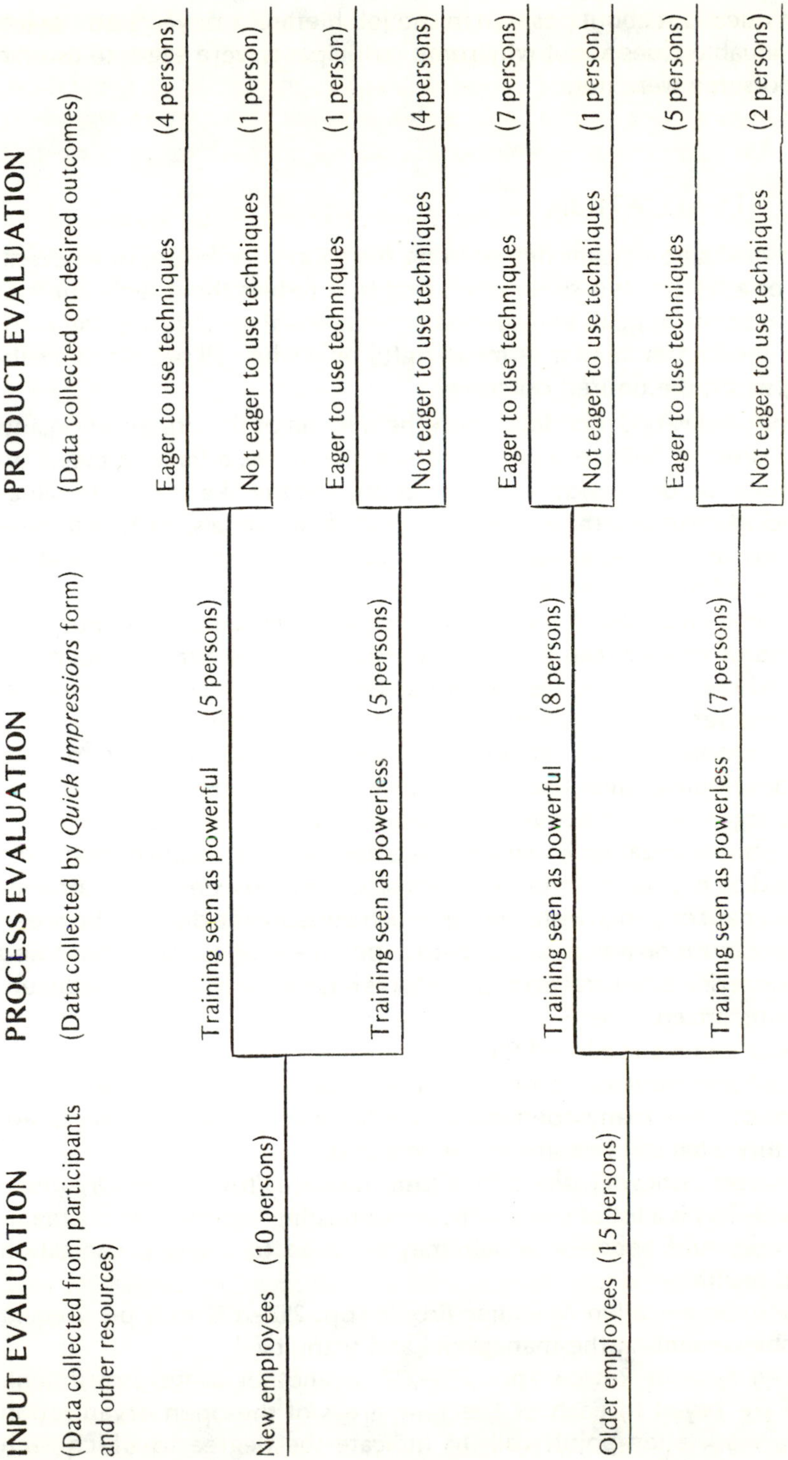

INPUT EVALUATION

(Data collected from participants and other resources)

New employees   (10 persons)

Older employees (15 persons)

PROCESS EVALUATION

(Data collected by *Quick Impressions* form)

Training seen as powerful   (5 persons)

Training seen as powerless   (5 persons)

Training seen as powerful   (8 persons)

Training seen as powerless   (7 persons)

PRODUCT EVALUATION

(Data collected on desired outcomes)

Eager to use techniques   (4 persons)

Not eager to use techniques   (1 person)

Eager to use techniques   (1 person)

Not eager to use techniques   (4 persons)

Eager to use techniques   (7 persons)

Not eager to use techniques   (1 person)

Eager to use techniques   (5 persons)

Not eager to use techniques   (2 persons)

Figure 28. Branching Analysis of the Success of a Training Event

case, input questions about position in the job hierarchy or years on the job provided valuable clues about why some participants were eager to use the training and some were not.

PRODUCT EVALUATION

Product evaluation means determining the success or failure of an event, a change, or a system. It is *summative,* that is, it judges the effectiveness of outcomes in terms of goals and success criteria established during the planning stage. Product evaluation is meaningful only when all people and subsystems agree on the desired outcomes.

Outcomes will vary depending upon the mission of the organization and the kind of product being evaluated: substantive goals, a training event, an entire consultation process, systems operation, and the like. Product evaluation may include assessing the job performance of individuals, the functioning of subsystems, and the achievement of organization goals. Such evaluation must be tailored to meet the specific situation.

In addition to the goals through which an organization achieves its purpose, another kind of product can be assessed—success in creating an open environment where problems are viewed as potential areas for organization growth, where pertinent data flows between the organization and society and between subgroups and individuals in the organizations, where people are viewed as developing rather than static. Here evaluation determines to what degree the organization is achieving a state of overall openness.

How can an organization know when it is approaching a state of openness characterized by high unity, internal responsiveness, and external responsiveness? It may adapt or design instruments which measure the distance between where the organization was, is, and aspires to be in relation to open and closed system characteristics. Several exemplary tools have already been introduced. They are summarized here:

Patterns of Open and Closed Organizations (Fig. 3, p. 19) lists contrasting structural and process features of open and closed organizations. It may be used to consider how many open characteristics an organization has gained, and to identify what still remains to be changed.

Some Characteristics of Unhealthy (Closed) and Healthy (Open) Organizations (pp. 213–217) is a list of twenty-three contrasting (open–closed) organization attitudes and behavior which may be used to assess organization climate and health.

The Open Organization Manager Profile (pp. 252–265) may be used to evaluate achievements at the managerial and team level.

The Open Systems Review (pp. 274–277) is another useful instrument. Statements are keyed to each of the nine areas of the open organization model. You mark a ten-point scale to indicate the degree to which each statement is true of you or your organization. The review is not intended to cover every possible aspect of organization functioning, but rather to suggest the kind of items that can be included in a customized instrument.

Product evaluation marks the end of one cycle of growth and the beginning of another. In an organization committed to knowledge-based development, a new perspective and sense of potential are gained from evaluating context, input, process, and product data. New energy is released which can be directed to produce a healthier, more productive organization.

PART IV

Action Tools

TOOLS FROM CHAPTER 1

A Leader Checklist

A Self-Appraisal Form

A LEADER CHECKLIST

_____ 1. I establish clearly defined *goals and priorities,* obtaining consensus from key persons.

_____ 2. I obtain appropriate *personal commitment* to these goals from key persons.

_____ 3. I develop *key performance objectives* from these goals.

_____ 4. I ask work groups to develop more *detailed performance objectives* and negotiate mutual understanding and commitment to these objectives.

_____ 5. I hold frequent "coaching" sessions in which *specific feedback* is examined regarding progress towards achievement of objectives.

_____ 6. I establish objectives designed to *"stretch" subordinates* and invite development of the whole person.

_____ 7. I achieve a *level of trust* which allows people to:
- deal directly with their concerns in face-to-face confrontation
- search for mutually satisfactory solutions
- establish working patterns that enable future satisfactory solutions of the same or similar problems

_____ 8. I give close attention to the *work group process* as well as outcomes:
- seek to establish relationship between staff persons' needs and program objectives
- ask for and obtain staff dedication to both process and outcome
- am willing to suggest improvements in program support systems, such as computation center, personnel office, or comptroller
- reach and maintain agreement with work group on position functions through role negotiation
- minimize and reduce, where possible, procedural buildup in the existing bureaucracy

A SELF-APPRAISAL FORM

DIRECTIONS

Circle the digit which comes closest to describing you.

1. How authentic am I? Am I fully aware, congruent, in myself?

1	2	3	4	5	6
Low		Average		High	

2. How expressive am I? Do I communicate unambiguously to others?

1	2	3	4	5	6
Low		Average		High	

3. How positive am I in my warmth, caring, respect for the others?

1	2	3	4	5	6
Low		Average		High	

4. Am I strong enough to be separate, respecting my own needs and feelings?

1	2	3	4	5	6
Low		Average		High	

5. Am I secure enough to permit others their full separateness?

1	2	3	4	5	6
Low		Average		High	

6. How fully can I enter into the private worlds of others, sensing their meanings and feelings with no desire to judge, to evaluate, to praise, to criticize, to explain or to alter them?

1	2	3	4	5	6
Low		Average		High	

7. Can I relate so that others feel me to be in no way a threat and so that they become less fearful of external evaluation from anyone?

1	2	3	4	5	6
Low		Average		High	

8. Do I encounter others as *becoming* rather than as fixed in past patterns?

1	2	3	4	5	6
Low		Average		High	

9. How clearly is my own self-image one of change, development, growth, emergence?

1	2	3	4	5	6
Low		Average		High	

TOOLS FROM CHAPTER 2

Values Survey

VALUES SURVEY

PART I: Terminal Values

DIRECTIONS

Below is a list of eighteen values arranged in alphabetical order. We are interested in finding out how important each of these values is for you as a guiding principle in your life. First, study the whole list carefully. Then rate how important each value is by placing an X in the appropriate column. Please do not leave any blanks.

	EXTREMELY IMPORTANT	VERY IMPORTANT	SOMEWHAT IMPORTANT	MILDLY TO NOT VERY IMPORTANT
A COMFORTABLE LIFE (a prosperous life)				
AN EXCITING LIFE (a stimulating, active life)				
A SENSE OF ACCOM-PLISHMENT (lasting contribution)				
A WORLD AT PEACE (free of war and conflict)				
A WORLD OF BEAUTY (beauty of nature and the arts)				
EQUALITY (brotherhood, equal opportunity for all)				
FAMILY SECURITY (taking care of loved ones)				
FREEDOM (independence, free choice)				
HAPPINESS (contented-ness)				
INNER HARMONY (freedom from inner conflict)				

From "More on the Protestant ethic" by A. P. MacDonald, Jr., *Journal of consulting and clinical psychology*, 1972, 39, 116–122. Copyright© 1972 by A. P. MacDonald, Jr. Reprinted by permission

	EXTREMELY IMPORTANT	VERY IMPORTANT	SOMEWHAT IMPORTANT	MILDLY TO NOT VERY IMPORTANT
MATURE LOVE (sexual and spiritual intimacy)				
NATIONAL SECURITY (protection from attack)				
PLEASURE (an enjoyable, leisurely life)				
SALVATION (saved, eternal life)				
SOCIAL RECOGNITION (respect, admiration)				
SELF-RESPECT (self-esteem)				
TRUE FRIENDSHIP (close companionship)				
WISDOM (a mature understanding of life)				

Now in each column in which more than one X appears we would like you to rank the Xs in order of importance. For example, if you have three Xs in the "Extremely Important" column you should read all three values and place a 1 next to the X for the value you consider most important of the three, a 2 next to the next most important, and a 3 next to the least important *within that column*. Then go on to the next column and so on until you have ranked the Xs in all columns that contain more than one X. Remember to give a rank of 1 to the *most* important value in *each* column.

VALUES SURVEY

PART II: Instrumental Values

DIRECTIONS

Below is a list of eighteen values arranged in alphabetical order. We are interested in finding out how important each of these values is for you as a guiding principle in your life. First, study the whole list carefully. Then rate how important each value is by placing an X in the appropriate column. Please do not leave any blanks.

	EXTREMELY IMPORTANT	VERY IMPORTANT	SOMEWHAT IMPORTANT	MILDLY TO NOT VERY IMPORTANT
AMBITIOUS (hard-working, aspiring)				
BROAD-MINDED (open-minded)				
CAPABLE (competent, effective)				
CHEERFUL (light-hearted, joyful)				
CLEAN (neat, tidy)				
COURAGEOUS (standing up for your beliefs)				
FORGIVING (willing to pardon others)				
HELPFUL (working for the welfare of others)				
HONEST (sincere, truthful)				
IMAGINATIVE (daring, creative)				
INDEPENDENT (self-reliant, self-sufficient)				
INTELLECTUAL (intelligent, reflective)				

From "More on the Protestant ethic" by A. P. MacDonald, Jr., *Journal of consulting and clinical psychology,* 1972, *39,* 116–122. Copyright© 1972 by A. P. MacDonald, Jr. Reprinted by permission

	EXTREMELY IMPORTANT	VERY IMPORTANT	SOMEWHAT IMPORTANT	MILDLY TO NOT VERY IMPORTANT
LOGICAL (consistent, rational)				
LOVING (affectionate, tender)				
OBEDIENT (dutiful, respectful)				
POLITE (courteous, well-mannered)				
RESPONSIBLE (dependable, reliable)				
SELF-CONTROLLED (restrained, self-disciplined)				

Now in each column in which more than one X appears we would like you to rank the Xs in order of importance. For example, if you have three Xs in the "Extremely Important" column you should read all three values and place a 1 next to the X for the value you consider most important of the three, a 2 next to the next most important, and a 3 next to the least important *within that column*. Then go on to the next column and so on until you have ranked the Xs in all columns that contain more than one X. Remember to give a rank of 1 to the *most* important value in *each* column.

TOOLS FROM CHAPTER 3

Group Membership Questions

GROUP MEMBERSHIP QUESTIONS

DIRECTIONS

After each group session, each person is to fill out this sheet. The group should then get a combined rating of all members and discuss why they gave themselves these ratings.

I. To what extent did I feel a real part of the group?

1. Completely a part of the group all the time.
2. Sometimes a part of the group.
3. On the edge of the group most of the time.
4. Mostly outside the group.
5. Generally outside except for one or two short periods.
6. On the outside, not part of the group the entire time.

II. How safe is it in this group to be at ease, relaxed, and myself?

1. I would feel perfectly safe to be myself—they won't hold mistakes against me.
2. I feel most people would accept me if I were completely myself, but there are some I am not sure about.
3. Generally I have to be careful what I say or do in this group.
4. I would be quite fearful about being completely myself in this group.
5. A person would be a fool to be him- or herself in this group.

III. To what extent did I have private thoughts, unspoken reservations, or unexpressed feelings and opinions that I would not have felt comfortable bringing out into the open?

1. Almost completely under wraps.
2. Somewhat under wraps.
3. Slightly more under wraps than free.
4. Slightly more free and expressive than under wraps.
5. Somewhat free and expressive.
6. Almost completely free and expressive.

IV. How effective were we, in our group, in getting out and using the ideas, opinions, and information of all group members in making decisions?

1. We didn't really encourage anyone to share ideas, opinions and information with the group in making decisions.
2. Only the ideas, opinions and information of a few members were really known and used in making our decisions.
3. Sometimes we heard the views of most members before making decisions and sometimes we disregarded most members.
4. A few members were hesitant about sharing their views on decisions, but we generally had good participation in making decisions.
5. Everyone felt his or her ideas, opinions, and information were given a fair hearing before decisions were made.

V. To what extent did the goals we were working towards, during this last session, have interest and meaning to me?

1. I felt extremely good about the goals of this session.
2. I felt fairly good, but some things were not too important to me.
3. A few things we were doing were of interest to me.
4. Most of the activity was a waste of time.
5. This session was a total waste of time.

VI. How well did the group work at its task?

1. Coasted, loafed, made no progress.
2. Made a little progress; most members loafed.
3. Progress was slow with spurts of effective work.
4. Above average in progress and pace.
5. Worked well, achieved definite progress.
6. Worked hard, achieved its goal.

VII. Our planning and the way we operated as a group were largely influenced by:

1. One or two group members.
2. A clique.
3. Shifted from one person or clique to another.
4. Shared by most members; some were left out.
5. Shared by all members of the group.

VIII. What was the level of responsibility for work in our group?

1. Each person assumed personal responsibility.
2. A majority of the members assumed responsibility.
3. About half assumed responsibility, about half did not.
4. Only two or three members assumed responsibility.
5. Only one person really assumed responsibility.
6. No one really assumed responsibility.

TOOLS FROM CHAPTER 4

Organization Norms That Affect You

Methods and Tactics to Secure Organization Support for Change

Power Strategies for Resolving Differences

ORGANIZATION NORMS THAT AFFECT YOU

DIRECTIONS

This form has been designed to help you become aware of norms that affect work life. List on the form some norms of an organization with which you are associated. List norms that help you use your strengths as well as those that crunch you. Assess these norms by the following criteria:

Visible or invisible?
Visible norms are formalized into policies and procedures. Invisible norms are ways people are expected to behave without being told.

Set by whom?
Do the persons affected by the norms set them, or are they set by others?

Negotiable?
Are the norms open for examination and reality testing?

Helping or hindering?
Do the norms help you use your strength, or hinder you from doing an effective job?

Norms	Visible or invisible?	Set by whom?	Negotiable?	Helping or hindering?
1.				
2.				
3.				
4.				
5.				
6.				
7.				
8.				
9.				
10.				

METHODS AND TACTICS TO SECURE ORGANIZATION SUPPORT FOR CHANGE

INTRODUCTION

Many persons in organizations have commented that arriving at a decision, plan, or innovative idea is much less difficult than selling the decision, plan or idea to their boss, management, or organization. It is often difficult to get change initiated and implemented.

Researchers in the organizational communication field have noted that top management has many downward channels available to communicate with and influence employees, but that the reverse is not generally true. When subordinates are asked to list ways they can influence their boss, management, or organization, they initially feel limited in choice of methods and tactics. Upon further reflection, however, they often discover that many choices are open to them.

This instrument is designed to help you examine ways you tend to confront and influence people in your organization. It is also designed to help you identify other influence options. (The techniques listed are ones that have been used by employees. The designer of this instrument does not present all of the techniques as being desirable or ethical.)

PART I: Methods and Tactics

DIRECTIONS

On the next pages you will find a number of methods and tactics which middle managers, supervisors, and staff personnel have identified as exerting influence. Read each statement carefully. To the left of each statement enter the appropriate letter, based on the code below, to indicate your use of the method or tactic described.

CODE:
  a. I normally always use this technique.
  b. I use this technique occasionally.
  c. I would use this technique only if I felt very strongly about the change effort.
  d. I consider this technique unethical and would never use it.
  e. This technique is not applicable to me in my job.

1. _____ Do good staff work, research, and documentation—put forth best effort I can.

2. _____ Get the boss to attend a training program, seminar, or professional meeting that supports my view of things, or get the boss on a program that will necessitate supporting my idea.

3. _____ Play the organizational game of presenting two alternatives, one which I know is unacceptable, or "massage" the data to support my view.

4. _____ Participate in a demonstration in or out of the organization if it supports some change I strongly believe is needed, even if that change is adverse to the organization's product, service or policies.

5. _____ Get consumer or client groups to bring pressure for my point of view.

6. _____ There's too much change in organizations. Wait. If the change idea is good, people will ultimately come around to it.

7. _____ Point out and emphasize advantages that will accrue to the organization, customers or clients, program, and staff.

8. _____ Maneuver so the boss will think the idea, decision, or plan is his or hers and will make him or her look good.

9. _____ Use the chronological reading file or routing slip to get my idea on record. The boss looks at it and often so does the boss's boss.

10. _____ Participate in a slow-down, sick-in, or walk-out, or join a union to bring about desirable change.

11. _____ Let my professional society or union bring pressure to support my idea.

12. _____ My ideas are often ahead of their time and I usually just have to wait for the organization to catch up.

13. _____ Use good timing. Show how my idea will help solve a current organizational problem.

14. _____ Instill in my boss fear of competition or other unpleasant consequences if the change idea is not accepted.

15. _____ Work through staff specialists and let them sell the idea.

16. _____ Take action while the boss is on vacation, or at lunch, so that when the boss comes back he or she is committed to a decision I have made.

17. _____ Try to persuade members of an outside organizational committee, board, or task force, and let them promote my change idea.

18. _____ If my idea is not bought, I assume that things must get worse before they will get better.

19. _____ Use rational argument, well thought out. Let facts speak for themselves.

20. _____ Socialize with the boss; join his or her informal groups.

21. _____ Use employee organizations and groups, including grievance or complaint procedures.

22. _____ Refuse to carry out a policy or regulation I don't believe in.

23. _____ Send a letter to the editor of the organization newsletter, local newspaper, or other media distribution system.

24. _____ Put the idea in official reports, correspondence, and channels. If the organization does not buy it, forget it—I have done my job.

25. _____ Prepare an excellent presentation or submission package, using visuals.

26. _____ Lobby through organizational friends of the boss—people to whom he or she listens.

27. _____ Use internal politics.

28. _____ Practice *malevolent obedience*—carrying out a policy or regulation to the letter to demonstrate the need for its change.

29. _____ Use an outside consultant or consulting firm to recommend what I want.

30. _____ Change is the responsibility of those in higher positions. As a subordinate, I should do my job and not try to make waves.

31. _____ Demonstrate how my idea will increase efficiency, cut costs, or provide a better service or product.

32. _____ Originate correspondence or reports over my boss's signature that support my position. It is not easy for a boss to tell a subordinate "no" when staff work is completed.

33. _____ Put the data or proposal in the organization's management information system.

34. _____ Mobilize a group of associates and others supporting the desired change and confront management directly.

35. _____ Get the boss's wife, husband, children, or friends to support my position.

36. _____ Wait for attrition or a reorganization to remove those opposing my idea.

37. _____ Use suggestion boxes, work improvement reward systems—the Benny Sugg system.

38. _____ Put the boss in a vulnerable position—for instance, by bringing up my idea when the boss's boss is present.

39. _____ Make an end run. Go directly to those in higher authority.

40. _____ Report my better idea to the internal audit system or inspectors.

41. _____ Place articles in commercial or professional periodicals and route them appropriately.

42. _____ Defer gratification from acceptance of my ideas. Eventually, I will be promoted, authority will be conferred, and I will have power to implement my own ideas.

43. _____ Let the organization have its way at the beginning on less important issues so I can become known as a "good organization person." Later, I will be able to carry out my own notions of excellence.

44. _____ Compliment the boss when he or she moves in the direction I want—especially in front of others who are in an influential position over the boss.

45. _____ Form coalitions and make reciprocal agreements with other departments instrumental in my plans. "You scratch my back and I'll scratch yours."

46. _____ Deliberately modify an assignment given to me so that it contributes to my desired ends.

47. _____ Arrange for representatives of other organizations to reveal their success with ideas similar to mine under conditions like those in my organization.

48. _____ Deliberately delay taking direct or aggressive action on potentially explosive matters. Unforeseen variables in organizational life often take care of the problem in a natural way.

49. _____ Set up formal feedback systems which enable me to evaluate and adjust current practices, as well as to find opportunities for expansion into new areas.

50. _____ Tie my idea in with an area of personal interest to the boss.

51. _____ Establish a working relationship with a board or external committee that oversees internal operations of the organization.

52. _____ Drag my feet on unacceptable tasks or decisions in order to get attention and a full hearing on my own alternative.

53. _____ Circulate literature favorable to my position.

54. _____ Put things in perspective. My project is probably only a ripple in the organizational sea.

55. _____ Establish a good "track record" of having been right in past proposals.

56. _____ Confront the boss in a nice way with several persons favorable to my proposal.

57. _____ Tie my unnoticed, unsupported, or untried proposal to a widely accepted program and ride its coat tails.

58. _____ Lobby with public officials or community action groups to gain new advantages for my organization and plans.

59. _____ Arrange with regulatory agencies to pressure the organization to adopt certain measures or to meet obligations.

60. _____ Organizations are bigger than the individual. I can't really influence the organization, so I don't "get my bowels in an uproar."

PART II: Tabulation and Analysis

DIRECTIONS

Now complete the tabulation below. For each of the sixty statements, place the appropriate code (a, b, c, d, e,) in the square containing that statement's number.

I	II	III	IV	V	VI
1	2	3	4	5	6
7	8	9	10	11	12
13	14	15	16	17	18
19	20	21	22	23	24
25	26	27	28	29	30
31	32	33	34	35	36
37	38	39	40	41	42
43	44	45	46	47	48
49	50	51	52	53	54
55	56	57	58	59	60

After you have entered the proper code in each box, examine the matrix to see in which vertical columns most of your a's, b's, c's, d's, and e's are clustered. The following is the key to analyzing yourself:

Column I: Methods most managers consider traditional, highly ethical, and generally desirable techniques to "sell" a change effort.

Column II: Direct attempts to influence your boss. He or she can then go to bat for your idea or oppose it directly.

Column III: Attempts to manipulate the organizational system and structure it to influence change.

Column IV: Aggressive, even militant, techniques to bring about organization change.

Column V: Influence attempts using resources and persons outside the organization to bring about change.

Column VI: A passive stance of waiting for the organizational milieu to change.

There is no "right" or "wrong" set of methods to gain acceptance of a change idea. The choice of methods depends upon the nature of the decision, plan, or idea being promoted. It also depends on the urgency involved, the kind of organization, external factors, and how much importance you attach to the change effort.

It is possible, however, that if most of your "a" and "b" checks fall in one or two change effort styles, you may be using too limited a range of change methods and tactics.

PART III: Group Assignments

1.   Share with each other the major methods and tactics which the analysis form indicated you use to bring about change.

2.   Is there a pattern within your group?
- If so, what is the pattern?
- Might this pattern be dysfunctional to your organization? In what way(s)?

3.   How can a person increase his or her repertoire of change methods?

4.   During the discussion, was a novel influence effort identified? If so, what was it?

5.   List the change methods considered unethical by more than one member of the group.
- Why are they considered unethical?
- Does everyone agree that they are unethical?
- Under what conditions might they be perfectly legitimate?

6.   Each participant will select his or her last initiation effort that failed. Using the analysis form, analyze the techniques and methods not used that might have changed the results. Share the analysis with each other.

7.   If participants are planning a change effort individually or as a group, use the analysis form to map a course of action. Individual plans will be analyzed and critiqued by members of the group. If the group is discussing only one change effort, its proposed course of action should be critiqued by another group.

POWER STRATEGIES FOR RESOLVING DIFFERENCES

SECTION I: Identifying Your Power Strategies

DIRECTIONS

In the space at the right, check the strategies you see yourself using in personal and professional life.

Veiled or Secretive Strategies	My professional life	My personal life
1. Controlling Information (Data) Having exclusive possession of Selectively imparting	————	————
2. Using Wealth Money and other real assets Control of wealth (i.e., budget officer) Contributions (i.e., largest contributor to an organization	————	————
3. Using Position Temporary or permanent positions (i.e., treasurer, secretary, committee chair)	————	————
4. Using Rank Hierarchical status (i.e., president)	————	————
5. Using Title Earned or honorary title (i.e., Doctor, Reverend, Your Honor)	————	————
6. Using Speaking Ability Ability to handle language Delivery Knowing language	————	————
7. Using Physical Characteristics Appearance Size	————	————

	My professional life	My personal life

8. Withholding
    Not moving
    Not talking
    Not giving, boycotting
    Behavior freeze-out
	_____	_____

9. Using Inducing Words
    Using words that can cause feelings of guilt
    or being dumb.
	_____	_____

10. Using Humor
    Keeping people laughing while getting what
    you want accomplished
	_____	_____

11. Using Organizational Norms	_____	_____
12. Structuring the Organization	_____	_____
13. Arranging the Physical Accouterments	_____	_____

14. Using Reputation
    Credibility (usually no title, but
    person is respected)
 	
    Visibility (being well known)
	_____	_____

15. Using Status
    Elite
    Majority
    Minority
	_____	_____

16. Associating with Special People	_____	_____

17. Using Sex
    Masculinity/feminity as power (i.e., woman
    who gets a management position under the
    banner of "women's rights")
 	
    Masculinity/feminity as a trade-off (i.e., man
    who gets access to information through
    sexual relationship with secretary)
	_____	_____

	My professional life	My personal life
18. Obligating Others 　　Developing feelings of obligation	_____	_____
19. Using Eyes and Facial/Body Affect 　　Steady eye contact or no contact	_____	_____
20. Using Body Language	_____	_____
21. Identifying with Significant People and/or 　　Organizations	_____	_____
22. Promising	_____	_____
23. Playing Victim (Poor Me) 　　"I'm helpless." 　　"I don't understand."	_____	_____
24. Using Disability 　　Using a real or supposed disability to get 　　　others to do something for you (i.e., "weak 　　　heart," "fragile female," "I've never been 　　　good in math.")	_____	_____
25. Being Mysterious 　　Being vague ("There are several people around 　　　here who . . .")	_____	_____
26. Trading Off 　　Actual 　　Potential or projected	_____	_____
27. Using Physical Force 　　Body (i.e., pushing, restraining) 　　Use of body (i.e., person hyperventilating) 　　Mechanical extension of body (i.e., paddle, 　　　stick, gun, auto)	_____	_____
28. Using Sound and Silence 　　Vocal 　　Other	_____	_____

	My professional life	My personal life

29. Dropping Names
    Calling on the name of a supervisor or
      well known person to support a position
      or get something done
	____	____

30. Using Experience
    Longevity with an environment
    Experience in a unique environment
	____	____

31. Using Age
    Older persons
    Youth
	____	____

32. Using Special Skills Selectively imparting skill or knowledge	____	____

33. Using Hooking
    Saying or doing things with the intention of
      calling forth old or loaded feelings
	____	____

34. Controlling Time
    Control of work or vacation schedules
    Structuring meetings to have your items brought
      right before scheduled adjournment
 	
    Being perpetually late
	____	____

35. Using Heritage	____	____
36. Using Touching	____	____

37. Using Seduction
    "Snowing" with words
    Behaviors (i.e., slap on the back,
      arm around the shoulder)
	____	____

SECTION II: Assessing the Effect of Power Strategies

DIRECTIONS

From the list (Section I) select five power strategies you most frequently use and evaluate their impact using the following scales and sentence completions.

Power strategy 1: _____
(name of strategy)

I use this power
strategy . . .   minimally   :   :   :   :   :   :   :   :   :   extensively
                                         1   2   3   4   5   6   7   8   9

When I use this
power strategy, I see   very   very
myself being . . .   ineffective :   :   :   :   :   :   :   :   :   effective
                                         1   2   3   4   5   6   7   8   9

When _____ sees me
use this power strategy
he or she sees me as   very   very
being . . .   ineffective :   :   :   :   :   :   :   :   :   effective
                                         1   2   3   4   5   6   7   8   9

When others use this
power strategy toward
me I feel _____.

Power strategy 2: _____
(name of strategy)

I use this power
strategy . . .   minimally   :   :   :   :   :   :   :   :   :   extensively
                                         1   2   3   4   5   6   7   8   9

When I use this
power strategy I see   very   very
myself being . . .   ineffective :   :   :   :   :   :   :   :   :   effective
                                         1   2   3   4   5   6   7   8   9

When _____ sees me
use this power strategy
he or she sees me as   very   very
being . . .   ineffective :   :   :   :   :   :   :   :   :   effective
                                         1   2   3   4   5   6   7   8   9

When others use this
power strategy toward
me I feel _____

Power strategy 3: _____
(name of strategy)

I use this power
strategy   minimally : : : : : : : : : extensively
                             1 2 3 4 5 6 7 8 9

When I use this
power strategy I see   very
myself being . . .   ineffective : : : : : : : : : very
                                                                 effective
                                      1 2 3 4 5 6 7 8 9

When _____sees me
use this power strategy
he or she sees me as   very
being . . .   ineffective : : : : : : : : : very
                                                                 effective
                                      1 2 3 4 5 6 7 8 9

When others use this
power strategy toward
me I feel _____

Power strategy 4: _____
(name of strategy)

I use this power
strategy . . .   minimally : : : : : : : : : extensively
                             1 2 3 4 5 6 7 8 9

When I use this
power strategy I see   very
myself being . . .   ineffective : : : : : : : : : very
                                                                 effective
                                      1 2 3 4 5 6 7 8 9

When _____sees me
use this power strategy
he or she sees me as   very
being . . .   ineffective : : : : : : : : : very
                                                                 effective
                                      1 2 3 4 5 6 7 8 9

When others use this
power strategy toward
me I feel _____

Power strategy 5: _____
(name of strategy

I use this power strategy . . .	minimally	:	:	:	:	:	:	:	:	:	extensively
		1	2	3	4	5	6	7	8	9	

When I use this power strategy I see myself being . . .	very ineffective	:	:	:	:	:	:	:	:	:	very effective
		1	2	3	4	5	6	7	8	9	

When _____ sees me use this power strategy he or she sees me as being . . .	very ineffective	:	:	:	:	:	:	:	:	:	very effective
		1	2	3	4	5	6	7	8	9	

When others use this
power strategy toward
me I feel _____.

SECTION III: Thinking About Your Use of Power

DIRECTIONS

Think about or talk with another person about what you have learned concerning your personal use of power.

- Are you limiting the number of power strategies you use?

- Are the ones that you do use effective for you?

- Is there a discrepancy between how you and others perceive the effectiveness of your use of power?

- What did you discover about how you feel when others use your favorite power strategies toward you?

- Is there a difference in the types of power strategies you use in your personal life and in your professional life?

TOOLS FROM CHAPTER 6

Some Characteristics of Unhealthy (Closed) and Healthy (Open) Organizations

SOME CHARACTERISTICS OF UNHEALTHY (CLOSED) AND HEALTHY (OPEN) ORGANIZATIONS

DIRECTIONS

Every organization is somewhere on a continuum between the extremes of "open" and "closed." Below is a list of contrasting closed (left) and open (right) behaviors. Please mark each scale to indicate where your organization is now on the open-closed continuum.

1. ORGANIZATIONAL OBJECTIVES

There is little personal investment in organization objectives except by higher management.

Members share objectives and put strong consistent energy into realizing them.

1	2	3	4	5	6	7	8	9

2. REACTING TO PROBLEMS

People in the organization see things going wrong and do nothing. Mistakes and problems are habitually hidden or shelved.

People feel free to admit difficulties because they expect problems to be dealt with and solved.

1	2	3	4	5	6	7	8	9

3. PROBLEM SOLVING

Status on the organization chart is more important than solving the problem. Nonconformity is frowned upon.

People are not preoccupied with status, territory, or second-guessing what "higher management will think." Much nonconforming behavior is tolerated.

1	2	3	4	5	6	7	8	9

Developed by Oscar G. Mink. Characteristics were adapted from *Managing with people: A manager's handbook of organization development methods* by J. K. Fordyce and R. Weil, pp. 11–14. Copyright© 1971 by Addison-Wesley Publishing Company, Inc. Reprinted by permission from Addison-Wesley Publishing Company, Reading, Massachusetts

4.   DECISION MAKING

Higher managers try to control as many decisions as possible. They become bottlenecks, and make decisions with inadequate information and advice.

Decisions are made by those best qualified in terms of ability, training, sense of responsibility, access to information, work load, and timing.

| 1 | 2 | 3 | 4 | 5 | 6 | 7 | 8 | 9 |

5.   ACCOMPLISHING OBJECTIVES

Managers feel alone in trying to get things done.

People work as a team in planning, performance, and discipline.

| 1 | 2 | 3 | 4 | 5 | 6 | 7 | 8 | 9 |

6.   RESPECT FOR PEOPLE'S JUDGMENT

The judgment of people in lower ranks of the organization is not respected outside the narrow limits of their jobs.

The judgment of people in lower ranks in the organization is respected.

| 1 | 2 | 3 | 4 | 5 | 6 | 7 | 8 | 9 |

7.   PERSONAL NEEDS AND FEELINGS

Personal needs and feelings are side issues.

The range of problems tackled includes personal needs and human relationships.

| 1 | 2 | 3 | 4 | 5 | 6 | 7 | 8 | 9 |

8.   COLLABORATION

People compete when they need to collaborate. They distrust each other's motives and speak poorly of one another. This situation is tolerated by management.

People collaborate freely. When individuals and groups compete, they do so fairly and in the direction of a shared goal.

| 1 | 2 | 3 | 4 | 5 | 6 | 7 | 8 | 9 |

9. **HANDLING A CRISIS**

In a crisis people withdraw or start blaming each other.

In a crisis people quickly band together and work until the crisis is over.

1 2 3 4 5 6 7 8 9

10. **HANDLING CONFLICTS**

Conflict is mostly covert and managed by office politics. There are interminable and irreconcilable arguments.

Conflict is dealt with in the open. People speak their minds and expect others to do the same.

1 2 3 4 5 6 7 8 9

11. **LEARNING METHODS**

People don't approach peers to learn from them, and get little helpful feedback from others. They have to learn from their own mistakes.

People learn much on the job because they are willing to give, seek, and use feedback and advice.

1 2 3 4 5 6 7 8 9

12. **FEEDBACK**

Feedback is avoided.

Joint feedback and critique of progress is a routine practice.

1 2 3 4 5 6 7 8 9

13. **RELATIONSHIPS**

Relationships are contaminated by maskmanship and image building. People feel alone and lack concern for one another. There is an undercurrent of fear.

Relationships are honest. People care about one another and do not feel alone.

1 2 3 4 5 6 7 8 9

14. ATTITUDE TOWARD TASKS

People feel locked into their jobs. They feel stale and bored but constrained by the need for security. Their behavior is listless and docile. The work place is not much fun.

People are "turned on" and highly involved by choice. They are optimistic. The work place is important and fun.

1   2   3   4   5   6   7   8   9

15. MANAGEMENT LEADERSHIP

The manager is a prescribing father to the organization.

Leadership is flexible, shifting in style and person to suit the situation.

1   2   3   4   5   6   7   8   9

16. MANAGEMENT CONTROL

The manager controls small expenditures tightly and demands excessive justification. He allows little freedom for making mistakes.

There is a high degree of trust and a sense of freedom and mutual responsibility. People generally know what is important to the organization and what isn't.

1   2   3   4   5   6   7   8   9

17. RISK TAKING

Minimizing risk has a very high value.

Risk is accepted as a condition of growth and change.

1   2   3   4   5   6   7   8   9

18. HANDLING MISTAKES

Mistakes are not tolerated.

Mistakes are viewed as learning opportunities.

1   2   3   4   5   6   7   8   9

19. EVALUATING PERFORMANCE

Poor performance is glossed over or handled arbitrarily.

Poor performance is confronted, and a joint resolution is sought.

1 2 3 4 5 6 7 8 9

20. ORGANIZATIONAL STRUCTURE

Structures, policies, and procedures encumber the organization. People use them to play self-interest games. They are difficult to change.

Structures, policies, and procedures are fashioned to help people get the job done and to protect the long-term health of the organization. They are readily modified.

1 2 3 4 5 6 7 8 9

21. TRADITION

Tradition encumbers the organization, hindering growth and progress.

There is a sense of order, yet high innovation. Old methods are questioned and often give way.

1 2 3 4 5 6 7 8 9

22. INNOVATION

Innovation is not widespread, but is left to a few.

The organization adapts swiftly to opportunities or other changes because everyone is anticipating the future.

1 2 3 4 5 6 7 8 9

23. FRUSTRATIONS

People swallow their frustrations: "I can do nothing. It's *their* responsibility to save the ship."

Frustrations are a call to action. "It's our responsibility to save the ship."

1 2 3 4 5 6 7 8 9

TOOLS FROM CHAPTER 8

Contracting

Organization Problem Analysis

Organization Diagnostic Survey

CONTRACTING

OUTLINE FOR LECTURETTE ON THE CONTRACTING PROCESS

1. Human beings as living systems exist within social systems—both systems are characterized by openness.

2. Open systems are characterized by profound transactions with the world. To people, other people are usually the most important part of that world.

3. People-to-people transactions are characterized by many things:
   - expectations
   - interdependence
   - wants, needs
   - offers, responses
   - ambiguities
   - conflicts, etc.

4. In this demonstration we will concentrate on:
   - Interdependence   Interdependence is rapidly increasing in our world today—which places a heavy stress on mutual goals and mutual need fulfillment.

   - Expectations   Almost all of us are constantly forming, negotiating, and re-forming expectations of many other people in our lives. Whether or not needs and expectations are met determines human fulfillment.

5. Expectations can be stated in contract form. A contract is:
   - a set of expectations or orientations
   - communicated to others
   - through writing or speech
   - which sets the conditions of an agreement that
   - can be and often is formalized, and
   - usually has some statement of sanctions against violation.

6. The term *contract* often connotes something binding, whereas *agreement* usually means a less formal, less binding arrangement.

7. The purpose of a contract is to regulate behavior in a relationship in order to maximize mutual goals (synergy).

8. Much unnecessary conflict can result from violation of contracts—especially implicit contracts—and from unstated assumptions.

9. There are many kinds of contracts—legal, learning, and interpersonal. We will concentrate on interpersonal (including group) contracts.

10. The general purposes of the interpersonal contract exercise are:
   - To increase skill in forming, negotiating and renegotiating interpersonal contracts
   - To maximize fulfillment of mutual goals
   - To minimize the unproductive components of conflict

11. The technique of the contract exercise places emphasis on:
   - *Clarity* and *explicitness*—especially anticipated consequences and action assumptions
   - Leaving contracts *open to change* and renegotiation
   - The kind of *mutuality* which does not violate *inner integrity* (inner integrity = self-contracts)
   - Enabling people to *examine the process* of contract formation experimentally

12. Cautions in the use of the concept of interpersonal contracts in a learning setting:
   - Jargon—indiscriminate use—superficiality
   - Freezing—emphasis on rigidity and binding features—closed to change and renegotiation
   - Premature contracts—before people are ready to state or form them
   - Overemphasis on "deals"—bargaining versus trust orientation.

13. The main model we use for this demonstration is:

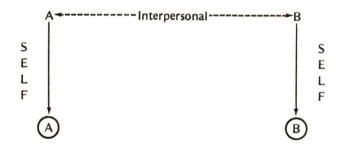

<u>A</u> and <u>B</u> stand for individuals or groups. <u>A</u> verbalizes what he wants from <u>B</u> and <u>B</u> verbalizes what he wants from <u>A</u> in interpersonal terms. <u>A</u> and <u>B</u> also form contracts in terms of what they want from themselves while in their relationships to one another.

14. The role-playing demonstrations are intended to illustrate the following issues:

- *Group boundaries* (inclusion-exclusion)—what does it take to become a bona fide member of a group? This exercise also examines implicit action assumptions and double messages from superficial contracts.

- *Role contracts*—the implicit expectations tagged on to a role. For example, "I expect a leader to be helpful (always)." Or "I expect a college dean to be establishment (and to be uptight)."

- *Group leader contracts*—the kinds of contracts groups might make with leaders and leaders with groups and some ways of renegotiating these contracts.

- *Contracts in pairs*—milling exercise as a warm-up, and brief demonstration of person-to-person contracts and contracts with self.

CONTRACTING

CONTRACT EXERCISES IN TEAM BUILDING: INSTRUCTIONS FOR GROUP LEADERS

When your group meets for its session, distribute contract forms and suggest that many people have found it valuable for learning purposes to write down these contracts, but do not push the writing aspect.

The contracts are intended in most cases for the life of your group, but some may involve more extended relationships. The pairing can be done conveniently in the same room or nearby. Procedures are the following:

Contracts with others

Each person in the group will pair for *ten minutes* with each other person, including the group leader or leaders.

One person of each pair begins by saying what he wants of the other, for about four minutes. The other then responds to this "bid" as to whether he feels he can meet the conditions or needs presented.

The pairs then reverse roles and the second person now tells the first what he wants. There is one minute to respond. Time-keeping is the leader's responsibility.

Explain the shortness of the time is intended only to begin the explicit contract work which can be continued as well as renegotiated later by individuals or in groups.

Contract with self

Each person is encouraged to write down what he wants *from himself* in each of his relationships in his group. He may or may not wish to declare his agreement with himself to his group. Disclosure trust is optional. Developing contractual trust is the objective.

Contract between group and trainers

After each person has had a chance to pair with each other person in the group, including the leader, the group as a whole will convene and the group and the leader together will negotiate a mutual contract.

NOTE: Explain that you will be available to answer questions which may arise. If people are reluctant or refuse to do the exercise exactly as given, don't be too concerned. The exact format is far less important than observing kinds of contracts, and skill practice in formulating *explicit* contracts with self and others. Emphasize also that these contracts should be open for renegotiation or expansion.

CONTRACTING

Name _____

Date _____

CONTRACT EXERCISE FORM

Contract Areas	GROUP MEMBERS			
	Name:	Name:	Name:	
What I want from him or her				
What he or she wants from me				
What I want from myself in this relationship				
Impressions				

CONTRACTING

CONTRACT QUESTIONS

1. What do you want (want to change)? Be specific. (Take it from the general to the specific.)

2. What are you willing to do to get it (to make that change)? What do you need to do to get what you want for yourself? (Specifically—actual, observable behavior.)

3. How will we (the work group or the manager and subordinate) know when you've gotten it? How will it be observable, behavioral, measurable?

4. How might you "sabotage" yourself? How might you not get what you want?

5. How might this contract apply here now? (In this work group or with the manager and subordinate.)

CONTRACTING

CONTRACT CRITERIA CHECKLIST

Indicate whether the contract meets the following criteria by checking "yes" or "no" by each item. Under each item write the portion of the contract referred to, or otherwise describe the rationale for your assessment.

		Yes	No
1.	Stated in "here and now"	_____	_____
2.	Stated in positive terms	_____	_____
3.	Written in one sentence	_____	_____
4.	Stated in first person	_____	_____
5.	Clearly stated behavior	_____	_____
6.	Written so that an eight-year-old child could understand	_____	_____

ORGANIZATION PROBLEM ANALYSIS

DIRECTIONS

In the space below, take a few paragraphs to describe an organization conflict in which you are currently involved. Describe the situation, the underlying causes, your role and the role of other principals who are central to it. After you have finished, turn the page and answer the questions which make up the Diagnostic Survey.

Reprinted by permission from *Reality consultation in organizations,* an unpublished manuscript by Jerry B. Harvey, Department of Management Science, The George Washington University, Washington, D.C. 20052. Copyright© 1979 by Jerry Harvey. All rights reserved

ORGANIZATION DIAGNOSTIC SURVEY

DIRECTIONS

For each of the following questions please indicate whether the conditions described *are* or *are not* characteristic of a conflict or problem of which you are a part.

Condition	Characteristic	Not Characteristic
1. Organization members feel angry, frustrated, unhappy and impotent when trying to deal with the situation.	_____	_____
2. Organization members spend a lot of time and energy in trying to deal with it.	_____	_____
3. Organization members place blame for much of the problem on others—other individuals, other groups, or the boss.	_____	_____
4. The problem is discussed among subgroups of trusted friends and associates during coffee, lunch, or informal "closed door sessions." During these sessions there is much agreement about the causes of the problem and an effective solution.	_____	_____
5. Attempts to solve the problem do not seem to work. In fact, such attempts seem to escalate the problem and make it worse.	_____	_____
6. People are looking for a way to "escape" from the tension generated by the problem. They may avoid meetings at which the problem is discussed, take sick leave and vacation, or look for jobs or organization affiliations elsewhere.	_____	_____
7. You frequently feel cautious, less than candid, or "closed" when talking to most people in your organization about the problem and your ideas for solving it.	_____	_____

TOOLS FROM CHAPTER 9

Confronting Organization Issues

Conflict Resolution: Strategy Questionnaire

Task, Group-Building, and Maintenance Functions

Analysis of Skills in Groups

CONFRONTING ORGANIZATION ISSUES

This exercise is designed to give you a more realistic "feel" of the process of confronting. Think of a current problem/situation/difficulty that you believe needs confronting in your organization. It must be one that involves *you*.

1. What is the problem/situation/difficulty that needs confrontation?

2. Who needs confronting?

3. What is now happening because the issue is *not* resolved?

4. Why have you thus far *not* confronted?

5. What would happen if the confrontation was successful?

6. What would *you* say at the confrontation?

7. Besides the gain to the organization or job, what would *you* personally gain by the confrontation?

CONFLICT RESOLUTION: STRATEGY QUESTIONNAIRE

	FREQUENCY OF USE OF STRATEGY	EFFECTIVENESS OF STRATEGY	HOW I FEEL WHEN THE STRATEGY IS USED TOWARD ME
1. Power/Authority			
2. Courtesy			
3. Presenting alternatives			
4. Withdrawal			
5. "Divide and Conquer"			
6. Isolating the problem or problem persons			
7. Bureaucratic procedures (hiding in the system or finding a crack)			
8. Absorption of hostility and momentary defeat			
9. Changing the structure of the organization			
10. Passive resistance			
11. Grievance committee			
12. Temporary truce or moratorium			
13. Negotiation or arbitration process			

TASK, GROUP-BUILDING, AND MAINTENANCE FUNCTIONS
OBSERVATION SHEET

TASK FUNCTIONS: Leader-member behavior required for accomplishing group tasks.

1. **INITIATING:** Proposing tasks or goals; defining a group problem; suggesting a procedure or ideas for solving a problem.

1	2	3	4	5
Poor				Excellent

2. **INFORMATION- OR OPINION-SEEKING:** Requesting facts; seeking relevant information about a group concern; asking for suggestions and ideas.

1	2	3	4	5
Poor				Excellent

3. **INFORMATION- OR OPINION-GIVING:** Offering facts; providing relevant information about a group concern; stating a belief; giving suggestions or ideas.

1	2	3	4	5
Poor				Excellent

4. **CLARIFYING OR ELABORATING:** Interpreting or reflecting ideas and suggestions; clearing up confusions; indicating alternatives and issues before the group; giving examples.

1	2	3	4	5
Poor				Excellent

5. **SUMMARIZING:** Pulling together related ideas; restating suggestions after the group has discussed them; offering a decision or conclusion for the group to accept or reject.

1	2	3	4	5
Poor				Excellent

6. **CONSENSUS-TESTING:** Sending up "trial balloons" to see if group is nearing a conclusion; checking with group to see how much agreement has been reached.

1	2	3	4	5
Poor				Excellent

GROUP-BUILDING AND MAINTENANCE FUNCTIONS: Leader-member behavior required for building and maintaining the group as a working unit.

7. **ENCOURAGING:** Being friendly, warm and responsive to others; accepting others and their contributions; regarding others by giving them an opportunity for recognition.

1	2	3	4	5
Poor			Excellent	

8. **EXPRESSING GROUP FEELINGS:** Sensing feeling, mood, relationships within the group; sharing one's own feelings with other members.

1	2	3	4	5
Poor			Excellent	

9. **HARMONIZING:** Attempting to reconcile disagreements; reducing tension through "pouring oil on troubled waters"; getting people to explore their differences.

1	2	3	4	5
Poor			Excellent	

10. **COMPROMISING:** When one's own idea or status is involved in a conflict, offering to compromise his or her position; admitting error; disciplining oneself to maintain group cohesion.

1	2	3	4	5
Poor			Excellent	

11. **GATE-KEEPING:** Attempting to keep communication channels open; facilitating the participation of others; suggesting procedures for sharing opportunity to discuss group problems.

1	2	3	4	5
Poor			Excellent	

12. **SETTING STANDARDS:** Expressing standards for group to achieve; applying standards in evaluating group functioning and production.

1	2	3	4	5
Poor			Excellent	

TASK, GROUP-BUILDING, AND MAINTENANCE FUNCTIONS
GROUP PROFILE

DIRECTIONS

For each member, place check marks in the column corresponding to the roles he or she has played most often in the group. Include yourself.

ROLES   MEMBERS

Task Functions

1. Initiator
2. Information- or opinion-seeker
3. Information- or opinion-giver
4. Clarifier or elaborator
5. Summarizer
6. Consensus-tester

Group-Building and Maintenance Functions

7. Encourager
8. Expresser of group feelings
9. Harmonizer
10. Compromiser
11. Gatekeeper
12. Standard-setter

Anti-Group Roles

13. Blocker
14. Recognition-seeker
15. Dominator
16. Avoider

ANALYSIS OF SKILLS IN GROUPS

DIRECTIONS

This form is designed to help you think about your attitudes and behavior in groups (staff meetings, committees). First, read over the scales, and on each one place a checkmark at the point that describes you when you are a member of a group. Label this mark "P" for "present." Do the same for the point that describes where you would like to be as an effective member of a group. Mark this check "F" for "future." After marking all the scales, pick out the three or four that you would most like to change.

1. Clarity in expressing my thoughts

0	1	2	3	4	5	6	7
Quite vague							Exceptionally clear

2. Ability to listen in an alert and understanding way

0	1	2	3	4	5	6	7
Very low							Very high

3. Ability to present ideas forcefully and persuasively

0	1	2	3	4	5	6	7
Very low							Very high

4. Ability to "stay with" the topic being discussed

0	1	2	3	4	5	6	7
Very low							Excellent

5. Tendency to trust others

0	1	2	3	4	5	6	7
Quite suspicious							Extremely trusting

6.   Willingness to tell others what I feel (express emotions)

0	1	2	3	4	5	6	7
Conceal everything							Reveal everything

7.   Readiness to accept direction from others

0	1	2	3	4	5	6	7
Very reluctant							Like to very much

8.   Tendency to "take charge" of the group

0	1	2	3	4	5	6	7
Don't try							Try very hard

9.   Usual behavior toward others

0	1	2	3	4	5	6	7
Cold							Warm

10.   Reactions to comments about or evaluation of my behavior

0	1	2	3	4	5	6	7
Ignore them							Take them very seriously

11.   Understanding the feelings of others (empathy)

0	1	2	3	4	5	6	7
Don't know what they feel							Really understand

12.   Understanding why I do what I do (insight)

0	1	2	3	4	5	6	7
Don't know							Really understand

13.   Tolerance for conflict and antagonism in the group

0	1	2	3	4	5	6	7
Can't stand it							Like it very much

14. Tolerance for expressions of affection and warmth

0	1	2	3	4	5	6	7
Can't stand them							Like them very much

15. Thinking creatively in groups

0	1	2	3	4	5	6	7
Seldom contribute ideas							High idea production

16. Tolerance of opposing opinions

0	1	2	3	4	5	6	7
Low							High

TOOLS FROM CHAPTER 10

Manager Role Checklist

Manager Functions

Individual Manager Needs

Getting Problem Statement

Open Organization Manager Profile

Open Systems Model of Manager Competencies

Needs of the Organization

MANAGER ROLE CHECKLIST

DIRECTIONS

For each manager role, please respond to both questions by circling "yes" or "no."

Manager Roles		Now Perform This Role?		Want to Develop in This Area?	
1. Advocate	Energizes, initiates, acts. Is an extra pair of hands.	Yes	No	Yes	No
2. Diagnoser	Finds facts, conducts studies, acts as a catalyst in helping team members pull together ideas, analyzes data.	Yes	No	Yes	No
3. Planner	Assists in setting up action plans and developing strategies.	Yes	No	Yes	No
4. Problem Solver	Helps get problems out where they can be clarified and analyzed. Explores, develops, and evaluates alternative action plans to resolve problems.	Yes	No	Yes	No
5. Team Builder	Provides teams with ways to increase their effectiveness.	Yes	No	Yes	No
6. Conflict Manager	Helps examine and reduce conflict situations.	Yes	No	Yes	No
7. Systems Analyst	Examines how such areas as structure, decision-making, communication, personnel procedures, rewards and punishments, and employee participation affect organization functioning.	Yes	No	Yes	No
8. Process Observer	Views, reflects, and analyzes individual or work group functioning. Raises necessary questions.	Yes	No	Yes	No
9. Change Process Expert	Gives information on the impact of change and ways to plan for it.	Yes	No	Yes	No
10. Informational Expert	Knows work content area. Knows chances for success or failure. Acts as technical interpreter and is able to give specific answers.	Yes	No	Yes	No

Manager Roles		Now Perform This Role?		Want to Develop in This Area?	
11.	Individual Developer — Helps individuals analyze, problem-solve, plan. Helps design career paths, acts as resource person, provides feedback.	Yes	No	Yes	No
12.	Organization Developer — Assists work groups, individuals, and organization in bringing about planned changes.	Yes	No	Yes	No
13.	Interpersonal Developer — Provides ways to enrich human interaction and enhance working relationships and climate.	Yes	No	Yes	No
14.	Skills Builder — Provides training for individual, work group, and organization growth using a variety of methods.	Yes	No	Yes	No

MANAGER FUNCTIONS
DIRECTIONS

After reading each manager function, please (1) mark the scale with an X at the point that represents your present skill level; (2) on the same scale, circle the number representing the skill level you want to reach; (3) circle "yes" or "no" to indicate whether there is a general organization need for training in this function.

X = now
O = want to be

	No skills						Very skillful	General Organization Need?	

I. Planning (Determining what work must be done)

1. *Defining roles and missions.* Determining nature and scope of work to be performed.	1	2	3	4	5	6	7	Yes	No
2. *Forecasting.* Estimating the future.	1	2	3	4	5	6	7	Yes	No
3. *Setting measurable objectives.* Determining results to be achieved.	1	2	3	4	5	6	7	Yes	No
4. *Developing strategies.* Deciding how and when to achieve goals.	1	2	3	4	5	6	7	Yes	No
5. *Programming.* Establishing priority, sequence and timing of steps.	1	2	3	4	5	6	7	Yes	No
6. *Scheduling.* Establishing time requirements for objectives and programs.	1	2	3	4	5	6	7	Yes	No
7. *Budgeting.* Determining and assigning the resources required to reach objectives.	1	2	3	4	5	6	7	Yes	No
8. *Policy-making.* Establishing rules, regulations, or pre-determined decisions.	1	2	3	4	5	6	7	Yes	No
9. *Establishing procedures.* Determining consistent and systematic methods of handling work.	1	2	3	4	5	6	7	Yes	No
10. *Analyzing problems.* Gathering facts, ascertaining causes, developing alternative solutions. Inviting recommendations from above, below, and laterally in the organization.	1	2	3	4	5	6	7	Yes	No

	No skills					Very skillful		General Organization Need?	

II. Organizing (Classifying and dividing work into manageable units)

11. *Structuring.* Grouping the work for effective and efficient production.

1	2	3	4	5	6	7	Yes	No

12. *Delegating.* Passing out work responsibility and authority to staff so that you can concentrate on managerial tasks.

1	2	3	4	5	6	7	Yes	No

13. *Integrating.* Establishing conditions for effective teamwork among organizational units.

1	2	3	4	5	6	7	Yes	No

III. Staffing (Determining work requirements and insuring availability of personnel)

14. *Determining personnel needs.* Analyzing the work for capabilities required.

1	2	3	4	5	6	7	Yes	No

15. *Creating position descriptions.* Defining scope, relationships, responsibilities, and authority.

1	2	3	4	5	6	7	Yes	No

16. *Selecting personnel.* Identifying and appointing people to organizational positions.

1	2	3	4	5	6	7	Yes	No

17. *Training.* Making new people proficient through instruction, practice, and facilitating the learning process.

1	2	3	4	5	6	7	Yes	No

18. *Developing personnel.* Providing opportunities for people to increase their capabilities to meet organizational needs. Providing counseling.

1	2	3	4	5	6	7	Yes	No

19. *Rewarding.* Praising, giving recognition for achievement.

1	2	3	4	5	6	7	Yes	No

	No skills					Very skillful		General Organization Need?	

IV. Directing, Leading (Bringing about human activity required to accomplish objectives)

20. *Assigning.* Charging individual employees with job responsibilities or specific tasks to be performed.
| | 1 | 2 | 3 | 4 | 5 | 6 | 7 | Yes | No |

21. *Motivating.* Influencing people to perform in a desired manner.
| | 1 | 2 | 3 | 4 | 5 | 6 | 7 | Yes | No |

22. *Communicating.* Achieving effective flow of ideas and information in all desired directions including upward, downward and laterally in the organization.
| | 1 | 2 | 3 | 4 | 5 | 6 | 7 | Yes | No |

23. *Coordinating.* Achieving harmony and effectiveness of group effort toward accomplishment of individual and group objectives.
| | 1 | 2 | 3 | 4 | 5 | 6 | 7 | Yes | No |

24. *Managing differences.* Encouraging independent thought; resolving conflict; understanding group behavior.
| | 1 | 2 | 3 | 4 | 5 | 6 | 7 | Yes | No |

25. *Managing change.* Stimulating creativity and innovation in achieving goals.
| | 1 | 2 | 3 | 4 | 5 | 6 | 7 | Yes | No |

26. *Making decisions.* Arriving at conclusions and judgments.
| | 1 | 2 | 3 | 4 | 5 | 6 | 7 | Yes | No |

V. Controlling (Assuring the effective accomplishment of objectives)

27. *Establishing reporting systems.* Determining what critical data are needed how, when, and where.
| | 1 | 2 | 3 | 4 | 5 | 6 | 7 | Yes | No |

28. *Establishing standards.* Devising a gauge of successful performance in achieving objectives.
| | 1 | 2 | 3 | 4 | 5 | 6 | 7 | Yes | No |

29. *Measuring performance.* Assessing actual versus planned performance.
| | 1 | 2 | 3 | 4 | 5 | 6 | 7 | Yes | No |

	No skills					Very skillful		General Organization Need?	
30. *Taking corrective action.* Bringing about performance improvement toward objectives	1	2	3	4	5	6		Yes	No
31. *Administering contracts.* Making proper application of the contracts as related to the employee's responsibility in the organization.	1	2	3	4	5	6	7	Yes	No
32. *Handling labor relations.* Understanding the history and role of unions, the obligation to bargain, management rights, and the limitations of unions and management.	1	2	3	4	5	6	7	Yes	No
33. *Taking care of legal responsibilities.* Ensuring that the individuals and the institution are in compliance with federal, state and local government legislation and regulations.	1	2	3	4	5	6	7	Yes	No

INDIVIDUAL MANAGER NEEDS

1. How would you describe yourself if you were functioning as an "ideal" manager? What would you be doing? Saying? Feeling?

2. How would you describe yourself *now?*

3. What forces are *helping* you move in your ideal direction? What persons, groups, resources?

4. What forces are *hindering* your movement toward your ideal functioning?

5. What action steps could you take to increase the forces helping you move in your "ideal" direction (items listed in question 3)?

6. What action steps could you take to decrease the effect of the restraining forces (items listed in question 4)?

7. What resources are available to you for carrying out these action steps?

8. How do you see a program of leadership and management competency development fitting into your own development scheme?

    a) **Types** of support:
- Large group?
- Small group?
- Work with you as an individual?
- Supply you with material to read, or other media?
- Other?

    b) **Areas** of support (be specific):
- Problem-solving strategies?
- Managing change and conflict?
- Evaluating programs?
- Other?

    c) **Times/dates** of support: What months of the year, days of the week, times of the day are convenient for you to attend such programs?

9. How will you know you got what you wanted?

Interviewee: _____ Position: _____

Date: _____ Interviewer: _____

GETTING A PROBLEM STATEMENT
(From Gripe to Goal in Five Minutes)

1. My gripe (frustration) is _____

_____

_____

_____

_____

2. My real concern is that _____

_____

_____

_____

_____

3. What I am really wishing for is _____

_____

_____

_____

_____

4. Therefore, my goal is to _____

_____

_____

_____

_____

If you do not know how to reach the goal, complete item 5:

5. Therefore, my goal is to find out how to _____

_____

_____

_____

_____

OPEN ORGANIZATION MANAGER PROFILE

MANAGER: _____ Date: _____

Supervisor completing form: _____

Subordinates' responses summarized on this form:

_____   _____
_____   _____
_____   _____
_____   _____
_____   _____

DIRECTIONS

This instrument is designed to help you look at your effectiveness as a manager. The dimensions listed are some of the more important ones with which the manager should be concerned. Please read each item and circle the point on the scale that describes where you are now on this item. A second scale is provided after each statement so that your supervisor may check where he or she now sees you. This person will not indicate where you should be; only you can make this decision. The third scale may be used to summarize responses from several of your subordinates.

Example: Is inconsistent. Associates never know what to expect from her. Arbitrary in applying rules and policies.

Is consistent. Associates know what to expect from her. Fair.

(self-estimate)

| 1 | 2 | 3 | 4 | 5 | 6 | 7 |

(supervisor's estimate)

| 1 | 2 | 3 | 4 | 5 | 6 | 7 |

(summary of subordinates' estimates)

| 1 | 2 | 3 | 4 | 5 | 6 | 7 |

This manager rates herself rather high on consistency; her supervisor sees her in the same way. Seven subordinates who completed a similar form (results are tallied here) differed considerably in their judgment about the consistency of their manager's behavior.

A. The effective manager possesses a sense of her own worth. She has a positive regard for herself. She is seen by others as being consistent. The manager possesses a set of qualities, values, beliefs that define her uniqueness.

1. Is inconsistent. Associates never know what to expect from her. Arbitrary in applying rules and policies.

Is consistent. Associates know what to expect from her. Fair.

(self-estimate)

(supervisor's estimate)

(summary of subordinates' estimates)

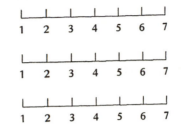

2. Is irresponsible. Does not fulfill commitments. Does not accept responsibility for decisions she has made.

Is responsible. The commitments she makes she keeps. Is trustworthy.

(self-estimate)

(supervisor's estimate)

(summary of subordinates' estimates)

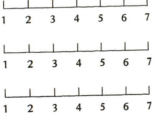

3. Is incompetent. Lacks knowledge of current developments in the field.

Is competent, knowledgeable and up-to-date in the field.

(self-estimate)

(supervisor's estimate)

(summary of subordinates' estimates)

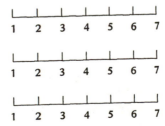

4. Is weak. Her stated con-
victions conform to external
pressures.

Is personally courageous.
Takes a stand for what she
believes.

(self-estimate)

|___|___|___|___|___|___|___|
1   2   3   4   5   6   7

(supervisor's
estimate)

|___|___|___|___|___|___|___|
1   2   3   4   5   6   7

(summary of
subordinates'
estimates)

|___|___|___|___|___|___|___|
1   2   3   4   5   6   7

5. Is despondent and bored.
Has no zest for life or work.

Is enthusiastic, alive, energetic,
interested, happy, concerned.
Has energy.

(self-estimate)

|___|___|___|___|___|___|___|
1   2   3   4   5   6   7

(supervisor's
estimate)

|___|___|___|___|___|___|___|
1   2   3   4   5   6   7

(summary of
subordinates'
estimates)

|___|___|___|___|___|___|___|
1   2   3   4   5   6   7

6. Is lacking in self-confidence.
Does not perceive herself as
being worthwhile.

Is confident. Sees herself as a
worthwhile person.
Secure.

(self-estimate)

|___|___|___|___|___|___|___|
1   2   3   4   5   6   7

(supervisor's
estimate)

|___|___|___|___|___|___|___|
1   2   3   4   5   6   7

(summary of
subordinates'
estimates)

|___|___|___|___|___|___|___|
1   2   3   4   5   6   7

B. The effective manager is aware of himself, his feelings, needs, motivations, defenses. He is able to acknowledge (own) his feelings and not project his feelings or frustrations on others. He allows others the freedom to be themselves.

1. Is intolerant of mistakes. Sees errors as sign of weakness, incompetence.

Is tolerant of mistakes. Realizes growth that can come from errors.

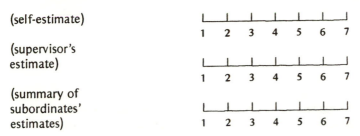

(self-estimate)

1 2 3 4 5 6 7

(supervisor's estimate)

1 2 3 4 5 6 7

(summary of subordinates' estimates)

1 2 3 4 5 6 7

2. Is blind to own deficiencies. Sees no need for building skills.

Is always looking for ways to improve himself and his skills. Realizes his deficiencies and acts to remedy them.

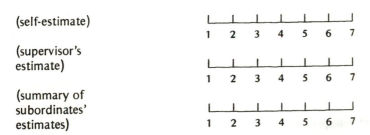

(self-estimate)

1 2 3 4 5 6 7

(supervisor's estimate)

1 2 3 4 5 6 7

(summary of subordinates' estimates)

1 2 3 4 5 6 7

3. Is not free to be himself. Acts in a contrived, artificial manner. Makes demands on others to be as he wants them to be.

Is natural. Is himself, allows others to be themselves.

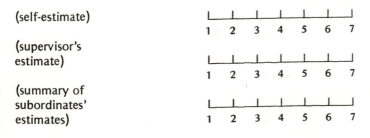

(self-estimate)

1 2 3 4 5 6 7

(supervisor's estimate)

1 2 3 4 5 6 7

(summary of subordinates' estimates)

1 2 3 4 5 6 7

4. Is "there and then" in his
responses. Dumps data from
past events at later, inappropriate times.

Is current with sharing feelings.
Does not store up negative (or
positive) feelings.

(self-estimate)

(supervisor's
estimate)

(summary of
subordinates'
estimates)

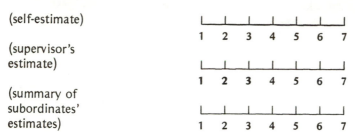

5. Is closed, secretive. Does
not share relevant data.
Dishonest.

Is open. Has no hidden
agendas. Acknowledges
where he stands and what
he feels. Is honest.

(self-estimate)

(supervisor's
estimate)

(summary of
subordinates'
estimates)

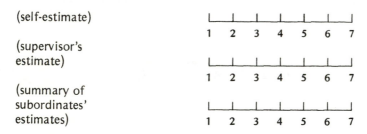

C. The effective manager hears and responds to others, listening actively. The manager is open to different persons, experiences and ideas. She has a plan for personal
and professional growth; she sees herself as constantly interacting with her environment and learning.

1. Is insensitive to statements
by others. Gives responses which
do not reflect understanding of
what others say or feel.

Is an active listener. Takes
time to hear associates and
respond in a relevant manner.

(self-estimate)

(supervisor's
estimate)

(summary of
subordinates'
estimates)

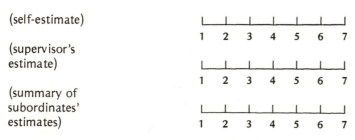

2. Will not hear feedback concerning herself. Denies negative and/or positive feedback. Does not act to correct deficiencies. Inflexible.

Hears feedback about herself. Acts to correct deficiencies; accepts positive feedback without denial or apology. Flexible.

(self-estimate)

(supervisor's estimate)

(summary of subordinates' estimates)

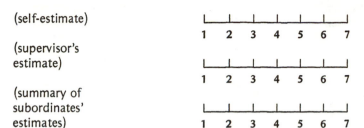

3. Talks down to associates. Speaks as a parent would to a child. Denies equality of other person. Often reprimands associates publicly.

Talks "with" rather than "to" associates. Treats associates as adults. Is nonjudgmental.

(self-estimate)

(supervisor's estimate)

(summary of subordinates' estimates)

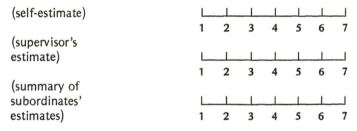

4. Communicates in an obtuse manner. Associates are never sure she understands what they are saying and are often unsure of what she is saying.

Communicates simply and clearly. Is clear with her expectations of others. Never assumes; checks her understanding of others and their understanding of her.

(self-estimate)

(supervisor's estimate)

(summary of subordinates' estimates)

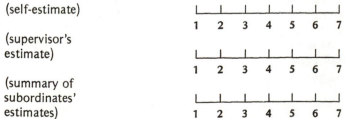

D. The effective manager promotes department (team) unity by identifying team goals. He builds cohesiveness by communicating these goals and relating each department (team) member's task to team goals. The manager focuses team energy on established goals. The manager involves the department (team) members in establishing and revising goals.

1. Shares no information on his goals for the department (team).

Makes explicit department (team) goals and objectives. Explains where he sees department (team) going.

(self-estimate)

(supervisor's estimate)

(summary of subordinates' estimates)

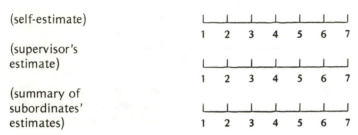

2. Makes all department (team) decisions concerning goals of department (team). Solicits no input from associates.

Involves all department (team) persons in planning of goals, objectives, and priorities. Everyone has "ownership" in program direction.

(self-estimate)

(supervisor's estimate)

(summary of subordinates' estimates)

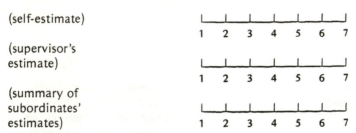

3. Works on individual assignments. Makes no attempt to relate his work to department goals. Makes fragmented assignments to associates; no sense of overall achievement of department (team) goals.

Constantly relates activities of himself and associates to over-all department (team) goals. Manages coordination of associates toward common goals.

(self-estimate)

(supervisor's estimate)

(summary of subordinates' estimates)

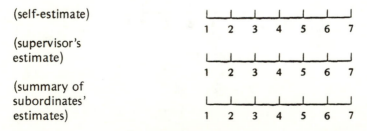

E. The effective manager functions as a team member. She facilitates interaction among team members. She allows herself and others to perform different group functions based on expertise rather than on an individual's position in the organization. She has a concern for team functioning to achieve task; she balances concern for team members and concern for task achievement. The manager facilitates personal and professional growth in the team members as an aid to better team functioning.

| 1. Makes no attempt to develop associates. Denies requests for training. Assigns routine tasks to persons. | Facilitates development of each associate. Constantly suggests training programs and offers assignments which allow associates to grow. |

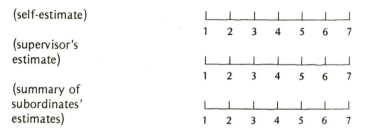

(self-estimate)

(supervisor's estimate)

(summary of subordinates' estimates)

| 2. Assigns tasks without regard to who is best skilled to accomplish task. | Knows unique skills of each department (team) member and uses each person's skills in department (team) problem-solving. |

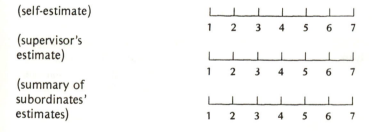

(self-estimate)

(supervisor's estimate)

(summary of subordinates' estimates)

3. Functions as sole team leader. Does not allow others to assume any leadership roles.

Functions as a team member. She and associates share leadership and team maintenance functions. Allows team members to share in effective leadership.

(self-estimate)

(supervisor's estimate)

(summary of subordinates' estimates)

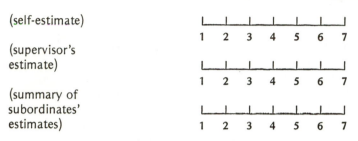

4. Allows only statements related to task to be made. Does not recognize interplay of interpersonal and task issues.

Allows confrontation to emerge in team sessions. Has skills to manage interpersonal agendas as they relate to team task.

(self-estimate)

(supervisor's estimate)

(summary of subordinates' estimates)

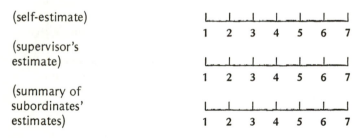

5. Supervises every detail of a task herself. Over-supervises.

Operates with management by objectives. Team members agree on assignments. Manager facilitates team accomplishments.

(self-estimate)

(supervisor's estimate)

(summary of subordinates' estimates)

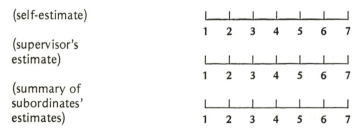

F. The effective manager gathers data concerning a department (team) task from all relevant sources and conveys it to his department (team) as an aid to problem-solving. He serves as a link between his department (team) and other departments within the organization so that his department's plans and decisions reflect all available organization data. He serves as a spokesperson for department decisions. He seeks data from the organization for his department and shares department data with others.

1. Does not pass on information from his department to others. No data flow outward. No acknowledgment of contribution of team members.

Takes department (team) products or decisions to superiors. Acknowledges contributions of associates.

(self-estimate)

(supervisor's estimate)

(summary of subordinates' estimates)

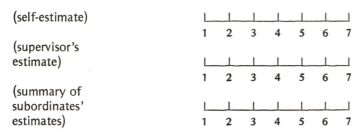

2. Does not seek data from sources outside his department (team) for problem solving. Unresponsive to external information.

Constantly seeks information from outside department (team). Brings information to department (team) for relevant problem-solving.

(self-estimate)

(supervisor's estimate)

(summary of subordinates' estimates)

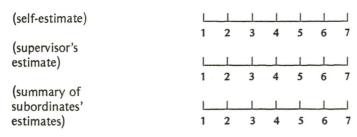

3. Department (team) decisions made in vacuum. His department (team) often viewed as "empire" unto itself.

Relates department (team) decisions and goals to overall organizational goals.

(self-estimate)

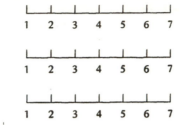

(supervisor's estimate)

(summary of subordinates' estimates)

4. Works on a day-to-day basis. Does not "look up" to see where he and department are going. Often responds to "crisis." Reactive manager.

Constantly works with department (team) on long-range goals (one to three years). Looks to outside sources for trends. Proactive manager.

(self-estimate)

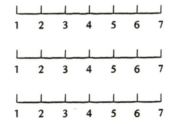

(supervisor's estimate)

(summary of subordinates' estimates)

G. The effective manager knows the overall organization goals. She promotes knowledge of organization goals and commitment to them. She realizes the need for organization identity.

1. Does not communicate understanding of corporate goals. Does nothing to make team feel a part of total corporate effort.

Communicates corporate goals. Sets objectives (and helps associates set theirs) consistent with corporate goals.

(self-estimate)

(supervisor's estimate)

(summary of subordinates' estimates)

2. Her department (team) policies are inconsistent with corporate policies and procedures.

Communicates corporate policies and procedures. Her department (team) policies and procedures are consistent with corporate policies.

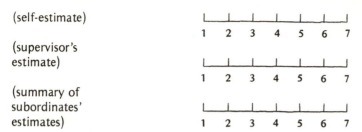

(self-estimate)

1 2 3 4 5 6 7

(supervisor's estimate)

1 2 3 4 5 6 7

(summary of subordinates' estimates)

1 2 3 4 5 6 7

3. Openly criticizes other departments. Fosters fragmentation within the organization.

Recognizes areas of fragmentation within organization and promotes cooperation to unify total corporate effort.

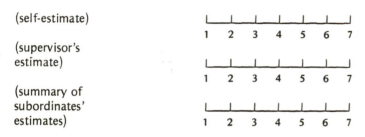

(self-estimate)

1 2 3 4 5 6 7

(supervisor's estimate)

1 2 3 4 5 6 7

(summary of subordinates' estimates)

1 2 3 4 5 6 7

H. The effective manager is able to see how all components of the organization function and affect each other. He has a grasp of the total organization and can suggest ways to improve internal efficiency.

1. Does not know how components of company are organized and work together.

Knows how corporate divisions and departments function and how they affect each other.

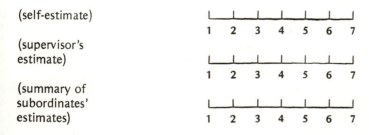

(self-estimate)

1 2 3 4 5 6 7

(supervisor's estimate)

1 2 3 4 5 6 7

(summary of subordinates' estimates)

1 2 3 4 5 6 7

2. Often duplicates work done by others.

Checks other departments before pursuing tasks to avoid duplication of effort.

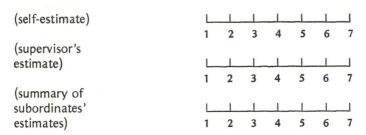

(self-estimate)

(supervisor's estimate)

(summary of subordinates' estimates)

3. Does not know skills and capabilities of other departments (teams).

Allocates tasks to other departments (teams) that are better prepared to deal with them. Knows boundaries and limitations of his department (team).

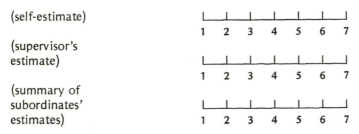

(self-estimate)

(supervisor's estimate)

(summary of subordinates' estimates)

4. Operates from a "win–lose" stance. Sees departments competing rather than cooperating.

Operates from a "win–win" stance. Fosters cooperation among departments.

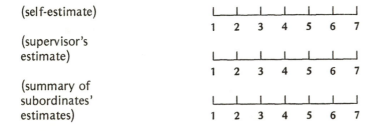

(self-estimate)

(supervisor's estimate)

(summary of subordinates' estimates)

I. The effective manager is part of the world outside the organization. She is able to gather and use information on the impact of the organization on the larger social system and the impact of the larger system on the organization.

1. Is not involved in government or community activities.

Participates in government and community activities. Aware of interplay between organization and community.

(self-estimate)

(supervisor's estimate)

(summary of subordinates' estimates)

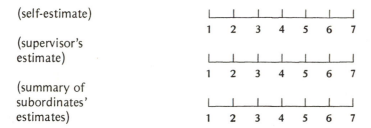

2. Is closed to data from outside the organization. Does not see larger societal trends. Often caught unaware by changes in environment. Products of her department (team) are often outdated.

Relates data from larger economic and social system to goals and objectives of organization. Products of her department (team) are timely.

(self-estimate)

(supervisor's estimate)

(summary of subordinates' estimates)

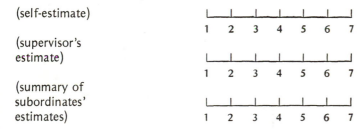

OPEN SYSTEMS MODEL OF MANAGER COMPETENCIES

DIRECTIONS

Each lettered block represents a cluster of manager skills at the individual, group, or organization level. Please rate your present overall skill level in each block by circling a number from 1 (low) to 7 (high) on the "Am now" scale. Circle the number on the second scale that shows the overall level you want to reach.

A I am clear about my basic beliefs. I know who I am. I have a positive self-concept. I am congruent and responsible. I am energetic.

Am now 1 2 3 4 5 6 7
Would like to be 1 2 3 4 5 6 7

B I am aware of my feelings, needs, wants. I express feelings. I am aware of my defenses.

Am now 1 2 3 4 5 6 7
Would like to be 1 2 3 4 5 6 7

C I hear and respond relevantly to others. I am open to ideas, experiences, people, and love. I am an active listener.

Am now 1 2 3 4 5 6 7
Would like to be 1 2 3 4 5 6 7

D I identify team goals and objectives. I build group cohesion.

Am now 1 2 3 4 5 6 7
Would like to be 1 2 3 4 5 6 7

E I facilitate development of personnel. I use the unique skills of individuals, and am able to manage divergent views. I facilitate interaction among team members.

Am now 1 2 3 4 5 6 7
Would like to be 1 2 3 4 5 6 7

F I gather and relate information from other groups in the organization to tasks of my team. I relate team decisions and goals to organization goals.

Am now 1 2 3 4 5 6 7
Would like to be 1 2 3 4 5 6 7

G I promote knowledge and commitment to organization goals. I communicate organization goals, policies, and procedures to my unit. I work for organization unity.

Am now 1 2 3 4 5 6 7
Would like to be 1 2 3 4 5 6 7

H I see ways all components of the organization function and affect each other. I check with other departments before pursuing tasks.

Am now 1 2 3 4 5 6 7
Would like to be 1 2 3 4 5 6 7

I I relate information from external economic and social systems to organization goals and objectives. I develop organization programs relevant to larger social and economic systems.

Am now 1 2 3 4 5 6 7
Would like to be 1 2 3 4 5 6 7

NEEDS OF THE ORGANIZATION

1. For this organization to be an outstanding institution _____
   _____
   _____
   _____
   _____

2. We could get a lot more done around here if _____
   _____
   _____
   _____
   _____

3. What this organization needs is _____
   _____
   _____
   _____
   _____

4. The job that needs to be done that isn't getting done is _____
   _____
   _____
   _____
   _____

5. People around here need skills in_____
   _____
   _____
   _____
   _____

TOOLS FROM CHAPTER 11

Quick Impressions

Open Systems Review

QUICK IMPRESSIONS
PARTICIPANT REACTION FORM

Program: _____ Program Coordinator: _____

DIRECTIONS

1. Respond to *all* items though some may not seem relevant.

2. Make a check between dots at the point closest to your immediate impression about this program.

3. Check as close to the word on either end of each line as is consistent with your impression.

EXAMPLE: COLD _____ : _____ : _____ : _____ : _____ : _____ : ✓ WARM

My overall immediate impression of this session is that it was . . .

IMPRACTICAL _____ : _____ : _____ : _____ : _____ : _____ : _____ PRACTICAL
POWERFUL _____ : _____ : _____ : _____ : _____ : _____ : _____ POWERLESS
SHARP _____ : _____ : _____ : _____ : _____ : _____ : _____ DULL
COLD _____ : _____ : _____ : _____ : _____ : _____ : _____ WARM
MOVING _____ : _____ : _____ : _____ : _____ : _____ : _____ STANDING
STRONG _____ : _____ : _____ : _____ : _____ : _____ : _____ WEAK
USEFUL _____ : _____ : _____ : _____ : _____ : _____ : _____ USELESS
BAD _____ : _____ : _____ : _____ : _____ : _____ : _____ GOOD
OUTSTANDING _____ : _____ : _____ : _____ : _____ : _____ : _____ ORDINARY
RELEVANT _____ : _____ : _____ : _____ : _____ : _____ : _____ NON-RELEVANT
UNDERSTANDABLE _____ : _____ : _____ : _____ : _____ : _____ : _____ MYSTERIOUS
UNREALISTIC _____ : _____ : _____ : _____ : _____ : _____ : _____ REALISTIC
CLEAR _____ : _____ : _____ : _____ : _____ : _____ : _____ CONFUSING

The part(s) of the day's activities I found most helpful were:

How would you change today's activities to make them more worthwhile?

General comments on the experience:

QUICK IMPRESSIONS
Participant Response Tally Sheet
DIRECTIONS

Use this tally sheet to record individual responses. Calculate an average score for each dichotomized pair.

Potency

Powerful |—1—2—3—4—5—6—7—| Powerless

Strong |—1—2—3—4—5—6—7—| Weak

Moving |—1—2—3—4—5—6—7—| Standing

Evaluation

Outstanding |—1—2—3—4—5—6—7—| Ordinary

Cold |—1—2—3—4—5—6—7—| Warm

Bad |—1—2—3—4—5—6—7—| Good

Understandability

Understandable |—1—2—3—4—5—6—7—| Mysterious

Clear |—1—2—3—4—5—6—7—| Confusing

Sharp |—1—2—3—4—5—6—7—| Dull

Practicality

Impractical |—1—2—3—4—5—6—7—| Practical

Useful |—1—2—3—4—5—6—7—| Useless

Unrealistic |—1—2—3—4—5—6—7—| Realistic

Relevant |—1—2—3—4—5—6—7—| Non-relevant

QUICK IMPRESSIONS

Summary Diagram

DIRECTIONS

This diagram may be used to obtain a profile of strengths and weaknesses at a glance for Potency, Evaluation, Understandability, and Practicality.

From the Participant Response Tally Sheet, take the numerical average for each word pair and write it in the corresponding square on the diagram. Notice that the pair of words are *not* in the same sequence as on the Quick Impressions Reaction Form. The positive values are all on the right.

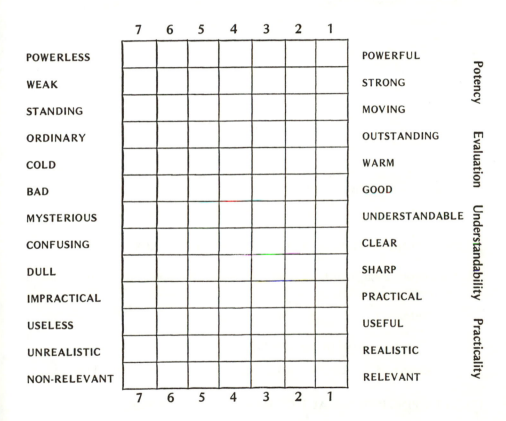

OPEN SYSTEMS REVIEW

ITEMS TAPPING INDIVIDUAL UNITY

1. I take responsibility for my own actions and make up my own mind, realizing my potential and operating in an integrated manner.

   Untrue   1   2   3   4   5   6   7   8   9   True

2. What I say and do is what I feel and believe.

   Untrue   1   2   3   4   5   6   7   8   9   True

3. I tolerate ambiguity well.

   Untrue   1   2   3   4   5   6   7   8   9   True

4. I believe that people are basically good and, given the right conditions, will move in positive directions.

   Untrue   1   2   3   4   5   6   7   8   9   True

5. I believe that every person is gifted and has untapped potential.

   Untrue   1   2   3   4   5   6   7   8   9   True

6. I believe that every human being (including myself) can live a much fuller life than he or she is currently experiencing.

   Untrue   1   2   3   4   5   6   7   8   9   True

ITEMS TAPPING INDIVIDUAL INTERNAL RESPONSIVENESS

7. I am strong enough to be a separate person, acknowledging and respecting my own needs and feelings.

   Untrue   1   2   3   4   5   6   7   8   9   True

8. My self-image is one of change, development, growth, and emergence.

   Untrue   1   2   3   4   5   6   7   8   9   True

ITEMS TAPPING INDIVIDUAL EXTERNAL RESPONSIVENESS

9. The organization I work for has specific long-range planning for what we are to achieve, and the whole organization is committed to this set of goals to produce the best possible product.

   Untrue   1   2   3   4   5   6   7   8   9   True

10. I see how present-day demands mean my job is growing ever more important.

   Untrue 1   2   3   4   5   6   7   8   9   True

11. Most of the time I am my own person—that is the way I function, and I let my friends know where I stand.

   Untrue 1   2   3   4   5   6   7   8   9   True

ITEMS TAPPING GROUP UNITY

12. People in my group are good about living up to their commitment to group goals. They get jobs done on time, are on the job when expected, and avoid unnecessary wrangling, so that team tasks are accomplished smoothly.

   Untrue 1   2   3   4   5   6   7   8   9   True

13. My group divides work according to what each of us does best, so we can all enjoy doing our work.

   Untrue 1   2   3   4   5   6   7   8   9   True

14. People in my group understand team goals and are committed to them.

   Untrue 1   2   3   4   5   6   7   8   9   True

15. The team members have a sense of loyalty and belonging to the group.

   Untrue 1   2   3   4   5   6   7   8   9   True

16. Group decisions are made by participation of all members, using consensus.

   Untrue 1   2   3   4   5   6   7   8   9   True

ITEMS TAPPING GROUP INTERNAL RESPONSIVENESS

17. When the boss of my group says he or she will do something, you can absolutely count on it, and that goes for the others in our group. Otherwise, we couldn't cooperate to get our work done.

   Untrue 1   2   3   4   5   6   7   8   9   True

18. The resources of individual group members are well used.

   Untrue 1   2   3   4   5   6   7   8   9   True

19. All group members at one time or another serve as leader.

   Untrue 1   2   3   4   5   6   7   8   9   True

20. Team members relate to each other with trust and openness.

   Untrue 1   2   3   4   5   6   7   8   9   True

ITEMS TAPPING GROUP EXTERNAL RESPONSIVENESS

21. When my group experiences conflict between work required of us by a leader and what we see as right and sensible, we confront the leader with the issue and negotiate.

    Untrue 1   2   3   4   5   6   7   8   9   True

22. I like my work and the friends I've made on the job. We often get outside materials and read up on doing the job better. When we have to work with other groups, we can usually see their problems.

    Untrue 1   2   3   4   5   6   7   8   9   True

23. My group works with other groups in an open way. We don't fear the risk of competition, because we know we're all part of the big picture.

    Untrue 1   2   3   4   5   6   7   8   9   True

24. My group makes an effort to examine its process (the *way* it operates and makes decisions) in order to improve functioning.

    Untrue 1   2   3   4   5   6   7   8   9   True

ITEMS TAPPING ORGANIZATIONAL UNITY

25. The goals of the organization are clear.

    Untrue 1   2   3   4   5   6   7   8   9   True

26. People are concerned about future planning: they dream, and they question existing procedures and assumptions.

    Untrue 1   2   3   4   5   6   7   8   9   True

27. Problem-solving is a positive process in which we explore the difference between "what is" and "what ought to be."

    Untrue 1   2   3   4   5   6   7   8   9   True

28. We take feelings as well as "facts" into account in making decisions and solving problems.

    Untrue 1   2   3   4   5   6   7   8   9   True

29. Concern with getting the job done is more important than whether we work exactly from 8:30 to 5:00 or take exactly one hour for lunch.

    Untrue 1   2   3   4   5   6   7   8   9   True

ITEMS TAPPING ORGANIZATION INTERNAL RESPONSIVENESS

30. My organization knows employees are an important resource and does its best to see we get as fair a break as possible within reasonable boundaries.

   Untrue 1   2   3   4   5   6   7   8   9   True

31. Information needed for effective decision-making flows easily between subgroups in my organization.

   Untrue 1   2   3   4   5   6   7   8   9   True

32. My organization makes an effort to assess and use the various skills of individuals, instead of having the same people doing everything.

   Untrue 1   2   3   4   5   6   7   8   9   True

33. Task groups are formed with persons having a variety of appropriate skills, in order to use differences creatively.

   Untrue 1   2   3   4   5   6   7   8   9   True

34. My organization makes an effort to exchange information with persons and organizations in the environment.

   Untrue 1   2   3   4   5   6   7   8   9   True

35. We use task·forces rather than standing committees.

   Untrue 1   2   3   4   5   6   7   8   9   True

ITEMS TAPPING ORGANIZATIONAL EXTERNAL RESPONSIVENESS

36. My organization does a good job of letting each group know about important items related to our work, including facts that should not be made public.

   Untrue 1   2   3   4   5   6   7   8   9   True

37. We just couldn't have a more open organization. We know what's what and there is little or no question, argument, or gossip about where we are going.

   Untrue 1   2   3   4   5   6   7   8   9   True

38. My organization plays an important part in the overall scheme of things. Our community or society needs our services.

   Untrue 1   2   3   4   5   6   7   8   9   True

39. My organization's goals are periodically reevaluated by representatives of constituent groups within and outside the organization.

   Untrue 1   2   3   4   5   6   7   8   9   True

References

Alderfer, C. P., and Ferris, R.   Understanding the impact of survey feedback. In W. W. Burke and H. A. Hornstein (Eds.), *The social technology of organization development*. Fairfax, Va.: NTL Learning Resources Corp., 1972.

Appel, V. H.   *Procedures for formulating instruments to measure setting-specific organizational goals*, 1978. Unpublished manuscript. (Available from Victor H. Appel, Ph.D., Department of Educational Psychology, The University of Texas, Austin, Texas.)

Appel, V. H., and Mink, O. G.   *High discrepancy/high importance institutional goals: a locus for focus*. Paper presented at the meeting of the American College Personnel Association, Denver, Colo.: April 1977.

Baker, G. A.   Participative structuring: a synthesis of individual and group goal-setting (Topical Papers and Reprints, No. 1). Newport, R.I.: Educational Planning Systems, 1973.

Barnard, C.   *Functions of the executive*. Cambridge, Mass.: Harvard University Press, 1962.

Bass, B. M.   A systems survey research feedback for management and organizational development. *Journal of Applied Behavioral Science*, 1976, *12* (2), 215–229.

Baumgartel, H.   Using employee questionnaire results for improving organizations. *Kansas Business Review*, 1959, *12*, 2–6.

Beckhard, R.   *Organization development: strategies and models*. Reading, Mass.: Addison-Wesley, 1969.

Beer, M., and Huse, E. F.   A systems approach to organization development. *Journal of Applied Behavioral Science*, 1972, *8*, 79–101.

Bennis, W. G.   *Organization development: its nature, origins, and prospects*. Reading, Mass.: Addison-Wesley, 1969.

Bennis, W. G.   Everything you always wanted to know about change (but were afraid to ask). *Environment, Planning and Design*, Summer 1971, 1–17.

Bennis, W. G., Benne, K., and Chin, R.   *The planning of change* (2nd ed.). New York: Holt, Rinehart & Winston, 1969.

Bennis, W. G., and Slater, P. E.   *The temporary society*. New York: Harper & Row, 1968.

Berne, E.   *Games people play*. New York: Grove Press, 1964.

Berne, E.   *Transactional analysis in psychotherapy: a systematic individual and social psychiatry*. New York: Ballantine Books, 1961.

Bogen, J. E.   Some educational aspects of hemispheric specialization. In M. Wittrock (Ed.), *The human brain*. Englewood Cliffs, N.J.: Prentice-Hall, 1977.

Bowers, D. G.   Organization development techniques and their results in 26 organizations: the Michigan ICL study. *Journal of Applied Behavioral Science*, 1973, *9*, 21–43.

Bowers, D. G., and Franklin, J.   Survey-guided development: using human resources measurement in organization change. *Journal of Contemporary Business*, 1972, *1*, 43–55.

Bowers, D. G., and Seashore, S. E.   Predicting organizational effectiveness with a four-factor theory of leadership. *Administrative Science Quarterly*, 1966, *11*, 238–263.

Chase, P.   A survey feedback approach to organizational development. In *Proceedings of the Executive Study Conference*. Princeton, N.J.: Educational Testing Service, 1968.

Deutsch, M.   Trust, trustworthiness, and the F scale. *Journal of Abnormal and Social Psychology*, 1960, *61*, 138–140.

Dreikurs, R. *Psychology in the classroom.* New York: Harper & Row, 1957.

Drucker, P. *The practice of management: tasks, responsibilities, practices.* London: Pan Books Ltd., 1968.

Dusay, J. *Ego grams.* New York: Harper and Row, 1977.

Etzioni, A. *The active society.* New York: Free Press, 1967.

Etzioni, A. *Complex organizations.* New York: Holt, Rinehart & Winston, 1961.

Evans, R., and Leppman, P. *Resistance to innovation in higher education.* San Francisco, Calif.: Jossey-Bass, 1968.

Fabun, D. The corporation as a creative environment. *Kaiser Aluminum News,* 1967, 3 (2), 12.

Ford, R. N. The obstinate employee. *Psychology Today, 1969, 3* (6), 32–35.

Fordyce, J. K., and Weil, R. *Managing with people, a manager's handbook of organization development methods.* Reading, Mass.: Addison-Wesley, 1971.

Forrester, J. W. *Industrial dynamics.* Cambridge, Mass.: Massachusetts Institute of Technology Press, 1961.

Forrester, J. W. *Principles of systems.* Cambridge, Mass.: Wright-Allen Press, 1968.

Forrester, J. W. *Urban dynamics.* Cambridge, Mass.: Massachusetts Institute of Technology Press, 1969.

Forrester, J. W. *World dynamics.* Cambridge, Mass.: Wright-Allen Press, 1971.

French, W. L., and Bell, C. H., Jr. *Organization development.* Englewood Cliffs, N.J.: Prentice-Hall, 1973.

Friedlander, F., and Brown, D. Organizational development. *Annual Review of Psychology,* 1974, 25, 313–341.

Frohman, M. A., Sashkin, M., and Kavanagh, M. J. "Action research as applied to organization development," *Organization and Administrative Sciences,* 1976, 7 (1–2), 129–161.

Fromm, E. *The revolution of hope: toward a humanized technology.* New York: Harper & Row, 1968.

Galin, D. The two modes of consciousness and the two halves of the brain. In R. E. Ornstein (Ed.), *Symposium on consciousness.* New York: Penguin Books, 1977.

Gardner, J. *Self-renewal: the individual and the innovative society.* New York: Harper & Row, 1964.

Glasser, W. *Reality therapy.* New York: Harper & Row, 1965.

Glasser, W. *Schools without failure.* New York: Harper & Row, 1969.

Glasser, W. *The identity society.* New York: Harper & Row, 1972.

Goldman, Katherine. Personal communication, spring 1977. Dr. Goldman is chairperson of the Human Development Program, Austin Community College, Austin, Texas.

Golembiewski, R. T., Billingsley, K., and Yeager, S. Measuring change and persistence in human affairs: types of change generated by OD designs. *Journal of Applied Behavioral Science,* 1976, 12 (2), 133–157.

Gould, J., and Kolb, W. L. (Eds.). *A dictionary of the social sciences.* New York: Macmillan Publishing Co., 1964.

Gross, E., and Grambsch, P. V. *University goals and academic power.* Washington, D.C.: American Council on Education, 1968.

Gross, N. Organizational lag in American universities. *Harvard Educational Review,* 1963, 33, 312.

Hall, C., and Lindzey, G. *Theories of personality.* New York: Appleton-Century-Crofts, 1957.

Harris, B. *Inservice education: improving staff performance.* Boston, Mass.: Allyn-Bacon, in press.

Harvey, J.   The Abilene paradox: the management of agreement. *Organizational Dynamics,* summer 1974, 63–80.

Harvey, J.   Eight myths OD consultants believe in...and die by. *OD Practitioner,* 1975, 7 (1), 1–5.

Hauser, D. I., Pecorella, P. A., and Wissler, A. L.   *Survey-guided development: a manual for consultants.* Ann Arbor, Mich.: Organizational Development Research Program, Institute for Social Research, 1975.

Hazard, W.   *Administrators as change agents: a role dilemma.* Paper presented at the 69th annual meeting of the Association of School Administrators, Atlantic City, N.J., February 1969.

Heller, F. A.   Group feedback analysis: a method of field research. *Psychological Bulletin,* 1969, 72, 108–117.

Herzberg, F., Mausner, B., and Snyderman, B. B.   *The motivation to work.* New York: John Wiley & Sons, 1959.

Jourard, S.   *The transparent self: self-disclosure and well-being.* New York: Van Nostrand Co., 1964.

Jung, C. G.   [*Psychological types*] (H. G. Baynes trans., revised by R. F. C. Hull). Princeton, N.J.: Princeton University Press, 1971. (Originally published, 1921).

Kahn, R. L.   Field studies of power in organizations. In R. L. Kahn and E. Boulding (Eds.), *Power and conflict in organizations.* New York: Basic Books, 1964.

Kast, F. E., and Rosenzweig, J. E.   General systems theory: applications for organization and management. *Academy of Management Journal,* December 1972, pp. 447–465.

Kelley, G. A.   *The psychology of personal constructs* (2 vols.). New York: Norton & Co., 1955.

Kerr, C., and Miller, R.   *Campus 1980.* New York: Dell Publishing Co., 1968.

Kessel, V., and Mink, O. G.   *The systems approach to organization development: formulating goals and deriving objectives.* Paper presented at the annual convention of the American Educational Research Association, New York, 1971.

Klein, S. M., Kraut, A. I., and Wolfson, A.   Employee reactions to attitude survey feedback: study of the impact of structure and process. *Administrative Science Quarterly,* 1971, 16, 497–514.

Knowles, H. P., and Saxberg, B. O.   *Personality and leadership behavior.* Reading, Mass.: Addison-Wesley, 1971.

Lawrence, P. R., and Lorsch, J. W.   Differentiation and integration in complex organizations. *Administrative Science Quarterly,* 1967, 12 (1) 1–47.

Lawrence, P. R., and Lorsch, J. W.   *Developing organizations: diagnosis and action.* Reading, Mass.: Addison-Wesley, 1969.

Lazarsfield, P.   *The social sciences and educational administration.* Edmonton: University of Alberta, 1963.

Lee, S. M.   *Goal programming for decision analysis.* Philadelphia, Pa.: Auerbach, 1972. 1972.

Lewin, K.   Action research and minority problems. *Journal of Social Issues,* 1946, 2, 34–46.

Likert, R.   *New patterns of management.* New York: McGraw-Hill Book Co., 1961.

Likert, R.   *The human organization.* New York: McGraw-Hill Book Co., 1967.

Lippitt, G.   *Organization renewal.* New York: Appleton-Century-Crofts, 1969.

Lippitt, G., and Lippitt, R.   *Consultation: roles, processes, and skills.* La Jolla, Calif.: University Associates, 1978. (a)

Lippitt, G., and Lippitt, R.   *The consulting process in action.* La Jolla, Calif.: University Associates, 1978. (b)

Lippitt, R., Watson, J., and Westley, B. *The dynamics of planned change.* New York: Harcourt, Brace & Co., 1958.

Lorsch, J. W., and Lawrence, P. R. *Studies in organization design.* Homewood, Ill.: Irwin, 1970.

Luft, J. The Johari window. In C. Mill (Ed.), *Selections from Human Relations Training News.* Arlington, Va.: National Training Laboratories, Institute for Applied Behavioral Science, 1969.

MacDonald, A. P., Jr. More on the Protestant ethic. *Journal of Consulting and Clinical Psychology,* 1972, *39,* 116–122.

MacDonald, A. P., Jr., Kessel, V. S., and Fuller, J. B. Self-disclosure and two kinds of trust. *Psychological Reports,* 1972, *30,* 143–148.

MacGregor, D. *The human side of enterprise.* New York: McGraw-Hill Book Co., 1960.

Mager, R. F. *Preparing instructional objectives* (2nd ed.). Belmont, Calif.: Fearon-Pitman Publishers, 1976.

Maslow, A. H. A theory of human motivation. *Psychological Review,* 1943, *50, 370–396.*

Maslow, A. H. A theory of metamotivation: the biological rooting of the value-life. *Journal of Humanistic Psychology,* 1967, *7,* 93–127.

Maslow, A. H. *The farther reaches of human nature.* New York: Viking Press, 1971.

McAlindon, H. Integrating the actualizing of individuals and organizational values. *International Consulting News,* 1976, *1,* (1), 1.

Meeth, R. *Power and authority in organizational life.* San Francisco, Calif.: Jossey-Bass, 1971.

Miller, E. J., and Rice, A. K. *Systems of organization.* London: Tavistock, 1967.

Miller, J. G. Toward a general theory for the behavioral sciences. *American Psychologist,* 1955, *10,* 513–531.

Miller, J. G. Living systems: basic concepts. *Behavioral Science,* 1965, *10,* 193–237. (a)

Miller, J. G. Living systems: cross-level hypotheses. *Behavioral Science,* 1965, *10,* 380–411. (b)

Mink, O. G., and Kaplan, B. *American's problem youth: education and guidance of the disadvantaged.* Scranton, Pa.: International Textbook Co., 1970.

Myers, I. B. *The Myers-Briggs type indicator manual.* Princeton, N.J.: Educational Testing Service, 1962.

Myers, I. B. *Introduction to type* (2nd ed.). Gainesville, Fla.: Center for Applications of Psychological Type, 1976.

Myers, I. B. *The Myers-Briggs type indicator manual* (2nd ed.). Palo Alto, Calif.: Consulting Psychologists Press, in press.

O'Banion, T. The junior college—a humanizing institution. In *A day at Santa Fe: a series of lectures presented at Santa Fe Junior College.* Unpublished manuscript, Santa Fe Junior College, Gainesville, Fla., 1971.

Ornstein, R. E. *The mind field.* New York: Pocket Books, 1976.

Osgood, C. E., Suci, G. J., and Percy, H. T. *The measurement of meaning.* Urbana, Ill.: University of Illinois Press, 1957.

Peak, H. Attitude and motivation. In M. R. Jones (Ed.), *Nebraska Symposium on Motivation.* Lincoln, Neb.: University of Nebraska Press, 1955.

Peterson, R. E. *College goals and the challenge of effectiveness.* Princeton, N.J.: Educational Testing Service, 1970. (a)

Peterson, R. E. *The crisis of purpose: definition and uses of institutional goals.* Princeton, N.J.: Educational Testing Service, 1970. (b)

Peterson, R. E.   *Toward institutional goal-consciousness.* Berkeley, Calif.: Educational Testing Service, 1971.

Peterson, R. E.   *Goals for California higher education: a survey of 116 college communities.* Berkeley, Calif.: Educational Testing Service, 1973.

Peterson, R. E., and Uhl, N. P.   *Institutional goals inventory, form 1.* Princeton, N.J.: Educational Testing Service, 1972.

Piaget, J.   *The psychology of intelligence.* New York: Harcourt, Brace, & Co., 1950.

Richman, B. M., and Farmer, R. N.   *Leadership, goals, and power in higher education.* San Francisco, Calif.: Jossey-Bass, 1974.

Rogers, C. R.   *Carl Rogers on encounter groups.* New York: Harper & Row, 1970.

Rogers, C. R.   *On becoming a person.* Boston, Mass.: Houghton Mifflin Co., 1961.

Rokeach, M.   *Beliefs, attitudes and values.* San Francisco, Calif.: Jossey-Bass, 1969.

Rokeach, M.   *The nature of human values.* New York: The Free Press, 1973.

Ross, J. E.   *Managing productivity.* Reston, Va.: Reston Publishing Co., 1977.

Rotter, J. B.   *Social learning and clinical psychology.* Englewood Cliffs, N.J.: Prentice-Hall, 1954. (Full scale may be obtained for research purposes only from J. B. Rotter, Department of Psychology, University of Connecticut, Storrs, Conn.)

Rotter, J. B.   A new scale for the measurement of interpersonal trust. *Journal of Personality,* 1967, 35, 651–665.

Rotter, J. B., Seeman, M., and Liverant, S.   Internal versus external control of reinforcements: a major variable in behavior theory. In N. F. Washburne (Ed.), *Decisions, values, groups* (Vol. 2). New York: Pergamon Press, 1962.

Roueche, J. E., and Boggs, J.   *Junior college institutional research: the state of the art.* Washington, D.C.: American Association of Junior Colleges, 1968. (ERIC Clearinghouse for Junior College Information, Monograph series.)

Rudolph, R.   *The American college and university.* New York: Random House, 1962.

Sanford, N. (Ed.).   *The American college.* New York: Wiley & Sons, 1962.

Santillana, G.   *The crime of Galileo.* Chicago, Ill.: University of Chicago Press, 1955.

Schiff, J.   *Cathexis reader: transactional analysis treatment of psychosis.* New York: Harper & Row, 1975.

Schutz, W. C.   *FIRO: A three-dimensional theory of interpersonal behavior.* New York: Holt, Rinehart & Winston, 1958.

Seashore, Charles N.   Personal communication, July 18, 1977. Dr. Seashore is a private consultant, at 4445 29th Street N.W., Washington, D.C. 20008.

Shepard, H. A.   An action research model. In B. Peek (Ed.), *An action research program for organization improvement.* Ann Arbor, Mich.: Foundation for Research on Human Behavior, 1960.

Smith, P. B.   Social influence processes and the outcome of sensitivity training. *Journal of Personality and Social Psychology,* 1976, 34 (6), 1087–1094.

Snow, J., and Mink, O.   *Survey of community college organizational functioning.* Unpublished manuscript, The University of Texas at Austin, 1977.

Steiner, G.   *The creative organization.* Chicago, Ill.: University of Chicago Press, 1965.

Stufflebeam, D. L.   The relevance of the CIPP evaluation model for educational accountability. *Journal of Research and Development in Education,* 1971, 5 (1), 19–25.

Tannenbaum, R., Davis, S., and Schmidt, W.   *Organizational frontiers and human values.* Belmont, Calif.: Wadsworth Publishing Co., 1970.

Taylor, J. C., and Bowers, B. G.   *Survey of organizations.* Ann Arbor, Mich.: Center for Research on Utilization of Scientific Knowledge, Institute for Social Research, 1972.

Taylor, J. C., and Bowers, B. G.   *Survey of organizations.* Ann Arbor, Mich.: Center for Research on Utilization of Scientific Knowledge, Institute for Social Research, 1974.

Trist, E. L. *The relations of welfare and development in the transition of post-indus-trialism*. Los Angeles, Calif.: Western Management Science Institute, University of California, 1968.

Uhl, N. P. *Encouraging convergence of opinion, through the use of the Delphi technique, in the process of identifying an institution's goals* (PR–71–2). Princeton, N.J.: Educational Testing Service, 1971.

Vollmer, H., and Mills, D. *Professionalism*. Englewood Cliffs, N.J.: Prentice-Hall, 1966.

Walton, R. *Interpersonal peacemaking: confrontation and third party consultation*. Reading, Mass.: Addison-Wesley, 1969.

Watzlawick, P. *How real is real? Confusion, disinformation, communication*. New York: Vintage Books, 1976.

Watzlawick, P., Weakland, J. H., and Fisch, R. *Change: principles of problem formation and problem resolution*. New York: Norton & Co., 1974.

Weber, Max. [*The theory of social and economic organization*] (2nd ed.) (T. Parsons, Ed. and trans., A. M. Henderson, trans.). New York: Free Press, 1957.

Whitehead, A. N. *Adventure of ideas*. New York: Macmillan Publishing Co., 1933.

PART V
Epilogue

Successful OD Change: Applying Open Systems Concepts in a Manufacturing Setting

by A. Robert Formosa, Carl R. Heinz, and Oscar G. Mink

BUSINESS PUBLICATIONS ARE REPLETE with accounts of organizations which have substantially improved performance. While some of those improvements are lasting and of long-term benefit to shareholders, many are not, because the improvement depends too heavily on the power of one seemingly heroic or charismatic individual or stem from actions that improve performance in the short term at the expense of the long term.

In this article, we present an approach to improved performance that balances short- and long-term achievements and perpetuates high performance levels. It depends primarily on changing the way the entire organization functions—a total systems approach—rather than on the influence of one or a few individuals, "miraculous" actions, or charismatic leadership.

WHAT TO INCLUDE IN A COMPREHENSIVE CHANGE EFFORT

We applied Open Systems Theory to practice during shared experiences at Joy Manufacturing. We worked together in various capacities over a period of years developing and implementing an approach for improving profitability and productivity through a process of planned change. The governing values of the planned change effort included free and informed choice at the "worksite," use of valid information and valuing good health in the organization. We came to recognize that the healthy individual is the first building block in achieving the goal of a highly adaptable organization that emphases quality products and services in a context of ever-changing technology, markets, and customer needs.

Our experience at Joy involved several business units. In each unit, we demonstrated that organizations, including those which already performed superior to their competitors, can still drastically improve performance.

In the Open Systems organization development model, performance is viewed as multi-level and multi-dimensional. Performance improvement is perceived differently at various levels in the organization structure, and at each level are a multiple of facets or dimensions that are critical to the organization's overall performance.

We suggest performance be viewed in the context of a hierarchy of levels, varying from owners to managers to employees. The roles and functions of each level in the hierarchy determine what dimensions of performance are relevant at that level in setting and measuring success (see Exhibit 1).

At the apex of the hierarchy, the primary concern is return on investment or equity. At the middle levels are concerns that vary in significance over time with product life: profitability, unit productivity, effectiveness, degree of alignment on common purpose, and team productivity. At the lower levels, other dimensions play key roles. Some, like labor turnover, absenteeism, and tardiness, are easy to observe and measure. Others, like collaborative working relationships between departments and levels, contribute to productivity, but are more difficult to assess. Job satisfaction variables, like quality of peers, supervision, involvement in decisions that affect one's work, quality of communications, and the work climate, appear to consistently relate to employee morale and performance.

This performance hierarchy corresponds to the organization structure. People at lower levels tend to focus on contributory aspects of performance, while executive management gives more time and attention to dimensions at or close to the pinnacle.

The dimensions of the various levels are interrelated: the relationships among them are often mutually interactive, sharing cause-and-effect relationships. Individuals at each level frequently fail to recognize the *systemic* effects of performance improvements that take place in other levels. Thus, when ROI and ROE performance improves, it is difficult for top leadership to attribute improved performance to organization development interventions that focus on influencing dimensions more frequently associated with lower levels of the Performance Measurement Hierarchy.

Organization Development (OD), by definition, needs to be comprehensive (multi-level and multi-dimensional), and hence tends to be complex. The impact of OD is gradual and occurs at various levels in the performance hierarchy at different times and in different degrees.

Some managers observe results key to their most immediate concerns and strongly endorse the OD effort. Other leaders and managers in the organization may fail to observe the systemic benefits of planned OD efforts, and may view these efforts as worthless.

Our experience at Joy convinced us that improvements at all levels in the performance hierarchy were attributable to the OD effort; albeit, some improvements, especially at lower levels, were easier to observe and substantiate than others. For example, when an OD intervention reduced labor turnover, we found that product quality improved and the number of employee contributions to our suggestion plan increased significantly.

A case study from our OD effort at Joy may clarify the kinds of results we achieved from applying the Open Systems Model to performance improvement.

The Joy plant in question had a very complicated new electronic machine called an electron beam (EB) welder, a laser application in manufacturing. The company was one of the first to put a EB welder in a machine shop. It was the first to try to make welds as deep as 1 1/4 inch, a capability made possible by this machine. Formerly, the deepest welds were 3/8 inch. After several years of experimentation, management remedied various mechanical problems and decided to buy a totally new machine to increase the plant's productive capacity.

Managers expected the machine to produce work faster in various ways. Of necessity, the new machine had to be enclosed in an air-conditioned room to insure air quality. Airborne particles in the electronic system would cause it to break down. As a result, both the operator and the machinery were enclosed in a chamber. This action induced severe morale problems for the operators in the "isolation" chamber. Originally a three-shift operation, the operator group was expanded to engage five workers instead of three. The new EB welder had the capacity to produce about twice as many parts (universals) as the company needed.

For the first two years of production, the output rate of the new machine never exceeded more than about 25 percent of standard. The company's top management was disappointed. The five operators turned out so few universals that management had to subcontract an inferior version of the part in order to meet customer needs. Something was "always broken" on the machine. The "model" workroom grew shopworn and dirty. Both the operators and their supervisors demonstrated signs of unhappiness—increased tardiness, increased absenteeism. Mistrust and anger between operators and supervisors abounded.

During the preceding few years, Joy had successfully applied team building to solve specific performance problems. At the suggestion of the plant manager, the deteriorating situation at the EB welder site was identified to the human resource management consulting group. Plant management recognized it should be getting much better results and agreed to explore what could be done to remedy the situation. With the advice of the consultant, a diagnostic study was performed using Open System audit techniques and a series of in-depth interviews with operators and line supervisors.

The study led to the development of a team-building program for the unit. The first step in the team-building effort required the supervisor to try doing the work of the machine operator himself. After two hours, the supervisor was so bored he could barely stick with it through the shift. But he did get the needed production. The supervisors and the operators began to meet with the consultant in a series of meetings. After a rocky start, a new level of trust began to build. The workers had plenty of suggestions. Some were so simple: "Let us have a radio." "Let us try our ideas for helping to keep the place clean." Several things were agreed upon to improve work climate that represented no-cost or low-cost modifications of the work station.

The team-building intervention dramatically increased productivity and created high morale. The consultant reported that both the supervisor and the operators had changed. The behavior of one operator had taken an about-face. Even his appearance had changed—from what could be described as "unconcerned" to obviously more clean-cut; he walked in a more erect position, lost 30 pounds via diet, and seemed happy with himself. His attitude became that of a proprietor.

The Plant Manager reported that the cost per weld dropped from $1.75 to 79 cents, and the new universal became more consistently available to match assembly schedules and satisfy customer requirements.

Another example of tremendous improvement occurred in the final assembly area for continuous miners. The figures, which speak for themselves, are dramatic. The audited cost savings were over $550,000 per month, with dramatic improvements in quality (see Exhibit 2).

LEARNING IN ACTION

Ours was a pioneering effort with false starts, wrong turns, avoidable delays, and inappropriate priorities. The OD effort itself does not constitute a recommended road map, but our experiences demonstrate how a comprehensive OD effort can succeed when based on a sound theoretical model. The undertaking at Joy, at the risk of overstatement, convinced us there is a way for organizations to break through to much higher levels of performance. As a consequence, businesses can compete much more effectively; better reward owners and other stakeholders; and better challenge, reward, and nurture employees; thereby leading to exemplary overall performance in the global marketplace.

We embarked upon a course of learning in action. We applied several concepts at Joy that seem to contain the necessary principles or requirements for transforming a traditional bureaucracy from a fairly closed, non-responsive organization to a more open, adaptive organization. Here are the guiding concepts selected and freely modified at Joy:

1. **An effort at organization transformation must be comprehensive.** It must consider the substance of the organization. The strategic foundation consists of: vision, mission, key goals, values, the mechanisms and processes for problem solving, ongoing strategic planning for decision making; the organization structure must be driven by function, yet the roles (i.e., responsibilities, duties, and authorities) of key members of the organization need to be negotiable; policies, procedures, human and technical systems must all be integrated and directed at the strategic outcomes. In a competitive environment, the time allotted any organization to integrate objectives and strategy to a given opportunity is clearly limited.

2. Because the approach is broadly comprehensive, **it is important that the undertaking have the informed interest and active support and understanding of all levels of management** and ultimately of the entire organization. Every employee must be able to discuss freely any perceptions or feelings related to any constraint, that might mitigate his or her work group's performance of their assigned tasks.

3. **Success depends heavily on education and training.** Most changes in organization performance require changes in human behavior. New organization behaviors typically require different knowledge, attitudes, and skills. Education becomes one vehicle to accomplish this. Much of the required learning needs formal support, but much important learning is informal and incidental, occurring in the context of the job and in critical social interactions like group problem solving.

4. **Successful organizational change efforts include attention to the human systems involved.** If the human systems are functioning well, the probability of success of any change effort is materially enhanced. Most organizations have some of the elements of the human system in place. However, there are usually inefficient interrelationships among the components and missing or weak components that prevent the overall system from operating at the required levels of effectiveness. Instead of high performance, poor human systems encourage non-work states.

5. It is important that **the organization's managers and key players in the OD effort understand the change process and be able to manage change efforts.** We used a variety of models, concepts, and practices drawn from research in the behavioral sciences and in management theory. However, we found that **total systems analysis techniques** were most useful. We learned that the most comprehensive approach to the actual management of the change process was our own hybrid, adapted to the unique characteristics of the organization. We coupled Kurt Lewin's work on Field Theory, particularly Force Field Analysis, as a diagnostic technique, with the Concerns-Based Adoption Model (CBAM). CBAM was developed at The University of Texas over a 10 + year period. It is a comprehensive system for managing change. We educated all managers in the use of the methods of Force Field Analysis and CBAM, including Stages of Concern (SoC) Levels of Use (LoU), action planning, and Innovation Configurations (ways to identify and describe the exact nature of a change to be implemented). We all learned how to plan or implement, manage, monitor, and evaluate change efforts.

During and since our experience at Joy, we have consulted with a number of other organizations. This has provided the opportunity to test and refine the concepts developed at Joy. Also, it has provided further evidence to support our opinion that significantly higher levels of performance can be achieved through a comprehensive, systematic OD effort coupled with tested change methodologies.

APPLYING THE CONCEPTS IN A MANUFACTURING SETTING

The remainder of this article presents our recommendations; it demonstrates how the five concepts we just reviewed can be used in practice. Given the comprehensiveness of the approach we are recommending, most organizations will have some components in place. To establish a starting point, estimate time and resources required, and develop an action plan or game plan. A careful analysis of what currently exists is required. The resources required to implement the approach can be predicted after a careful comparison of the current situation with the idealized plan has been made.

HOW WE APPROACHED CHANGE

The efficiency any organization can achieve is, in large measure, greater than or equal to the sum of the efficiency with which each individual and each department performs. It follows, therefore, that any approach to improve the performance of the organization must be "bottom up" as well as "top down." Each individual in every level of the organization must be considered. The appropriateness of his or her skills and abilities, the quality of the available information needed, and the tools and resources available to do the job are all important factors. Organization climate must be appropriate to support the tasks to be performed. For example, if risk taking is required, then errors must be corrected in supportive, non-punitive ways.

Similarly, it is necessary to keep sub-groups (i.e., departments) in mind. Are department and individual goals compatible? Do their policies and procedures make for productive interaction? Are the departmental organization structures in the best interest of the total organization? Are departmental incentives aligned with the larger goals of the entire organization?

SITUATIONAL ANALYSIS—THE STARTING POINT

To establish a starting point, we begin with a broad situation analysis. The situation analysis encompasses the organization's vision, mission, goals, values, key strategies, key roles (organization structure), and policies and procedures. The reason for the comprehensiveness of the approach is our belief that the elements we include are independent and intervening variables in the network of factors that influence productivity. A less comprehensive approach, or one that fails to recognize how these variables interreact, will be suboptimal because the benefits of an improvement in one variable may be mitigated by another variable that is not addressed.

For example, if we were to disregard the importance of having a clear definition of *roles* by not analyzing them for task appropriateness and by not negotiating them toward optimum coordination, the benefits of upgraded vision, mission, goals, and key values could be significantly mitigated in the area of plan execution. Where role responsibilities and authorities are unclear, or where voids and duplications exist, inefficiencies ensue. Similarly, upgrading the organization's technical competence through the introduction of CAD/CAM systems may prove to be a poor investment if the human systems do not provide for necessary retraining and job security needed to allay the fears of affected employees. People who feel the resultant improvement in productivity may threaten their jobs will find ways to delay change efforts.

To assess the organization's current level of performance, we use the Open Systems Model (see Exhibit 3). The Open Systems Model, based on research by Oscar Mink and others, defines individual, group, and organizational effectiveness in three dimensions—all indicators of openness in human systems. Derived from general systems theory and emphasizing adaptability, this model provided the framework for all diagnostic activities. From an organizational change perspective, the Open Systems approach views managers as change agents who examine the organization in terms of (1) its levels of proficiency in meeting the expectations of stakeholders, (2) the levels of performance of relationships among groups (units) that comprise the organization's internal responsiveness, and (3) the efficiency of the interactions among the organization's individual employees.

The processes for gathering information related to the dimensions of this model include one-on-one interviews, discussions with groups, and various questionnaires. The information is gathered in the following categories:

1. The nature of the industry the business serves, including such elements as the basis of competition, and description of customers and competitors.

2. The competitive position and financial performance of the business, currently and historically.

3. Current vision, mission, values, and strategic goals, formal or informal, explicit or implicit.

4. Major opportunities and threats.

5. Hopes and values of the leader and key managers.

6. Outside influences that affect the organization's performance, i.e., technological developments, government regulations.

7. How change has been managed to date.

8. An analysis and description of the human resource management system and an evaluation of how it performs.

EDUCATION:
REVEALING THE POTENTIAL AND HOW TO ACHIEVE IT

Education is a critical part of the process. It is designed to meet five interrelated objectives:

1. Create a belief that the organization's potential to function at a high level can be realized.

2. Explain the process for realizing the potential.

3. Establish and gather information regarding where the organization currently stands and where its leaders would like to take it.

4. Establish a plan of action and get commitment to implement it.

5. Observe the competency of the group and individuals.

Success in broad systemic change processes requires a strong commitment over a long term. Education is a key factor in maintaining that commitment over time. It is unlikely key managers will sustain the commitment unless they are convinced that higher levels of performance can be reached and that the process they are undertaking will produce this improvement. Through involvement in education and by actively demonstrating support for the program, managers and the leadership team must make a sustained commitment of themselves and the organization's resources to this undertaking.

OD PROCESSES

Once the success of other organizations is understood and appreciated with a high degree of manager involvement, managers should have high-level interest in defining a change process or course of action. The critical points about these processes are their comprehensiveness and high degree of logical integration.

We measure the comprehensiveness of a program using three dimensions: (1) the extent to which it addresses all levels of the organizational hierarchy, (2) the degree to which it relates to both long- and short-term goals, and (3) the scope of the organization's opportunities and threats that it addresses. The need for comprehensiveness is explained by the Open Systems Model. The broad goal of the process is to improve external responsiveness (i.e., the way the organization satisfies stakeholders, especially customers) by improving the way units of the organization work with one another and as individual entities. These working teams and individuals and their relationships and the work of these groups are influenced by and reflected in the direction the business is moving (i.e., vision, mission, key goals); the way it intends to get there (i.e., strategies and related or key programs); the tools the organization uses (i.e., human and technical systems); the way resources are organized to carry out strategies and tactics, and, finally, the way roles (duties, responsibilities, and authorities) are synchronized to achieve efficiency.

It is important to gain consensus among key managers, including the leader, regarding the organization's current level of performance, areas of strength and weakness, and specific objectives for improving performance. The Open Systems matrix displayed in Exhibit 3 is useful in achieving this end.

Education is directed toward an analysis of organizational factors and an appreciation of various types of organization climates, why they exist, their effects on performance, and how to change. Using a questionnaire, such as the Organization Openness Profile developed by Mink, Mink, and Owen, may be one way to establish how each manager views the organization and to provide the basis for a discussion to achieve consensus on this topic.[1] Once the organization's current performance is described in terms of the matrix, goals can be set for each dimension of performance (i.e., each cell of the matrix). The gap between the current status and the goals is addressed by the action plan.

The action plan can be developed in a workshop setting. The participants are the leader and key mangers. The assistance of professional facilitators is typically required. The situation analysis and the key manager's consensus about the organization's current status are used to determine the action required. The plan would vary significantly from organization to organization because of difference in current performance.

The following discussion of the elements of the Organizational Development process that we developed at Joy Manufacturing demonstrates how we applied Open Systems theory to practical organizational change.

PLANNED CHANGE TO FIT THE PARTICULAR SITUATION

The process is constructed from a standard group of elements (i.e., undertakings) to meet the particular needs of an organization in a specific time frame. The elements are standard in a generic sense, e.g., strategic planning; however, the details and the sequence in which they are integrated into the process would be tailored to meet the specific needs of an organization, e.g., quality and current status of existing planning and strategic thinking. The action taken must fit the needed outputs.

We have discovered that the degree of difficulty in the OD undertaking is directly influenced by the efficiency of the commitment of the top leadership team to make a difference in the performance of the organization, the work capacity and quality of the leadership team, and the existing human systems.

It is important that the organization's vision, mission, goals, and key cultural values be developed and/or identified through the participation of the leader, his or her key associates, and other members of the organization who have unique contributions to make or whose position in the organization requires that they have insight into the process for developing them.

The process can be most readily explained by a descriptive listing of its elements. Following the list, we will comment further on considerations required to arrange and detail the elements of the process.

ELEMENTS OF THE PROCESS

• **Create, state, and communicate a vision for the organization.** The vision expresses the hopes of the leader(s), their ideal image of the organization in the future. It deals with what the organization will be doing and achieving in the future. It has a strategic quality. It is practical and it contains an underlying nobility of purpose. It is concise, relevant, and easily understood at all levels of the organization. It is fundamental in setting the direction of the organization. In a sense, it is to the organization, the equivalent of Russell Ackoff's "idealized design" in product development. In a change effort, the creation of the idealized future and current situational analysis provides the foundation for action plans to bridge the gap, or discrepancy, between the ideal and the actual.

• **Create, state, and communicate a mission statement.** This statement clarifies the purpose and general scope of operation, identifies the target industry(ies) and how they will be served, and indicates the mode of operation to achieve these goals. It has some of the same characteristics of the vision statement; however, it is much more specific because it states the reason for the organization's existence and what it must do to succeed. It sets the boundaries, guidelines, and realm in which opportunities are sought. Basically, the mission statement clarifies what product(s) or service(s) the organization provides and to whom.

• **Establish, state, and communicate goals and objectives for the organization; both long- and short-term, as well as strategic and operational.** The goals serve to provide focus to the vision and mission and help establish standards of performance against which to measure progress. In our view, thinking through the business environment, and from it, deducing and defining the organization's opportunities is a prerequisite. We also believe that a thoughtful description of strengths, weaknesses, opportunities, and threats (SWOTS) is needed. The opportunities and strengths establish a range and arena for improving performance. The threats and weaknesses define the potential barriers or factors limiting success.

• **Identify key governing values of the organization.** Shared values form the fundamental organizer for all of an organization's behavior. These must be surfaced, clarified, and clearly communicated to each person in the organization. They *must* be emphasized by all leaders at all levels, and in all programs of the organization.

• **Develop strategies and actions to achieve the goals and the vision.** Strategies and action plans are aligned to the vision, mission, goals, and values. This planning provides a step-by-step process that will achieve the key organizational objectives. To be effective, they must be communicated clearly to the organization.

The preceding elements of this process are more than an exercise in strategic thinking. They are critical because they set the direction in terms of where the organization will go and how it well get there. They also provide the opportunity to build alignment and establish the prerequisites of subsequent commitment and empowerment of individuals and groups in their efforts to achieve.

The following elements pertain to the capability of the organization to move in the intended direction.

• **Have a method for gathering data to evaluate the competency of the leadership team, both in terms of group and individual performance.** These evaluations may be done in several ways, as follows:
  - Listening to the opinion of the organization's leader(s) and members
  - Interviews
  - Tests, surveys, questionnaires
  - Discussions and observations in educational sessions designed to draw out the data needed

• **Identify and address problems before they become crises.** It is important to be able to identify and bring to the attention of the leadership group any shortfalls in competency that will seriously hinder the process. Keep the leaders informed of progress and of your ability to achieve a recommended course of action that is clearly defined, agreed upon, and instituted.

• **Evaluate the organization structure to determine if it contributes to or hinders team functioning (i.e., carrying out the processes performed by the organization).** Building a structure that promotes openness based on the fundamental concept that "Structure Follows Function" is critical.[2]

• **Examine and evaluate the way the organization processes and performs in the following areas:**
  - Organization purpose and approach to planning
  - Time perspective
  - Organization focus (i.e., survival, goal directed, mission achieving contribution to society)
  - Management orientation in decision making
  - Management of change
  - Effectiveness of technical systems
  - Effectiveness of business systems

• **Assess the effectiveness of human systems and the focus of human development.** Without effective human systems in place, the OD undertaking becomes more difficult.

Human systems include policies, procedures, and supporting functions that produce manpower plans; influence the selection of new employees and of current employees for promotion; establish employee compensation, benefits, and other rewards; appraise performance and potential; establish the need and/ or qualifications for development; provide opportunities for development; keep employees informed; and provide the organization with an accurate picture of the human resources. Both human resources capability (*skill* data) and functioning (*will* data) are critical to this assessment.

The climate is right for a comprehensive OD effort when these policies, procedures, and functions can be integrated into a congruent, logical system that readily provides believable information to the organization, clearly conveys management's interest in the development and effective utilization of people, rewards performance, focuses work effort on the task at hand, builds collaborative relationships between groups, and establishes trust in communications and working relationships. Where these conditions for organizational effectiveness do not exist, the OD function may more effectively focus on laying the groundwork for improved organization effectiveness by cultivating these capacities in the system.

For example: If consistent, honest communication is unprecedented in the organization, it is doubtful that a comprehensive OD effort that depends heavily on communication and trust can succeed. In this instance, OD may focus on trust-building activities like "owning up to past mistakes," open dialoguing, and group brainstorming and problem solving. When these objectives have been achieved, the organization will be ready for a more comprehensive OD effort.

• **Review roles of key managers to determine how well they support the organization's function and structure.** Are these roles consistent with the organization's processes; are the roles clear? Are roles or functions duplicated? Do gaps exist between what a job should be as dictated by the organization structure and/or procedures (i.e., what the incumbent thinks it is, and the expectations of the person to whom the incumbent reports)? These variances make for confusion, reduce the organization's overall performance, and often adversely affect the careers of employees. The process we recommend for clarifying roles is the assessment of job dimensions. This is an approach to describing a job by describing the knowledge, skills, and attitudes (competencies) needed, and key activities performed by a successful candidate. There are usually several categories of dimensions, i.e., interpersonal, technical, managerial. The dimensions are described through a collaborative process involving the incumbent, the incumbent's boss, the incumbents boss's boss, a technician, peers, and subordinates.

The design of this process follows the situation analysis and uses the elements described above. It meets the particular needs of the organization. It is intended to move it from the current state, as revealed by the situation analysis, to a higher level of performance—closer to the idealized state.

The process is manifested in an action plan developed by the leadership team with the assistance of a professional who can facilitate the development of the plan. The time to implement the plan and achieve higher levels of performance varies, depending on the aptitude of the organization, the extent to which the aspects of team functioning addressed by the elements of the process are absent or malfunctioning. The nature of the organizational unit in a structural context is also a factor. Small, single-location units can move more rapidly than large, multi-unit organizations.

It is important to note that improvement in performance most likely will be incremental, and, in the context of the performance hierarchy described earlier, occurs at different rates in different places and levels in the organization. We have observed that early improvements frequently result from the educational message that *leadership believes improvements can be achieved and has adopted a logical, systematic approach.* Initial observable improvements frequently occur in the following areas:
- The top leadership team processes more efficiently.
- A positive attitude regarding the future permeates the entire leadership hierarchy.

It is important to note that embarking on this undertaking elevates expectations. As employees are educated or otherwise exposed, they come to expect more. And while the costs associated with doing this work may, at first glance, appear to be significant, the gains the organization can experience are exponential. Due to elevated expectations, it should be noted that the price of aborting the effort or doing it poorly is tremendous. We need to keep in mind that attempting to compete in a world-class marketplace (global economy) in the 21st century with 19th-century management rigidity just doesn't make sense, and, more importantly, it won't work!

SUMMARY

An OD program that is applied systematically, is comprehensive, and is tailored to the current condition and specific needs of an organization will produce significant measurable and lasting improvements in organization performance. The rewards easily justify the cost. Management's ongoing commitment and consistent allocation of the required financial and human resources is necessary.

The effort must be carefully designed and skillfully implemented through the involvement of the leader and all key personnel. Education can be critical in maintaining organization-wide commitment.

The income statement and balance sheet will show the benefits. Observable results will also be produced in the areas of employee morale and productivity, customer satisfaction, and investor confidence.

REFERENCES

1. Oscar Mink and Keith Owen. *Open Organization Profile* (Austin, Texas: Catapult Press, 1987).
2. Henry Mintzberg. *The Nature of Managerial Work* (New York: Harper & Row, 1973).

Exhibit 1. Performance Measurement Hierarchy

Levels	Dimensions
Financial Stakeholders, Leadership, and Upper-Level Management Concerns	• Return on Investment (ROI) or • Return on Equity (ROE)
Middle-Level Management Concerns	• Profitability • Degree of Alignment • Effective Team Efforts and Productivity Effectiveness ("Doing the right things right")
Lower-Level Management Concerns and Hourly Workers	• Efficiencies: Doing Things Right and • Various Other Factors, e.g., Organization climate, tools, supervisors, peers, degree of empowerment or autonomy in "Doing the best job that I know how to do" • Labor Turnover • Absenteeism • Collaborative Working Relationships (Vertical & Horizontal)

Exhibit 2. Manufacturing Assembly & Teams

When Joy Manufacturing installed individualized Work Centers and used a Team approach to product assembly, these results were achieved:

Year	Event	Number of Workers	Target Hours	Rework
1	Baseline	400	15% over	157 pieces (Additional 10% missed)
2	Introduced effort	400	8% over	132 pieces
3	Work Centers operational	200	5.8% under	18 pieces

Exhibit 3. Defining Characteristics of Open Systems

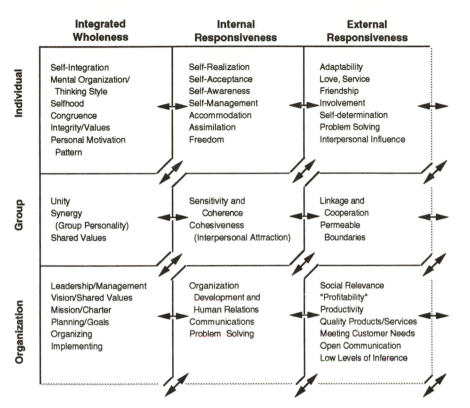

	Integrated Wholeness	Internal Responsiveness	External Responsiveness

Individual	Self-Integration
	Mental Organization/
	  Thinking Style
	Selfhood
	Congruence
	Integrity/Values
	Personal Motivation
	  Pattern
		Self-Realization
		Self-Acceptance
		Self-Awareness
		Self-Management
		Accommodation
		Assimilation
		Freedom
			Adaptability
			Love, Service
			Friendship
			Involvement
			Self-determination
			Problem Solving
			Interpersonal Influence

Group	Unity
	Synergy
	  (Group Personality)
	Shared Values
		Sensitivity and
		  Coherence
		Cohesiveness
		  (Interpersonal Attrraction)
			Linkage and
			  Cooperation
			Permeable
			  Boundaries

Organization	Leadership/Management
	Vision/Shared Values
	Mission/Charter
	Planning/Goals
	Organizing
	Implementing
		Organization
		  Development and
		  Human Relations
		Communications
		Problem Solving
			Social Relevance
			"Profitability"
			Productivity
			Quality Products/Services
			Meeting Customer Needs
			Open Communication
			Low Levels of Inference

Levels of Open Systems